# Reader Reviews of
## *Dance from the Heart*

I enjoyed this installment as much or more than the first two. Well written, good characters, accurate horse facts.

—Kindle reader

A fun, enjoyable story about girls, the horses they love, and the sport of Dressage. It would be fun if the author took Jane to the Olympics.

—Kindle reader

Love this series!

—Jordan Webberly

I don't want it to end! I want to see what happens with Jane and Cory…is the Olympics in her future with Santos? How does Mandy grow up and honor her mother, Erica's, memory? Please don't leave your fans hanging…

—Susan E. Mcintosh

I like that she grew up and found her way. Wish it would continue with their lives in another book.

—Karen Hunter

# Dance from the Heart

BOOK THREE IN THE *Dancing With Horses* TRILOGY

## TONI MARI

tonimaribooks

All characters in this book have no existence outside the imagination of the author and have no relation whatsoever to anyone bearing the same name or names. They are not even distantly inspired by any individual known or unknown to the author, and all incidents are pure invention.

Cover design by Tatiana Villa

Visit the author at http://www.tonimaribooks.com

ISBN-13: 978-1537223957

ISBN-10: 153722395X

*For my mom, Marie J. Palaia, who loved*
*to read books that made her laugh out loud.*
*She is my inspiration, my conscience,*
*and my guardian angel.*

*And for my grandmother, Natalie Valenza,*
*who shared her love, her wisdom*
*and her books endlessly.*
*When I grow up, Grandmom,*
*I want to be just like you.*

# Acknowledgements

I would to thank my readers who took the time to write reviews, engage with me on Facebook and sent me messages via my website. Your encouragement and responses fueled my motivation to write not one but three novels. I have learned a lot in the process and thanks to you and your support, will continue to write more.

*CHAPTER*

# 1

The tall black horse's coat glistened in the sun as his knees bent and his belly hit the dirt. A grunt burst from his lips as his hind end flopped against the ground. He groaned and rolled onto his back, spindly legs waving in the air. Throwing them from side to side, he wiggled his spine into the turf, rubbing his neck back and forth. With a twist, his hooves clicked together and toppled to the ground with a thud. He released a mighty breath, and his muscles went slack. His body was motionless.

"Windsong!" I called. My chin rested on my arms as I leaned on the gate. "Couldn't you stay clean for five minutes? I just finished bathing you."

The black head rose slightly and one eye opened lazily. Then he settled back onto the warm earth. Nap time, I guessed.

I knew how he felt. I sank into the grass, stretching my legs out and sighing heavily. I pulled the folded letter from my pocket and read it for the millionth time. Closing my eyes, I let my shoulders fall back, weeds tickling my neck.

I was physically and mentally exhausted. I couldn't decide what clothes to pack for college let alone make a big decision like this one.

*Congratulations on becoming the North American Junior Individual and Team Champion.* The words jumped around in my head while I tried to make them feel real. Nothing had penetrated the numbness I felt since Erica Flame had died in a highway accident a month ago. The letter was from EMA Rescue, an organization that Erica had founded, sponsored, and supported. They were asking me to be their spokesperson. *In her place.*

1

Spokesperson. That meant publicity, appearances, my name and photograph in magazines and newspapers, maybe even television commercials. Me. Jane Mitchell, shy, insecure, scared of my own shadow. I read the first line of the letter again. The tone was hopeful, delicate, cajoling, as if I was a celebrity to be persuaded.

A shadow fell across the sun and I lowered the letter.

"Hello, darling." Cory's deep, warm voice rolled over my body and I trembled. "Do you want company?" He was still treating me like fragile glass, and had been since the funeral. I had lived with Erica and her family for only a month while training for the championship, but they had felt like real family. I missed them.

I nodded silently. He lay down on his side next to me, long, denim-clad legs stretched out, dusty cowboy boots crossed at the ankle. He pushed his white cowboy hat back and propped his head on one hand, putting the other on my hip. Blue eyes the color of the late summer sky fixed on the letter. "What's that?"

I handed it to him. Inspecting his chiseled profile and strong, square chin, I saw no change as he read. He put it on my stomach when he was done.

"What do you think?"

"It's a good cause."

I sat up. "I know. Besides saving so many abused and neglected horses, they educate owners on proper horse care. It seems odd that they asked me to fill Erica's shoes. She was an icon; I'm just a high school kid." I folded the letter into a small square and pushed it back into my pocket.

Erica Flame was my idol, and I planned on becoming a world-class rider like her, but I was just starting my riding career. I needed to win some big, prestigious titles to gain the recognition to become influential in the sport of dressage and in the equestrian world in general. Once I had some championships to my name, becoming a spokesperson made sense, because people would know what I was capable of and respect me.

Cory's eyes sparkled. "You mean 'a college kid.'"

I cocked my head at him, "What?" It took me a second to rein back my thoughts from my future career to our conversation. "Right. Tomorrow, I enter the hallowed halls of North Carolina State. Another thing that seems odd to me. I'd rather stay home near you and ride Windsong." I was wondering how living at college was going to fit into my training schedule for upcoming Regionals.

Luckily, my parents had given me a car as a graduation present, and, boy, was I going to rack up some miles driving back and forth from the barn to school.

"And give up a college education? You would be crazy to do that. And you would be crazy to say no to this offer." Cory tipped his cowboy hat back to look up at me, his gaze thoughtful. "I keep thinking about all the horses you would be helping. Horses like Lakota, who deserve a chance to live in safety and comfort. He may not have gotten that chance if not for EMA Rescue saving him and the others at that farm last year."

"Even though it's pure publicity?" Cory had been on the World Reining Gold Medal Team a year ago, so he knew about fame. I thought for sure he would be against me doing this. "You always say you hate publicity, and that's all this would be."

"But you would be representing a good cause, not just promoting yourself." He took my arm and drew me down next to him. He kissed me gently on the lips.

Smoothing the soft curls at the base of his neck between my fingers, I murmured, "So, you think I should do it? I do want to help the horses, but think I would be a better spokesperson in a few years, after I become the best Grand Prix rider in the country."

My phone buzzed in the pocket of my tight breeches, the vibration causing me to jolt up and bump my forehead on Cory's. He sat up, rubbing the spot.

I worked the phone out of my pocket. It was a text message from Shawn Delaney. Averting my eyes, I pressed my lips together and quickly typed a response. I shot a look at Cory, and then busied myself standing and dusting off my pants. "I have to go."

Cory hopped up. "It's from him?"

My face heated. "It's not what you think." I started walking toward the barn. "He asked to meet for ice cream. I haven't seen him since the funeral. He's still my friend." I raised my voice defiantly.

"Just so he knows I'm still your boyfriend." Cory caught up to me and, taking my chin, tipped up my lips. He kissed me deeply, pulling me close and holding me in strong arms. "Don't forget. Our last dinner together before you leave for school is tonight."

CHAPTER

2

I pushed through the glass door of the diner, setting the brass bell tinkling. I scanned the booths, spotting Shawn's spiky blond head halfway down the aisle. His back was to me, and I took a deep, steadying breath.

I slid onto the bench opposite him, keeping my eyes on the closed menu and off of his. "Hi, Shawn."

One arm on the table, the other stretched along the seat back, he slouched comfortably across the booth in that way he had. He bobbed his head, bleak brown eyes rising lazily to mine. "You look good, Jane."

I smoothed the loose tendrils away from my face and tightened my ponytail. "Not really, but thanks. How are you?" I said pointedly.

His hair, always on the messy side, was showing dark roots and half covered his ears. He had bags under his eyes and his skin was pale. Finally, I wrenched my gaze from his dry, chapped lips—lips that I had kissed—to his eyes.

One eyebrow lifted as he tried for jaunty. "Just dandy." He failed. He glanced out the window. "According to the standing bet, I owe you an ice cream sundae."

"Technically, you don't, because the bet was that I had to beat Erica's score, and she never ..." His jaw stiffened, and I bit my lip. Summoning a fake smile, I said, "You know what? I'll take that sundae. I'll probably owe you one after Regionals."

He studied me for a minute and then signaled a waitress. After she took our order, he drummed his fingers on the table. "How's Cory?"

"Fine—we're fine," I stuttered.

4

He nodded. He pushed a folded newspaper across the table. I didn't touch it. I didn't need to. The headline was practically shouting at me:

**Multiple Vehicle Crash Claims 4 Lives Including Olympic Equestrian**

The picture showed her truck and trailer lying on their sides, a mangled compact car wedged underneath. The words blurred as moisture tingled the corners of my eyes, but not before I picked a few out. "Horrific accident." "Tragic deaths." I squeezed my eyes shut, closing out the image, and a hot, salty tear trickled down my cheek and pooled on my lip.

Shawn leaned forward and wiped it off with the pad of his thumb. "I talked to Mark. He could barely speak. He is still devastated." Sitting back, he tapped the table with his fork. "Mark is having the rescue people disperse all the horses. He's selling the whole place."

I turned the paper over. "Oh no. Where will you go?" Plucking a sugar packet out of the little square box under the window, I shook it back and forth, staring at the tiny print. Silently repeating *Domino sugar, Domino sugar,* I fought back the sting in my eyes while I waited for his response.

He shrugged. "I moved Donner to Rainbow Ridge, Melinda's barn, for now. I don't feel much like riding."

"What about Tucker? And Mandy? How's Mandy? She hasn't answered any of my texts." I choked up thinking of the twelve-year-old without her mom.

"Mark and Mandy moved to New York City. The two of them can't stand being in that house. I guess Tucker's going with the rest of the horses. I don't know."

The waitress set our ice cream in front of us.

"I wish I could see Mandy. Maybe I'll try again. Set something up." I stabbed at the sundae absentmindedly.

"She'd like that. To see you." His gaze intensified.

I squirmed, dropping my spoon with a clatter, and then sat on my hands. To steer clear of the implications of that gaze, I blurted out the first thing that came to mind. "Did you get a letter from EMA?"

Again, the lackluster lift of one shoulder. "No, for what?"

"I thought you would have." Then I snapped my mouth shut. It struck me that he may not like the idea of me benefiting from Erica's death. I casually lifted my spoon with a little shake of my head. "Oh, nothing, actually, just congratulations and stuff."

A small smile touched his lips. "You suck at lying. What was in it?"

He always was too perceptive when it came to me. Scraping the softened ice cream from the edge of my dish, I spooned it into my mouth. "I don't get why it was me. It should have been you. This spokesperson thing. For EMA."

His eyes bored into mine, his hot gaze holding me riveted. My stomach lurched.

Without looking, I scooped deep into my sundae and shoved the spoon in my mouth. A searing pain from the cold shot into my brain. I winced, slapping a hand over my mouth and bouncing on the seat until it passed.

When I finally opened my eyes, a full-blown smile creased Shawn's face. "You're a nut." A hint of his old confidence and swagger emerged. "Good to know I can still fluster you."

"It was brain freeze from the ice cream, nothing to do with you!" I denied immediately, back to the old habit of never admitting he affected me. "Anyway, they should have asked you to replace Erica as spokesperson since you've known her longer."

Trying again to capture me with his eyes, he quirked that charming eyebrow and whispered, "I'd forgotten."

Rolling my eyes, I pretended to be unaffected. I took a tiny bit onto my spoon and licked it. "What?"

"First, how everything you do can turn me on. But, second, how goody-goody and modest you are."

I gritted my teeth. "And I forgot what a pushy idiot you are."

He laughed out loud. "But you love me."

I shot him a warning look and he continued more seriously. "Jane, you are the number one junior rider in the nation. And you are beautiful and a good person. Erica would think you are the perfect spokesperson for EMA. She would laugh if they suggested me, saying I would make bad press."

"Why would she say that? Erica loved you. You were always the best rider on the team. You just didn't ride that last class, so I won."

Tipping his head and scratching an eyebrow, he sighed. "Erica knew me well, but she saw something in you. We all did—do. Anyway, you still would have beaten me."

"I doubt it."

He threw a twenty on the table and slid out of the booth. "I know it. Anyway,

I plan on doing my best to create bad press in college. I'll see you around."

I watched him walk out and climb into his little sports car. One thing was true, he knew Erica better than I did, so when he said he thought she would like me to be the new spokesperson, I believed it.

I snapped the cap on my mascara and looked at the poster of Erica hanging on the wall beside my bureau. Santos, Erica's majestic chestnut gelding, was standing in a perfectly square halt, head up and ears pricked forward. Erica's tall, elegant frame, in her tailcoat and top hat, leaned forward as she patted his gleaming auburn neck. Her face was tipped in the direction of the camera, beaming at an unseen audience. The sheer presence of the pair radiated from the poster giving me goosebumps even after months of looking at it.

I picked up the blusher and feathered my cheeks, studying my reflection. I closed my eyes and imagined me in my show clothes and Windsong shiny in the stadium lights, saluting in the halt. It was a pretty picture, sure, but worthy of a poster? Dabbing my lips with gloss, I smiled at myself. Nope, not charismatic.

I picked up the letter from my dresser and unfolded it again.

*EMA Rescue will benefit greatly from your representation.*

It said it right there in print. They wanted me, and it would help a lot of horses.

Cory stood behind the plush, U-shaped sectional couch in the living room, hatless. I hopped off the last step onto the cold, marble floor of the foyer and swept past the antique side table, touching the white felt cowboy hat that sat on it.

My father had turned down the volume of the big screen television, arms crossed as he spoke intently to Cory. His collared shirt and dress slacks were a direct contrast to Cory's T-shirt and jeans. At least he wasn't wearing a tie, his one concession to comfort on a Saturday.

Cory ran a hand through his dark curls, making them adorably messy. "No, sir, I'll plan a visit another time."

Sir? Cory was using his manners for grown-ups. His straight, stiff shoulders and serious expression showed that he was trying to be especially impressive for my father.

"I'm ready," I announced to interrupt their conversation.

"We were just talking about you leaving for college tomorrow. Why isn't Cory coming with us?" Dad asked, hands moving to his hips.

I darted a glance at Cory. Talk about putting me on the spot. I hadn't invited Cory because college was a sore spot with him. His mother was a waitress; he didn't have the option of spending another four years in school. He had to work. "I thought he would be bored, all the checking in and unpacking."

"I can't wait to see the campus after all these years. College was one of the best times of my young life," my father reminisced. His lips tipped up, making the skin crinkle around his eyes and softening the stern lines of his face.

Wanting to change the subject quickly before he got into some story from his school days, I held up the letter. "I wanted to show you this, Dad. Maybe you can help me draft an acceptance letter? I am excited to get involved with this organization."

After reading through it, my father folded the paper in half. "You know, you won't have time for something like this. You'll be busy with extracurriculars at school. We'll turn this down."

I resisted the urge to stamp my foot and cross my arms, resisted the urge to whine like I did when I was little and wanted another piece of candy. Swallowing, I mimicked Cory's formal tone. "But it's a good cause. I really want to do it."

"Jane, I know from experience, you won't have much time for the horses once you get involved at school. Besides, this is just doing media hype. You're smarter than that. Once you have your degree, you're going to be the business owner who hires a cute girl like yourself to market it." He handed the letter back to me. "Tell them no thank you. You kids have a nice dinner." He turned and sat back down, pointing the remote at the television and increasing the volume.

Closing my mouth before a childish protest came out, I faked a smile. "Guess we're leaving." When my father was done discussing something, he was done. And no amount of whining or begging would sway him. In fact, if I tried too hard to argue, he often became more stubbornly dug in. I looked at the letter again, trying to figure out what he was thinking. Even though it was associated with horses, the letter was professional and flattering, It would only advance my riding career. Unless he thought I would make a mistake and it would damage it by giving me bad publicity. I folded the letter into a small square and shoved it in my purse. I would have to talk to him about it later.

Cory took my hand, twining his fingers around mine. Shrugging one shoulder, he tugged me into motion. "C'mon," he whispered. "I have a surprise for you."

Allowing him to distract me from my troubling thoughts, I let him guide me to his truck. He opened the door with a flourish and closed it with a grin. He got in the driver's side, turned the key, started it up, and pulled away without speaking.

Wiggling my leg through the whole slow ritual, I finally grabbed his elbow and shook it. "What's the surprise?"

"Do you mind if we skip the restaurant? I have something set up for us at our special spot on the farm."

"Something special? I don't mind at all." Warmth spread from my core, and my shoulders relaxed.

Cory patted my leg. "Let's enjoy ourselves tonight. Your dad's pretty smart, and if he doesn't think you should work for EMA, he's probably right. Let it go and let's have fun."

His complete turnaround from encouraging me earlier to agreeing with whatever my father said put a chink in my anticipation. He turned his hand up on my thigh and I put mine in it. He squeezed and I let his promising smile distract me from exploring that feeling.

CHAPTER

3

Cory lifted the two suitcases into the back of my blue SUV. "Are you sure that's all you need?" he asked, eyebrows drawn together in doubt. I glanced at the front door of the house. My mother had asked me the same thing when I carried them down the stairs. "I'll be home this weekend; if I need anything more, I'll get it then."

He reached up and closed the hatch with a solid thud. I leaned against the driver's door, my arms crossed and my gaze on my boots.

Was it too much to hope that I could slip into my assigned dorm room, shove my clothes into the closet, and brood alone on the bed? My father wanted to hike around campus, see if he ran into any old classmates, and take us to lunch at the burger joint that used to be his favorite hangout. I was supposed to be bubbling with more excitement than him. But I wasn't interested in breathless introductions and tours of the campus or exclaiming how beautiful and fun it would be.

Plus, though he never admitted it, Cory wished he was going away to college, too, and knowing that I would easily give it up when he would kill to be going made it impossible to talk to him about my feelings. I wished he was going to be there today holding my hand, but I didn't want Cory to have to hide his jealousy as we found my dorm and lecture halls. I wasn't going to put him through leaving me on campus. I would rather do the goodbye thing here.

Cory's legs appeared, standing in front of me. "Wish I was going."

"I'll be home in three days. And every weekend." I summoned a smile.

He pulled off his hat and ran fingers through his dark curls. "I know, but I'll still miss you." He put his hat back on and grabbed both of my hands, swinging them gently.

I squeezed his fingertips. "In that case, I'll stay here." I lifted my eyebrows.

"Right. Your dad would never notice." He shook his head. "College is fun, and important, you'll be glad you went."

I straightened up, slipping my arms around his waist, and pulled him between my legs. "You're right, as usual. It's only an hour and a half drive. I'll miss you too, that's all."

He pushed his hat back and gathered me close. "I'll be holding my breath until you're back." His kiss was a promise, a tease—a brand. "Three days."

The front door slammed and my father interrupted us. "Let's go, Jane," he called. "We have a long drive and I want to have plenty of time to show you everything."

Cory pulled back, straightening his hat and smoothing his shirt. "Your dad's ready to go," he stated unnecessarily.

I rolled my eyes at his discomfort.

Rubbing his morning stubble, he assumed the straight-backed distance he portrayed around my parents. Even his voice became less intimate.

Purposefully, I put my hand behind his neck and pulled him close for one more sweet kiss. His lips were stiff and he put his hands on my hips, holding me back. "Bye, baby," I whispered, watching him look over his shoulder at my parents. They were busy getting in their car and were not paying any attention to us. That didn't keep the red color from creeping up Cory's neck into his cheeks.

"I'll see you this weekend." He pressed his lips together. "Call me."

Smiling, I climbed behind the wheel, never breaking contact with those incredible eyes as I started the car and waited for my father to back out of the driveway. Cory's truck appeared in my rearview mirror, and with one last wave, we turned in opposite directions at the end of the street.

An hour and a half later, I joined the queue of cars behind my parents' SUV at the entrance to campus. Inching forward, I started to roll down the window so I could show the attendant the postcard with my dorm assignment, but my dad's arm came out the window, pointing ahead. The attendant waved me through.

Dad parked in the lot but told me to take my car in front of the building to unload.

Eyeing the volume of double-parked vehicles up by the dorm, I pulled in next to his car. "I have only two suitcases, Dad. We can carry them in."

A line of kids were waiting at the sign-in table. It reminded me of the secretary's stand at a horse show, except the volunteers were handing out room keys instead of show envelopes. The bright chatter and tentative greetings bounced over me. I was wishing for wooden fences and sand arenas instead of brick walls and glass windows.

Mom elbowed me. "Be friendly. Say hi. One of these kids might be your roommate," she whispered, short blond bob bouncing with enthusiasm. She grinned at a haggard mother balancing a crate of odds and ends; bulging bags hanging from her shoulders. Oblivious of her crisp skirt set and heels, my mother held out a perfectly manicured hand. "Can I take something?"

The woman smiled broadly, shaking her head in response to my mother's offer to help. "I think she brought everything from her room at home. But her brothers are here to help. Thanks."

I handed my new ID to the student volunteer with the clipboard.

"Jane Mitchell. Oh, we just checked in your roommate," the smiling girl said as she handed me back my card and a key chain with two keys on it.

"Great," with a meager smile, I took the keys.

"She seemed nice," the girl reassured me, misinterpreting my lack of enthusiasm. "Don't worry."

Dad carried my suitcases down the hall, greeting anyone who looked his way. The door to the small cinder-block-lined room bearing the number that matched my key was open. Bodies blocked the opening, so I stood outside, reluctant to draw attention to myself.

"Hello," my father boomed from behind me.

All the bodies turned at once.

"Ooh, sorry. Do you need to come in here?" A tall, broad-shouldered man stepped to the side. "Carly, I think your roommate is here."

A squeal sounded from the other side of the wall of people. "Oh my God! Move Gabe. Let her in. There are way too many people in this room."

Amazingly, the crowd parted and a tiny dark-haired girl came hustling through. The grin on her face was filled with joy and excitement. Almost more than I could have handled at the moment. A spear of nerves pinned me to the spot, my mind blank. I gave a shaky little wave.

Carly kept coming, nothing shy about her. She didn't hesitate but put her arms around me. "I'm Carly. You, of course, are Jane. We are going to be such great friends and have the best time ever!" Her voice went up in a little scream.

I patted her back awkwardly, nodding wordlessly.

"Carly, let the girl in so we can all meet her." The woman from the lobby with the overloaded arms grinned at me as she gently pushed the four tall men to the side. "I am Mrs. Diamond, Carly's mom." She also didn't hesitate but pulled me in for a hug.

She gave a screech when she saw my mother, and they hugged like old friends. Carly took my arm. "This is my dad, Mr. Diamond." She used a teasing, falsely formal tone.

A sweet-looking man threw an arm around her shoulders as he held out his hand to my father, who towered over him by a good six inches. His soft hazel eyes crinkled and he patted my shoulder. "So nice to meet you, Jane."

Carly kissed his cheek affectionately and pointed to the three tall young men huddled in the corner. "And my three brothers, Gabe and Nat and Chuck."

They were all big and in their late twenties. "Hello." "Nice to meet you." "Hi." I looked at Carly's parents, both shorter than me, and wondered where her brothers got all that height.

Dad dropped my cases next to the empty bed, since the other one was overflowing with clothes and bags. He shook hands with the boys, announcing that he had lived in a room just down the hall when he attended.

As he described his room and bragged that his roommate became a Fortune 500 CEO, Carly spoke softly to me, "Do you have more stuff? My brothers can help you unload."

"No, that's all I have."

Carly grinned at me. "I think I brought everything from my room at home."

I stared at the giant mound on and around her bed, and then looked at my two bags. "I couldn't figure out what to bring."

She put her hand on my arm, instantly making me feel warm and comfortable. "We'll figure it out."

"Thanks. We can make a list and I could get it this weekend when I go home to ride my horse."

"A horse? I love horses! I don't ride or anything. I love all animals. I'm going to be a vet. What's your major?" She spoke with calm certainty, and despite the fashionable clothes and painted nails, I didn't doubt that she would do it.

With a sigh and a shrug, my response was not anywhere near that confident. "Business."

Dad clapped his hands. "Who wants to take a tour? If it hasn't changed too much, I should be able to point out all the hot spots. And some of the academic buildings, too." He chuckled.

Carly's mom smiled politely. "We better stay here and help Carly put her things away so the girls will have someplace to sit and sleep tonight. Thanks though, and have a good walk."

The campus was beautiful, all rolling green hills and shaded paths between brick and glass buildings. Not much had changed, according to my father.

He groaned. "There's the math building, none of us liked getting up early on Monday mornings for Statistics there. After freshman year, we did our best to schedule as many classes as possible later in the day." He laughed. "Despite the early hour, my classmates hated me, because I kept breaking the curve and acing the exams. What can I say? I'm a math whiz. You'll probably do the same thing, Jane. You're great in math." He rambled on, describing his favorite memories as we walked.

It did sound like he had fun. I couldn't summon up any enthusiasm for it, though. When I was walking along the lovely path, down the steep incline and past the pond with four geese floating on it, would I be missing Cory? And as I sat in the two-story brick building on a hard plastic seat with a smooth, cool desk to rest my elbows on, would I be wishing I was riding a canter half pass? Would Windsong pace the fence, wondering where I was and when he was going to get his treats? But, hey, I would be getting smarter, right?

I followed my parents across a parking lot, calculating the hours until I was back home.

My belly full of french fries and a burger, I kissed my parents and waved as they drove out of the parking lot. I stood for a moment watching the sun sink behind the math building, turning the red brick to bright orange. The crush of cars was gone and there weren't as many parents around. I used my key for the first time to let myself into the dorm.

My room door was open and Carly was kneeling on her bed, taping posters of puppies and kittens to the wall. Her family was gone, but two girls perched on the edge of my bare bed.

"Hey," she said as I closed the door behind me. "This is Linda and Colleen. They are two doors down that way."

"Hi, Jane."

I finger waved. I put my suitcase up on the bed and unzipped it. "Your side looks great, Carly."

It did. Her bedspread, the posters, and some extra furniture made it look like a real bedroom. I tugged out my sheets, and the picture frames I had tucked in between the folds fell onto the bed.

Linda scooped one up. "Wow, is this guy real? He looks like the model that comes with the frame."

I took it back from her, setting it on the table close to where my head would lay so I could wake up and see it. "That's my boyfriend, Cory."

"Seriously? He is hot." Colleen picked the photo up and handed it to Carly.

Carly studied it for a few moments. "Now I know why you want to go right back home. Me, I'm staying for all the weekend parties."

As I took out the next one, she held out her hand to exchange pictures. "And who is this one?"

I smiled. "That's my other boyfriend, Windsong."

Her eyes met mine. "How could you ever leave two gorgeous guys like these?"

I shrugged, and then mimicking my father's deep voice, I expounded, "Getting an education is the most important thing you can do, Jane." They giggled but didn't disagree. Then I unfolded my poster. "Can I borrow your tape?"

As I fastened it to the painted cinder block wall, Carly said, "That's Erica Flame. Isn't it just horrible what happened to her?"

Linda nodded. "It was all over the news. I really thought she was going to the next Olympics. What was her horse's name?"

Smoothing tape over the last corner of the poster, I pictured the giant, regal head as he took a treat from my hand. "Santos."

"Right. Did he die in the accident too? I don't remember them saying."

The newspaper photo with the trailer lying on its side flashed into my mind and my breath caught in my throat. No one ever said it, but Santos must have been severely injured when the trailer flipped. The poor thing. I touched the lightning blaze on the poster and then turned and sank down on to the bed.

I would have still been training with Erica if there hadn't been an accident. Her support and encouragement made me believe I could achieve my dream of becoming a top dressage rider like her. And now, I faltered at every decision I had to make—from answering EMA to whether I should ride Windsong on a ten-meter circle or across the diagonal. That sounded dramatic and I knew it, but the heavy feeling in my brain took more strength to lift than I had right now. I felt like a freak, an alien among these kids, with their excitement during this brand-new adventure. I wished I was home, getting ready to go to the barn, to Windsong. My lips curved down.

"Jane." Carly stopped unrolling posters to look at me. "Are you okay? What is it?"

I wanted my voice to sound normal, but it hitched as I tried to answer. "I trained with Erica over the summer. She was going to teach me to be as good as she was. I still want to be just like her, but I don't know how I will without her." I stared at my sneakers, doing a decent job of controlling my quivering lips. Blinking rapidly, I raised my chin to wave off the grief, but the exaggerated sympathy on their faces made me crumple into my pillow. "I'll be okay in a minute," I mumbled. I had to be, and I had to find a way to do it on my own, because Regionals were just four weeks away.

Linda rubbed my back. "Girl, what you need is a distraction. The boys down the hall told me where there's a party tonight. Let's go."

CHAPTER

4

My phone buzzed itself right off the front seat of my car and landed with a thud on the floor. I considered leaning over and trying to get it, but that seemed like a bad idea at sixty miles an hour on the highway. It was probably just Carly. I admitted to myself that she had made the first three days of college interesting, even if they seemed like the longest three days in history. If she hadn't dragged me to every planned freshman orientation event, I would have stayed by myself in our dorm room. But she was a ball of fire, and now I knew where every building on campus was and which clubs to join, and we had hit almost every party that would let freshmen in. Carly even had a crush already; granted the guy was a drunk junior lacrosse player who had flirted with every girl who walked near him and who next week wouldn't remember meeting us.

I was supposed to have left the night before, but Carly wouldn't hear of me missing the Friday night parties. Bad enough, she said, that I was going to miss Saturday night. I was running on four hours of sleep, and I had skipped breakfast at the dining hall to get a good start home. I did stop for a large cappuccino. I reached for a sip, savoring the yummy goodness of the hot drink.

Sliding the cup back into the holder, I turned up the radio, smiling to myself. I was going straight to the barn to ride Windsong before heading home for dinner with my parents. Cory was the first thing on my priority list, though. I pressed my foot on the accelerator, flicking on my blinker and switching to the fast lane. I was looking forward to getting home, getting back to him.

When I pulled off the highway onto the familiar roads of my town, the butterflies that lived in my stomach woke up and started to flutter around. My ears burned, and electricity danced through my veins. I was getting closer to Cory and it was a good thing I knew the way by heart, because my mind stopped thinking of anything but his blue eyes, his strong arms, and …

A blaring horn shrilled in front of me. I jumped in my seat, wrenching the wheel to the right, swerving the car back over to my side of the yellow line. Opening my mouth, I sucked in deep breaths. Taillights of the car I had nearly hit glinted in the rearview mirror. My heart still pounded as I reached to turn down the radio. Wow! I needed to keep my eyes on the road and my mind on what I was doing.

I turned into the farm driveway and cruised slowly past the pastures, bumping gently over ruts until I got to the dirt area by the barn. After I shoved the gearshift to park, my phone started buzzing and ringing so I unclipped my seat belt. I dove headfirst toward the furthest corner of the floor where the phone was wedged under the dash, my rear end up in the air as I scrabbled to grab the vibrating thing before it stopped ringing.

So this was the first view Cory got of me in three days. He grabbed my hips and pulled me out of the car and against his chest. "Darling."

Dropping the phone with a screech, I twisted in his arms and kissed him, smacking my forehead into his hat. All the butterflies, all the electric sizzles, and all the buzzing in my brain calmed under his touch. I sank into his warmth, feeling like I was in the right place for the first time in nearly a week.

After a moment, he pulled back and kissed my forehead. "I couldn't think of anything else but you all morning."

I squeezed his waist. "Me neither."

His gaze roamed over my face and body and then locked onto my eyes. Mischief danced across his lips as he lifted my hand and laid it on his chest. He whispered, "You still do this to my heart."

The strong, rapid beat pulsed against my palm, and I hated college all over again.

"Let's take lunch up on the hill in our favorite spot," I suggested, needing him all to myself.

"You bet." Just as he released me, my phone started buzzing and jumping all over again. I grabbed it and swiped, ready to tell Carly to get her own love life. "Hey, girl."

"It's me, Shawn. Hi, Jane."

I darted a look at Cory and turned my back to him. "Hi?"

"Where are you? I've been trying to get you all day."

I bristled at his impatient tone. What was he, my father? "None of your business. Why?"

"Mark and Mandy are meeting me for dinner and you need to come, too."

I put a hand on the car roof and pressed my lips together. Part of me wanted to see Mandy, but a bigger part of me wanted to avoid the whole difficult thing. I blew out a noisy sigh. "I'm at home. It would be a two-hour drive."

"It's not until six o'clock. You can make it."

"I just got here." I could hear the whine in my voice, and, glancing at Cory, I shook my head at his concerned look.

"Jane, I need you to come. I'm not sure I can handle it by myself. Please." He said the word softly, but it squeezed my chest. He sounded so different from when we stayed with Erica. Where was the guy who didn't take anything too seriously? That guy would have demanded with cocky confidence that I drive to him, joking away my protests.

I swallowed, closing my eyes as I said, "Okay. I'll come."

"Just you, Jane. I can't deal with you *and* Cory tonight."

"Okay." I hung up after he gave me the details.

"Where do you have to go?" Cory stood, arms crossed, face tight.

I couldn't meet his eyes, so I busied myself taking the fast-food bag out of the passenger seat. "That was Shawn. Mark has invited Shawn and I to dinner. I have to go. I need to see Mandy," I quickly added as his eyes narrowed.

"Fine. I'll drive. What time?"

I couldn't help tucking a strand of hair behind my ear and biting a fingernail. "Just me. Mark said."

Cory lifted his hat, combed his fingers through his hair, and placed the hat back on. His eyes were angry, but he didn't say anything.

"I still have time for a quick lunch." I slid my arms around him again.

"Lucky me," he mumbled and took the bag of food, pulling out of my arms. "Let's eat."

As I drove to the restaurant, I considered calling Cory and asking him to come despite Shawn's specific request to not invite him. This was not going to be a great time, and I wanted Cory's naturally charming personality to make things go smoothly. But then I thought about the last time Shawn, Cory, and I were together and ditched the idea as stupid. With all of our emotions so close to the surface right now, I could just imagine Cory and Shawn having a fist fight and getting us all thrown out of the restaurant.

Mental head slap. The only way to escape this situation would be to turn around and head right back home. But I couldn't do that to Shawn. I had already treated him badly enough by choosing Cory over him. I couldn't turn down his request for help without a major case of the guilts. I had plenty to feel guilty about, so I resolved to make it through one not-so-great dinner. And maybe Mandy would feel better after seeing Shawn and me. The three of us had had such a good time hanging out together before the Junior Rider Championships at the beginning of the summer.

Blowing out a huge breath, I braced myself, smoothing my hair with one hand and clearing my mind of gloomy thoughts. I would be positive and chipper and keep everyone talking of the good times. Then it would be over, I'd give everyone a tight squeeze, and zoom right back to Cory's arms.

I should have gotten credit for good intentions. I slid into the chair Shawn held for me. Across the table, Mark's crisp button-down and tailored business suit were in sharp contrast to his unkempt hair and pale, haggard complexion. His grief reached out like a hand, pressing down on my shoulders. Keeping a smile—or at least the corners of my lips tipped up—I unfolded the cloth napkin on my lap.

Shawn shook Mark's hand and then sat down next to me. "Hey, Mandy," he said softly, never quite looking at her. I looked. Her golden blond hair was dull and hung limply around her round face. Her gaze was riveted on the menu, and she didn't respond to anyone, not even the waitress who asked for her drink order.

"She'll have a lemonade," Mark said automatically.

After the bustle of ordering drinks and choosing dinners, I tried to draw Mandy out. "So, Mandy, is the city exciting compared to living on a horse farm?"

Her head lifted slowly and hazel eyes laced with wrath pierced mine.

I was so unprepared for the pure anger that radiated from her that I lapsed into stunned silence, staring at her face with my mouth hanging open. Where was the vivacious little girl that scolded her pony for dumping her and then proceeded to mount back up and win the class? Where was the coy flirt who had an adorable crush on Shawn?

With a noisy swallow, I glanced at Shawn, but he was pretending to read the drink specials card and refused to return my look. The waitress set my freshly squeezed lemonade in front of me, and I took a fortifying gulp, coughing and sputtering as the icy fluid tickled my throat and dripped into my lungs.

Shawn seemed relieved to have something to do and pounded my back for all he was worth. I held up a hand to get him to stop and sucked air through my mouth until my throat warmed up and my air passage cleared. I had to stop using cold substances to cover my anxiety.

"Excuse me." The waitress stood behind me, a plate of salad in each hand. "Are you ready for this?"

I almost said no, I wasn't ready to handle this tension, but then I realized she meant the salad. I nodded.

Once we settled into eating, no one spoke, no one looked at each other, and no one tried to ease the situation with words. The silence built like cars piling into a traffic jam at rush hour. I squirmed in my seat, anxious to accelerate the conversation.

"My horse Windsong is doing really well this fall show season. Mandy, how are you doing with your riding?" I cautiously asked, stupidly forgetting that horses don't live in New York City.

"I don't ride anymore," she bit out.

I winced at her curt tone. I couldn't tell whether she meant by choice or by circumstance. Not wanting to push the issue, I turned to Shawn. "How's Donner?"

Shawn darted a guilty look at Mark. "I haven't been riding, either."

I pushed back, my fork clattering against the ceramic plate. "Why not? Regionals are coming up, and you have to prepare."

His eyes narrowed and his jaw clenched. "I haven't felt like training," he said stiffly without moving his lips, rolling his eyes toward Mark.

I glanced at Mark, who was intently moving lettuce around on his plate. It didn't look like he was listening, but I didn't pursue that subject.

The silence was broken next by the sound of the ketchup bottle as Mandy drowned her fries. The tension was thick enough to cut with the knife I was using to cut up my meat. I wished someone would just say something, anything. I scrabbled for another subject to fill the void, and I thought of the letter from EMA. Mark was a board member for the charity, and it occurred to me that he may have suggested or agreed to the idea of me as representative.

"Mark, I received the letter from EMA asking me to be the new spokesperson for the rescue. Thanks for thinking of me."

Mark set his fork down. His brow wrinkled as he made an effort to return his thoughts from wherever his mind had been to the table. "EMA? What letter?"

"They asked me to represent them in their advertising campaigns. Me and Windsong. Posters, appearances, interviews."

Mark rubbed his forehead. "I haven't been paying attention to much with the rescue lately. Erica usually was the one who did the posters and appearances."

Mandy's glare burned a hole in my forehead. "They can just use the posters with my mother and Lucky. Everyone knows those posters." Mandy turned to her dad. "*She*," she said with a condescending tilt of her head toward me, "shouldn't be on the posters. It should be Mom, right? It was Mom's rescue."

Erica had named the rescue organization EMA, which stood for Erica, Mark, Amanda, her family. She had built it up from a local nonprofit to a renowned, national one.

"Erica really loved that rescue." Mark's voice broke. He reached for his mug of beer and took a big swallow.

"That's why they should use the posters with Mom. Right, Dad?" Mandy was clearly voting no for my taking the position.

Mark shrugged. "I don't know."

As Mark struggled to regain his composure, Shawn stared down at his plate.

Apparently, no subject was safe. I tried to put the question to rest. "My father doesn't want me to say yes, either. He says it would be too difficult since I'm starting college. Don't worry, I'll refuse the position. How's your chicken, Mandy?"

More glaring and no answering. I concentrated on my plate and didn't open my mouth until the waitress asked if we wanted dessert. Violently shaking my head, I rose. "I have a long drive. It was good to see you all," I lied.

As I walked to my car, my shoulders sagged. That dinner didn't do any one of us any good. The hurt was too raw, and we all just reminded each other of who was missing. I dug through my purse for my elusive keys and then shook it in frustration. They always disappeared into the murky depths of the darn thing. I threw it on the ground. My keys spilled out, along with sunglasses, lip balm, and loose change. I stooped to scoop it all back in and jumped at Shawn's voice.

"I had a lovely time in there. We should do it again soon. Not!"

I grabbed the keys and twisted up to my feet. "I miss you all so much, but we can't even manage to be together for one dinner. What happened to how close we were? We should be able to comfort each other. But I couldn't manage to say one thing right tonight."

Shawn took my keys and unlocked the car door for me. He rubbed my shoulders. "It's not your fault. It's not anyone's fault. Things are just different now. We can't go back."

"No." I sank into the driver's seat and started the car. "But forward isn't looking that great either."

"I hear you." He kissed my cheek and closed the door.

CHAPTER

5

Lifting my cheeks to the sun, I closed my eyes and savored that sweaty horse smell. I leaned forward and ran my hand through Windsong's silky, short mane, digging my fingers into the firm muscles of his arched, elegant neck. He cocked his delicately chiseled head back, enjoying the caress. His jet black ears flicked back and forth between me and the scary world. A horse can enjoy being rubbed and still keep an eye out for danger.

I sniffed at my shirt, wondering if Windsong thought the smell of sweaty human was pleasant. He liked the taste of my salty skin because he licked it all the time, so maybe he did.

Windsong's ribs lifted my legs gently, and I admitted to myself that touching him was all the therapy I needed after the stress of that awful dinner. I rubbed his velvety coat, the damp warmth welcome on my palm. This was what it was all about. A good, honest workout on my horse, focusing on the figures and making my muscles quiver with effort. After a deep, cleansing breath, I sat up, ready to pick up the reins and end our walk break.

My brow creased. Windsong's ribs were still pushing against my legs and his head drooped at the end of his long neck. I tugged the rein and tilted his face to the side so I could see his nostril. Yep, it was still flaring widely. Was he tired already? I had only been riding a few minutes. Granted, they were a glorious few minutes.

I pulled the phone out of my pocket and clicked it on. Twenty-two minutes had passed since we had entered the arena. This was our second walk break.

Was it possible that I had been working him too hard? Panic skittered through my veins. How could I know what was too much? I pressed my lips together.

Windsong's head flew up. Loud snorts erupted from his nose. Next thing I knew, we were dashing sideways and I was fighting to stop his flight. As I gained control, I stared into the distance, trying to find what Windsong had thought threatened his safety. Nothing, nothing that my naked eye could see. But Windsong continued to prance and yank at the bridle, bouncing up and down with his head almost higher than mine.

"Was I boring you, worrying about your health? Are you too macho to admit you might be tired, lunatic?" I crooned affectionately as I pushed him into a trot. Asking for some circles and figure eights, I firmly made him behave. As soon as he was listening, I jumped off. Although I didn't want to quit after a silly spook, I also didn't want to push him too hard. The cardiac veterinarian had said we could continue to train, but no one knew how much Windsong's damaged heart valve could take.

As I was about to lead Windsong to the hose, Cory's long, lean silhouette appeared at the other end of the barn aisle. When he caught up to us, his blue eyes twinkled as Windsong nuzzled his flat stomach.

"Looks like you had quite the workout, big guy," Cory drawled. He took the lead rope from my hand to hold Windsong still while I sprayed the water over his sweaty body. Windsong lifted his skinny legs, dancing away from the tickly drips, not looking tired or droopy at all. Maybe I hadn't given him enough of a workout after all.

Sighing, I turned off the spigot. "Cory, I'm constantly worrying about overworking Windsong. Sometimes it overshadows everything I do with him."

"You can't make yourself crazy."

"But he's so goofy. What if I can't tell when too much is too much?"

"You *will* know. Give your paranoia a rest."

Was I being overly paranoid? My phone buzzed, so I dried my hands on my pants and answered it. The voice on the other end made me stop moving.

"Jane? It's Michelle. Did you get the letter I sent you from EMA?" Michelle had been Erica's groom. She had gone with us to the Junior Rider Championships to help Shawn and me with our horses.

"Are you the one that sent it?"

"Yeah, it was me. I am the director here now that Erica is," she hesitated, and then finished lamely, "not."

"With college starting, I haven't had much time to think about the offer," I lied.

"I'm in your area tomorrow. Let me take you to lunch so we can talk about it. The board is anxious for a response, and I told them I would meet with you."

"Michelle, I'm sorry, but I can't do it. My father is against it. I talked to Mark about it. Mandy and he hated the idea. I have to say no. I am honored that you asked me, though. Thank—"

She cut me off. "We really think you would be great for us. Please, let me take you to lunch and explain."

My instinct was to help, like I did when Erica had asked me to do things. But really, my face on posters, speaking on commercials, and being adored by the public—I couldn't see the reality of it. Maybe after I graduated and had a few professional dressage titles under my belt, but right now, I was still a nobody. My father might be right about not having time for it. And I didn't want to see that look of horror on Mandy's face ever again. The right thing to do was to say no.

"Michelle, I don't want to waste your time. I have to focus on school, and I just don't feel that it is the right thing for me at this time."

"Nothing I can say will change your mind?" Her tone matched that of the letter, cajoling and hopeful.

I pinched the bridge of my nose. "No, I'm sorry. But you can call me to help out on a rescue any time."

A loud whistling breath hissed through the phone's speaker, and I held it away from my ear. "Fine. I was so excited about the idea, but I guess college is important, too. Okay, I'll talk to you soon."

I pressed end and stared at the screen. Cory came back from turning Windsong out. "Bad news?"

"Not for me. I just told Michelle I wouldn't take the spokesperson position. She was really disappointed."

"She'll get over it. Let's head to your house. Remember, your mom told us to be there for dinner by five."

Michelle would get over it and find another representative because that was her job. Me, on the other hand, I had just closed the door on my dream job. I was making a mature decision, for my future, right? Then why was I dreading going back to school, and why did I want to call Michelle right back and say yes?

I inhaled the smell of the perfectly cooked roast and creamy mashed potatoes, heaping a third helping onto my plate. That was another reason to hate college, the lousy food.

My mother's mouth fell open. "You're eating like a football player. Don't you eat well at school?"

My father laughed. "I remember the dining hall food, so I don't blame you, baby. Load up because you may not see a home-cooked meal again for weeks."

I scooped up a forkful of mashed potatoes. "One week, anyway. I'll be home next week to ride."

My father rubbed his chin. "This is your future, Jane. You had your fun with the horses, now you need to focus on your education. Your college degree will ensure you get a good job, be successful. I don't want you coming home every weekend. Once a month should be enough. Heck, I stayed until they kicked us out for Thanksgiving."

"But, Dad, you don't understand. I have to ride Windsong. Regionals are coming up and—"

He cut me off, slapping his hand on the table. "I am talking about your real life, your career. I played sports, too. Do you think I became CEO of a global company by worrying about my game scores? Get your mind off the horse and into your books, like it's supposed to be."

I froze with my fork halfway to my mouth. "What?"

His voice softened. "It's time to put the riding aside. Schedule your training for around the holidays. It's only four years, and then you can ride all you want when you have a real job. No homework then, you know?"

"Jane, I agree with your father," my mother chimed in, using her best lawyer voice. "It's time to put the horses aside and concentrate on your studies. This is important, for your future."

Slowly, I lowered my fork to the plate. I heard their words but they weren't making any sense. "Are you saying stop riding for four years?" Give up the time I needed with Windsong? Kate and I already had a plan for Regionals, and we had sent my entries in. I was going.

"Not give it up, but stop showing so much. There are a lot of things in college that you may find you like just as much. You won't know unless you try them out. I want you to cut back on the horse stuff and explore some other school activities."

I looked back and forth between my parents, Were they serious? "I'm not interested in other activities. *Riding* is my sport. Besides, I spoke to Michelle from EMA Rescue, like you told me to. I said that I couldn't take the spokesperson position because of school. So, I gave that up. How can I give up riding, too?" I pushed my plate back, the aroma not smelling so good anymore.

My father was nodding approval. "Good girl. You did the right thing. Pass the salad, please." He took the bowl that I handed him.

I kicked Cory under the table. "Help me. Say something," I mouthed silently. He gave a tiny shake of his head, unwilling to challenge my father.

As he picked through the greens, my father went on, oblivious to the effect his words were having. "That's a start, Jane. Cut back on the riding. Stay at school for the next few weekends, get involved. You won't regret it. College is your chance to make connections that could last the rest of your life."

Was that an order or a suggestion? I studied his stern face for a clue. None of this was making sense to me. My father had encouraged my riding and showing throughout high school; now, it seemed that all of a sudden, they were telling me to stop.

He arched his brows. "I'm being a protective, loving, caring, thinking-of-your-future parent, and you're my beautiful, precious, supersmart, ambitious daughter, who has unlimited potential that I don't want her to waste in a barn." His eyes crinkled as he used our favorite pastime of listing as many descriptive adjectives as we could think of to persuade the other in an argument.

Pressing my lips together, I relented, more for the peace of our meal than because I agreed. I rose and took my full plate and Cory's scraped-clean one to the kitchen.

Cory helped me carry the boxes I had packed and load them in my car. I nodded silently when he asked if we had everything.

Mom hugged me tight, even though my arms hung limply at my side, and said, "I'll miss you, but call me. I put money in your purse and paid your credit card bill. Let me know if you need more, okay?"

"Drive safe." Dad gave me a squeeze and then shook Cory's hand.

I glared at Cory for being so polite, but he didn't get it. When they went inside, I turned to him.

Cory slid an arm around my shoulders. "I guess there are some road trips in my future because I don't think I can wait a month to see you."

"You won't have to. In fact, this is your lucky day. I'm coming home with you tonight."

His eyebrows lifted and his arm dropped off my back at my sharp tone. "What?"

Pulling him to me by the belt buckle, I tilted my chin up. "Pretend you're kissing me goodbye, and then climb in your truck. I'll follow you home. We need to talk. I can go back to school tomorrow."

He threw a look toward the house, holding his head up so my lips couldn't reach his. "That's lying and that's not right."

"Are you saying I'm not welcome at your house?"

His hands covered my tank top and warmed my ribs. "'Trailer,' and you're always welcome, but I don't think I could lie to your father."

"It's not lying. I'm an adult and so are you. What's the difference between sleeping on your couch or sleeping in my dorm room?"

"Nothing, I guess. I'll be the one on the couch, though."

"It will be perfect. I'll go to the barn early in the morning, ride Windsong, and then make it to school for my classes." My last class of the day, anyway. I'd get the Statistics notes from Carly. No problem.

# 6

Cory set a glass of iced tea in front of me on the small, wobbly kitchen table in his tiny trailer. I slid my fingers up and down, smearing the moisture droplets on the clear glass. "Why didn't you speak up at dinner tonight? You know how seriously I take my riding. My dad might have listened to you."

Cory folded his long legs under the table as he sat, but his knees still banged into mine. "Right, like he would listen to someone who works in a barn. Your dad is really smart. He knows what he's talking about. He's done it all."

I bumped my leg against his. "He hasn't done everything. He's never won a World Reining Championship like you did. You could have told him how that improved your character and your life."

His stony glare had me biting my tongue. "Well, mostly improved your life, if we don't count losing Jet." I reached across the table and took his hand.

He turned it up, curling his fingers around mine. "Sometimes I think that was the worst thing that happened to me because, if I never went to France, things might have worked out completely different."

I sighed. "Different, but not better. You have a title and a reputation that people know about and that establishes you as a trainer. You have a credential."

He pressed his lips together. "But a college degree is your ticket to anything you want. Only horse people think mine is important. You should at least think about what your father said. Try out some activities at school."

"Maybe. But I'm not going to stop riding. I have to prepare for Regionals."

My pen scratched across the paper, and I listened closely to the professor, but what he said made no sense. Since skipping Monday's class, I hadn't had a chance to copy the notes from Carly. And not having done any of the reading either, I was completely lost.

I kept writing down everything the monotonous bearded guy rambled on about. My notebook page was full, crammed with partial phrases and extra jottings in the margins. I looked over at Carly's.

Neat bullet lists were printed in her very legible handwriting. She was going to have to take lessons from me in scribble scrabble if she expected to have any credibility as a veterinarian. Her writing was just too perfect. I glanced at my chicken scratch again and decided to just copy her notes from this lecture as well.

Relieved of the responsibility of taking notes, my mind wandered back to the farm. Right after this class, to Carly's disappointment, I was heading straight to the barn to ride Windsong. Cory didn't know it yet, but I was staying at his house again this weekend.

My stomach grumbled. Carly giggled, causing me to laugh, too, and my stomach groaned louder as it shook. Definitely a stop at the coffeehouse on my way off campus was in order.

In no time at all, I was on the highway, sipping a warm cappuccino and munching a zesty panini.

My cell rang, and I poked speaker phone. "Hi, Mom."

"How are you, sweetie? I just wanted to make sure you were okay on funds."

"Fine. I don't have to pay for food, you know? The dining hall is free."

"Not really free since the cost is included in your tuition, but I'm just used to worrying about you. Are you going out with friends tonight? Just remember to do some studying this weekend."

"I will, absolutely." I swerved around a pothole and the car in the lane beside me beeped. Really? I threw the driver a dirty look; I had barely crossed the white line.

"Where are you? It sounds like you're driving."

Was that a suspicious tone? I couldn't tell her I was on the way to the barn. "The mall." I blurted out and then winced. I just told her I didn't need any money. "I'm picking up underwear. And socks. I need a pair, a couple pair."

I bit my lip hard, but she answered trustingly. "Okay, I won't keep you on the line if you're driving. Be careful and have a good weekend."

I slumped in the seat. I was not a good liar. It would be best to avoid conversations unless I had a better story prepared.

One, two, three, four, skip, a flying change. One, two, three, four, change back the other way. Kate barely moved in the saddle, making it look easy when she rode the canter zigzag on Windsong. He lifted his front end as he moved from right to left and back again with a lightness that was breathtaking.

Since I was the one riding him most of the time, I forgot how mesmerizing watching him could be. His long, dainty legs powering him across the ground with graceful, ground-covering strides. His body elastically bending at the change of direction, his muscles rippling under his smooth, sleek black coat. I couldn't take my eyes off of him, and I wanted to tell Kate to keep going.

She halted, though, and slid down his side, her feet dangling for a split second before she landed solidly in the glistening sand of the outdoor arena. She unbuckled my helmet and handed it back to me, shaking out her blond ponytail. "You have to give much more on that dominant right rein when you do the flying change back to the left-lead canter," she instructed me.

I stamped my foot. "I hate my right hand." I held it up in front of my face and spoke to it as if it were a separate being. "Right Hand, why can't you stop trying to take over everything? Calm down and listen to what I say."

Kate smirked.

I brought Windsong to the mounting block, not wanting to twist his back by hauling myself up from the ground. I lifted the leather stirrup straps and lowered the stirrups three holes from where Kate had them buckled for her shorter legs.

I signaled the canter and guided Windsong along the rail. Turning down the quarterline of the arena, I recited the count in my head, except instead of saying *Turn my shoulders*, I said, *Release my right hand.*

My hips and seat rocked along with Windsong's smooth, collected canter, but I kept my shoulders back and slightly rotated to the side. With the lightest touch of my calf, Windsong bounded sideways. I could feel his quicker response as a result of Kate's gentle but firm corrections. I told myself to relax another degree, trust his response.

I purposefully moved my right fist forward a quarter of an inch toward

Windsong's ears, cocked my shoulders back to the left, and asked for the flying change with my leg. Windsong effortlessly skipped to the left lead and took four strides to the side. Really concentrating, I turned my shoulders, adjusted my hands, and we skipped to the right. I grinned.

One more time and then, whooping, I turned back onto the rail of the arena and let Windsong speed up. I slowed him before he reached the next corner and brought him back to the walk.

"It took all my concentration, but I see what you mean. I will really, really work on that," I told Kate as I leaned forward, patting the horse's neck. Windsong shook his head and walked energetically.

I watched his nostrils as we turned the corners, making sure he quickly recovered his breath. He seemed fine, but I figured we should end our lesson on that great note.

"You rode well today. The canter zigzag is coming along," Kate said from behind her desk in the indoor arena office.

I chewed and swallowed, setting my sandwich down on my lap, before answering. "Thank you. I felt like I understood what you were telling me with my head, but now I have to practice making my right hand understand."

"You will, I'm sure of it. By the way, I received confirmation that your entry for Regionals was received. I was thinking that you should declare your intention to ride at the U.S. Dressage Finals in Kentucky." She grinned, sliding her eyebrows up. Her casual tone didn't match the excitement glittering in her eyes.

Tucking half-chewed turkey in the side of my cheek, I leaned toward her. "Only the top five can be nominated to go, and I'm showing in a whole new division, Intermediate I, which is two levels above the level I rode at the Junior Championships in July. I've only performed this freestyle two times."

"Yes, and you scored really well at the two qualifying shows. And didn't I just say you had improved? We have a whole month to keep working it out."

"But this level is so much harder, and it's an open class, not for juniors. Can I score in the top five in the open classes? I think not."

"I think so. Besides, declaring doesn't cost anything and you don't have to go. But if you don't declare ahead of time, you can't go even if you win the division. It's one form. We'll fill it out today and send it." She tossed a sheet of paper across her desk.

My father wouldn't like this, I thought as I picked up a pen and started filling in the blanks. The chances of me beating the likes of Robert Peterson, a multiple Olympic medal winner, or another professional were slim, so it wouldn't hurt to send in the declaration. It was just paperwork.

I paused. "We're having another lesson tomorrow, right?"

Kate laughed. "Absolutely."

The increased difficulty of this new level and the fact that seasoned professional riders would be competing against me made my chances of placing in the top five pretty slim. But the competitor in me wouldn't sit back and accept the current odds. As Kate had said, we still had a whole month to train, and I was going to use that time to maximize any chance that I might have.

Chewing my fingernail, I pushed my father's words way into the back of my mind and considered my schedule. "I can come home right after class on Fridays and leave for school after I ride on Monday mornings, so that will give me four rides per week, including Saturdays and Sundays. Can you ride him once in the middle of the week?"

With a nod, Kate raised her plastic water bottle. "Absolutely."

"With that schedule, Windsong and I will be so prepared, those pros won't know what hit them." Grinning, I signed the bottom of the form with a flourish.

# CHAPTER

# 7

Kate sure knew how to motivate me. It was still dark as I led a blinking Windsong to the outdoor arena on Monday morning. I mounted and pushed Windsong forward with my legs as I tugged my gloves on. There was a damp chill to the late summer air, reminding me that fall had nearly arrived. The lower temperature for this early-morning workout would be better for Windsong anyway. The heat had seemed to be affecting him more.

I stroked his muscled neck. "What do you think, big boy? You feel like you can win Regionals?" He tossed his head up and down. Even though it was in response to me shortening the reins, it was enough of an agreement to have me grinning.

After a while, we were both dripping with sweat despite the cool morning, and I loosened the reins so Windsong could relax. The sky was a gorgeous blue, with pink streaks over the trees. A vehicle bumped down the driveway toward the barn and multiple horses greeted their caretaker with hungry whinnies. Windsong's ears perked up as he watched the car park, and he softly nickered.

"Hungry? I'll take you in now so you don't miss your breakfast."

After rinsing him off, I put Windsong in his stall and went to get his grain and supplements. I left him with his nose slamming the bucket sideways on its hook and chewing noisily.

After an uneventful commute and a tall cappuccino, I tiptoed into the lecture hall and slid in my usual seat next to Carly. The professor didn't pause but sent me a disapproving look. I tried to look apologetic, but I was too exhilarated from my weekend. With a roll of her eyes, Carly pulled her arm back so I could see her notes. I blew her a kiss and started copying.

Carly breezed into our dorm room and tossed her books onto the bed. "I'm starving. You ready to go get some lunch?"

I slammed my textbook closed. After the third try, I still couldn't recite the dates of the significant events that led up to the Great Depression. I might as well get some sustenance; maybe food would make my brain function better. "Sure, let me grab my raincoat."

My schedule on Wednesdays was weird. I had one course first thing in the morning and then one evening course after dinner. The dorm was quiet during the day when most kids were in class, but today because of the rain, it was busier than normal. Rain was as good of an excuse to skip class as any other, and kids took advantage of it. I couldn't concentrate. Every shout I heard or person who walked past my room snagged my attention.

I had done well in high school, always As and Bs. I didn't remember having to study—I just did the homework and took the tests they gave me. That didn't seem to be working very well for me in college. I had actually failed two quizzes. Failed, as in *F*. And I had an American history quiz tonight, but I couldn't seem to relate to the Great Depression.

After lunch, when my brain was food stimulated, I would start at the beginning, copying out the sequence of events.

My phone chimed as we were running down the path to the dining hall. Once we were in the door and had caught our breath, I pulled it out of my pocket and swiped in my passcode. My jaw clenched as I read the text from Kate.

Carly shook the umbrella and closed it. "Your face just turned white. What's wrong?"

"I have to call Kate. She thinks Windsong is sick." Kate was supposed to ride him today. Could something have happened while he was working? Did Windsong crash to the ground in midstride? I could see his slim body stretched out flat and his chest shuddering to a stop. My throat closed, and I put a hand to my stomach as I forced air past my lips. I leaned on the wall to the side of the vestibule and dialed Kate with a shaky finger.

"What happened?" Not exactly good manners, but this was Windsong we were talking about.

Kate was just as urgent. "I'm not sure, but he didn't finish his morning grain or hay and is already lying down. Not his usual routine."

"Is he colicking?"

"I don't know. He has normal manure in his stall, and he drank from his bucket while I was watching him. Then he just sank to the floor. He's still lying down now."

"Call the vet. I'll come right home."

"Normally, I would say don't bother to come, but with his condition, I tend to worry. I would rather take him to the clinic, to the heart doctor, if that's okay with you."

"If you're worried, I'm panicking. Make an appointment. I'm on my way."

My heart racing like a jackrabbit's, I ran straight for my car. I stopped long enough to text my parents, and then took off.

Sitting in the same plastic chair that I had sat in the first time we brought Windsong to the hospital, I chewed my nails instead of the candy bar in my hand. I put the soda bottle to my lips but couldn't make myself swallow. It felt like a rerun watching Dr. Clark's tall, lanky form amble toward Kate and me in the clinic's waiting area—except this time my anxiety was doubled because I already knew Windsong had heart disease.

The vet slumped into a chair, looking more exhausted than the last time we saw him. Of course, it had been nearly eight thirty in the evening by the time we arrived at the hospital with Windsong. He had agreed to stay after hours and wait for us.

Icy cold sweat dampened my sweatshirt under my arms.

"Well, ladies. It's all good news, relatively speaking. Everything looks exactly the same as the last time we did all the tests. He's basically fine."

"Why do you think he was acting so dull and unlike himself?"

"I can only guess, because all his vitals are normal right now. Maybe he had a minor colic that passed on its own. Sometimes in the fall, the changes in the weather cause colic episodes. Intestinal gas from the new growth in the grass, or cramps due to unexpectedly cool nights. Or he could just be tired. Did you change his routine? Riding him more?"

I thought about my weekend rides. Did I work harder than normal? I didn't think so, but training for upper-level dressage was difficult and physical. "I did ride him early in the morning on Monday. I don't usually ride then."

The doctor shrugged. "He could just be tired. Cut back a little and see how he does. His heart hasn't sustained any damage at this point."

Pulling a stethoscope from his side pocket, the doctor continued, "I would like to teach you how to check his vital signs. I'll give you a chart to write the numbers on, and then you will build a history. When you have questionable moments, you can take his vital signs and have an idea whether things are abnormal or not."

Kate stood up. "That's a great idea, Doctor."

"I'm also going to give you a prescription for a mild sedative. When his heart rate is at certain levels, the sedative will act to relax him and lower the strain on his heart. You can't, however, use it before a horse show because it will show up in a drug test and is disallowed in competitions."

He scribbled on a prescription pad and handed the blue slip to me.

"Thank you, Doctor." I couldn't understand the words he had written, and I thought of Carly's neat handwriting with a smile.

"Windsong's malformed heart valve makes managing his condition difficult. There are no specific symptoms. I am glad you brought him in and still encourage you to do so if you have any doubts. Now let's show you how to use this stethoscope."

As I walked Windsong back onto the trailer, I sighed. After Kate helped me secure the ramp, I asked, "Umm, Kate?" I shifted my weight from one foot to the other, clasping my hands together and pressing my knuckles to my mouth. "Is there any way you could keep all of this to yourself? I mean, I'll explain the emergency visit, but could you not tell my parents about the vital signs and," in a small voice that crept through my hands, "the training?" I braced my shoulders for her answer.

Kate's eyebrows sank toward each other, causing two straight lines between her eyes. "I don't really talk to them much, except at shows. What's going on?"

"They want me to quit riding while I'm in college."

"Oh." Another line appeared on her forehead and the corner of her lip lifted as if I had given her a rotten tomato to taste.

"Exactly. So, I'm kind of not telling them anything about Regionals and Finals and stuff."

Kate blew out a long, loud puff of air. She got in the truck and started it before she said anything. "I won't lie if they ask me something."

"Of course not," I agreed, on the edge of the seat, my knee bouncing.

"Keep the chart in your tack trunk so I can fill it in when I ride Windsong." She put an arm over the back of the seat and turned to watch the trailer as she backed out of the parking spot.

I smiled.

*CHAPTER*

# 8

C ory held his hat brim down low over his eyes as he shouldered through the line of people at the front entrance gate to the rodeo grounds. He lifted it slightly to catch the eye of the girl behind the glass of the ticket booth. She smiled and waved us in.

The teen put her lips to the opening and her voice sounded like she spoke from the bottom of a bottle. "Come on in, Cory. Hi, Jane. Good to see you. Congratulations on your gold medal!"

Surprised that she knew about my win, I smiled over my shoulder and waved with my free hand. "Thanks!" Cory clutched my hand and moving fast, kept his hat low and his back to the people. I stumbled over Cory's feet when he stopped suddenly. Furrowing my brows, I asked in a low voice, "Do I know her?"

Cory didn't answer. The crowd was thick on this beautiful Saturday night, and this was the last rodeo of the season. Many fans were milling around the souvenir carts and the food truck. The wooden grandstands rocked with thumping feet as people made their way to seats.

Cory spun on his boot heel, ducked behind the bleachers, and strode toward the chutes, still keeping the visor of his hat pulled down. The crowd was thinner back there, and he sped up. I had to jog to keep up.

"Are you late or something? Geez, Cory! You're hurting my arm."

He immediately dropped it, apologizing, and I rubbed my wrist.

"I was just trying to get in the back before we were spotted."

"Spotted?" What was he talking about? "By who?"

Finally, he stopped. With a deep sigh, he explained, "Ever since I came back here, people mob me. It sometimes takes me thirty minutes to get from the gate to the chutes if I walk down front through the crowd."

I stared at him. He lifted his hat, ruffling his hair before putting it back on. He avoided looking at me. "People? Your friends?"

"Autographs," he spit out. "They want me to sign all kinds of things. I'd rather just get on my horse."

With a laugh, I gave him a quick hug. "This is what I meant before when we talked. Your hometown fans love you. You are a World Champion, and they're proud of it."

His discomfort was amusing. He never liked to be fussed over but was nevertheless charming and warm to anyone who approached him. It had been over a year since he was on the U.S. Reining Team that won gold at the World Games, but his fans didn't forget him even if he wanted them to, proving just how lasting a win like that could be.

We rounded the far side of the bleachers and a girl called, "Cory! Hi!" There was a roar of applause and whistling as more people recognized him.

My mouth dropped open and I started laughing. Cory grabbed my arm and pulled me through the high, solid gate to the back workings of the rodeo, letting it slam shut behind us. The look of relief on his face had me laughing harder.

He adjusted his hat and glared at me. "I actually thought about not coming."

Stretching up on tiptoes, I kissed him. "You deserve all that recognition."

He slid his arms around my waist and pressed his lips on mine. "I wish they would forget. I just want to ride horses and do this." He blew in my ear and nibbled the lobe.

"Hey, none of that back here." A familiar voice interrupted us. "This is a family rodeo. Show a little restraint."

Cory swung me to the side, placing his body between me and a tall blond cowboy. "Jealous, Brandon?"

My face burned, and the hairs on the back of my neck rose. Cory's throat worked and he directed a cold stare at his former friend, pulling me close beside him. Apparently, he hadn't forgotten Brandon's advances toward me in the past and the harsh words they had exchanged about Cory's treatment of me.

I slipped an arm around Cory's waist, prepared to hold him back if things got heated. I'd seen how fast Cory could jump a guy, and Brandon wasn't one of his favorite people.

"Easy, nimwit. You roped the best girl at the rodeo." Brandon lifted my free hand to his lips, a mocking glint in his eyes. "How are you, Jane? I read all about your win. Good job, sweetie."

I tugged my hand away, pressing closer into Cory. "Thanks, Brandon. It's good to see you. Not competing tonight?" Keeping my tone impartial, I hooked my thumb into my belt loop and out of reach.

"My events are coming up. Since this guy hasn't entered calf roping," he said, indicating Cory, "maybe you could cheer *me* on. I might even have a shot if the calf lines up tonight." His dimples when he smiled were almost irresistible.

Cory's hand tightened painfully on my waist and he leaned forward, holding up his fist. "Jane's not the cheering type."

My eyes widened, but Brandon bumped his knuckles on Cory's, his dimples deepening as he turned to me. "I know for a fact how supportive Jane can be. She waited around all those months for you, didn't she?" Brazenly, he leaned forward and gave me a brief, one armed hug. "Good to see you, girl. If you ever need anything, you know how to find me." He sauntered away unaffected by Cory's hostility.

I twisted out of Cory's tight grip and rubbed my side. "Geez, Cory. Lighten up. He was just saying hello."

With a cold glare, Cory swung easily into the saddle of the sturdy gray gelding he was borrowing from Dale, the rodeo's owner. Leaning toward me, he hissed, "That wasn't all he was saying. You didn't need to encourage him."

He sat up, waiting for me to respond, but I was speechless. Encourage him? Seriously?

"Ahh, forget it, I gotta ride." He turned the horse away without another word.

I threw my hands up. What did I do? I was just standing there. "I'll be fine, don't worry about me," I mumbled to his uncaring back. I turned and pushed the heavy wooden gate open. This wasn't the first time I had seen Cory's jealous streak. He didn't believe that I would choose him over someone else, anyone else. He couldn't stand it when I talked to Shawn on the phone, either.

After hitting the snack stand, I climbed into the bleachers.

"Over here, Jane!" a bubbly blonde called, waving her cowboy hat to get my attention.

I grinned. It had been a long while since I had talked to Brenda. She was great. "Where's Jill?" I asked as I slid onto the bench next to her.

"Working. Real life, you know." Brenda rolled her gray eyes. Her wholesome, peachy complexion and cheery nature were more attractive than the smooth good looks of a television actress. "So, how are you? I heard you did great, won a gold medal and all. Congratulations."

"Thanks. You heard about that?"

She bumped her shoulder into mine. "Yeah, I don't live at the rodeo, you know. Of course I keep tabs on my fancy riding friend."

I laughed; it was good to be here with her simple friendliness. I offered my nachos, and she told me what was going on in her life as we munched.

The noise of the crowd drowned out the thundering hooves of Cory's horse as he raced through the gate and galloped a lap around the arena, one arm in the air waving his hat. Golden hunks of sand leapt out from under the gelding's hooves as he slid to a stop in front of us. Cory put his hat back on, using two hands to fix it in place, sending me a steely glare from under the brim.

The crowd was still making noise for him, but my blood pounded in my ears under his gaze and I could no longer hear it. Through the sturdy chain link, my eyes locked onto his doubtful blue ones, and there was more distance between us than that stretch of sand and fence. How could he doubt me still? Didn't he know how much of a hold he had on my heart?

Never breaking eye contact, I lifted my hand, touched two fingers to my lips, softly kissing them. I pointed to him and stretched my mouth to exaggerate the words. "I love you." For an endless moment, I pressed my hands over my racing heart, hearing only the whoosh of it in my head.

Slowly, finally, he grinned; his icy blue eyes warming to the color of the sky on a hot summer day. With a flick of his fingers on his hat brim, he wheeled the gray around and trotted to the center of the arena to prepare for the first bucking bronc to come flying out of the seven-foot-high slatted gate.

Brenda sighed. "He is something else. They should put him on a calendar. I bet he could sell a million."

I chuckled. Brenda was right. Besides mouthwatering looks, Cory had that special something, that charisma, which made people love him. But somehow, he didn't know that about himself. I couldn't imagine wanting anyone but him, but lately, it seemed it didn't take much for me to make him angry.

My body still tingled and I nodded. "He still makes my knees weak, not that he believes it."

Brenda patted my leg. "Every couple has rough spots, but his eyes don't lie, and I can see the love he has for you shining like a beam of light."

I giggled at her southern drawl.

An instant hush fell over the crowd as that first gate flew open and a wild-eyed buckskin came careening out, mouth open and ears laid flat back. Brenda and I leaned forward, hands on our knees, like the rest of the crowd. A silent second passed, and then folks started yelling encouragement.

Suddenly, the cowboy's shoulders fell forward, his body folding like a ragdoll's. The savvy horse twisted his ribs and kicked out his hind feet in the opposite direction. The guy couldn't hold on and flew off the side of the spinning horse. He collapsed into the dirt of the arena, and I winced because I knew what that kind of impact felt like. But he was already standing and dusting off his chaps when the startling buzzer sounded. Sadly, he would receive no score to console him while he nursed his bruises.

Three rides later, I clutched Brenda's arm when they announced Len, another of Cory's buddies, as next up. The gate burst open and a monster bay horse sprang out. With his nose down between his thick, strong legs, the horse threw his square, muscular rump up hard and high, twisting from side to side, trying to get Len off. Each leap in the air was punctuated by a grunt of effort, and spittle dripped from the thick, furry muzzle. Dirt sprayed as high as Len's beige hat.

"Holy cow! That horse can buck. Stay on, stay on, Len!" I bit my lip, shaking Brenda's arm. Despite the glare of the stadium lights, I could make out the fierce determination in the lanky cowboy's dark, gentle eyes.

With his palm high in the air, his legs bent and flopping by the horse's shoulders, Len matched the tough-looking horse's efforts, staying centered and as balanced as a rider could be on a leaping, kicking beast. His hat tumbled off and rolled under the horse. A massive hoof slammed down on it, crushing it.

The buzzer screamed. Len made it! I winced when Len let go and flew through the air, surprisingly landing on his feet and stumbling into the rodeo clown's arms. When he gained his balance, he swept up his hat and punched the dents out of it, and then jumped in the air, hooting and pumping a fist.

I screamed, smacking my hands together. What a good ride.

Cory chased the bay through the wide-open gate at a corner of the arena, and the attendant slammed it closed behind the flicking black tail. Cory circled back toward the center of the arena, slapping Len's open hand as he passed. Len climbed the fence and perched on top, waiting for the giant digital scoreboard to show his score.

The announcer's voice boomed with enthusiasm. "Good job, cowboy! That ride was enough to put him in first place with a seventy-two."

Len snatched his hat off and whooped it up, catching himself before falling back into the ring. Showing every one of his perfect white teeth, his grin was electrifying. Brenda and I squeezed each other's arms in excitement for him.

Len held on to first place and proudly came out to collect his oversized check and pose for a picture.

There was a pause in the action while the crew set up for the next event. The announcer filled the silence. "Folks, we have one of our hometown heroes here with us tonight. While this pretty little gal doesn't ride rodeo, Jane Mitchell won a gold medal for the North American Junior Rider Individual Dressage Championship. Where are you, Jane? Stand up and let the folks congratulate you!"

My breath stopped in my throat, and I grabbed Brenda's arm. "Huh?"

"Stand up, silly." Brenda shoved me up, grinning and whooping along with the people in the stands.

I rose slowly as heat flooded my face and gave a shaky wave. My eyes flew to the big display screen where my image appeared. I reached up to smooth my messy ponytail and watched my hand in giant detail. My oversized sweatshirt wasn't as flattering as it was comfortable. I stood a little straighter, tugging down the hem, and smiled wider. Luckily, my image disappeared before that awkward expression was up there too long.

"There she is. Jane, you may not ride a quarter horse, but we love you anyway. Congratulations." His chuckle trickled out of the speakers.

There was polite applause. My smile grew as I looked around. I sat as the cheering faded, my body humming, and I found it impossible to stop grinning.

That was totally unexpected. Brenda put an arm around my shoulders and squeezed.

"My very own celebrity friend." She threw her head back and laughed. "I love it!"

I grinned at her, willing my heartbeat to return to normal. I loved it, too.

Celebrity. I glanced around. People were still watching me. I brushed the nacho crumbs from my shirt and rolled on some lip gloss. I assumed a serious expression, deliberately sitting tall and straight. I hoped the glow I felt was charisma radiating out to my fans, not just nacho breath.

When Cory rode out of the ring, I told Brenda I was going to find him. I stumbled past knees and tried to avoid stomping feet as I made my way to the end of the row, mumbling, "Ooh, sorry. So sorry."

They answered, "That's okay, Jane. And congratulations." "No problem, Jane. Good job." One woman whom I had never seen before even said she was proud of me as she yanked her foot out from under mine.

Straightening my ponytail when I finally reached the end of the row, I admitted that I radiated klutz more than charisma.

I slipped through the back gate, looking for the gray horse or Cory's hat. He was just sliding off when I reached him.

"Hey."

"The look on your face was priceless. Just saying." Cory quirked an eyebrow.

"I was surprised, that's for sure. Did you put him up to introducing me?"

"No, I wouldn't do that to my worst enemy." Cory pulled the leather girth strap through the ring on the saddle, dropping the girth, and lifting the saddle off the gray's sweaty back.

"Right. Like you really hate when people cheer, screaming your name." I was proud of the attention Cory drew; I liked walking with him as people called his name.

Picking up a handful of hay, I rubbed at the gelding's matted, moisture-darkened hair.

"I don't like it. They expect too much of me. I'm just me."

"Yes, but you won a World Championship and that makes you special." I ducked under the horse's neck to rub the other side.

Cory stopped moving and looked at me over the horse's withers. "Is that what you think? I don't think the gold medal changed anything. I'm still at the same rodeo, and these people have been cheering like that every time I made the bell or roped a steer since I started."

"Right, and that's why they love you because you're a winner and more talented than the others." I gave the silver hair one last swipe and patted the quiet gelding's shoulder.

Cory led him through a gate and released him into a holding pen. Shaking his head, he stared at me as the horse sauntered away. "That's not it at all. It's not about one big show, or one shiny medal. It's about being here, week after week. It's about blood, sweat, and guts."

"I know." He didn't have to tell me how hard it was to train yourself and your horse to win something like that. He didn't have to tell me that the actual medal wasn't what was important. It was a symbol of what a person was capable of. It showed that they had put in the blood, sweat, and guts. It was the proof. How could I explain to him what I meant?

Before I could find the right words, Cory's intense face smoothed into a polite mask as he spotted someone over my shoulder. Easing me to the side with one hand, he held out the other. "Speaking of sweat and guts, here comes a real cowboy. Congrats, dude. Dinner on you tonight?"

Chuckling, Len grabbed Cory's hand and pulled him close for a man hug, slapping his back. He was six inches shorter but wiry and tough; his simple happiness radiated from his face. "Yeah, dinner for two. It's our one-month anniversary." He reached for the hand of a beautiful, glittery barrel racer, her felt hat as red as her rhinestone-studded chaps. Fringe swung from her red vest as she hugged Len's arm to her chest.

Cory's grin dimmed as he turned toward her. "Hello, Doreen. Jane, do you remember ... ?"

"I remember," I interrupted him, surprised by the instant hostility that clenched my fists. "I didn't realize you two were together." My eyes met Len's, and I smiled warmly at the genial cowboy. "Hi, Len."

He dropped Doreen's hand and gave me a hug, squeezing my shoulders and making me glad he didn't do the whacking thing on my back.

I whispered in his ear, "Guess the big checks got her attention, huh?"

He rolled his eyes but gave a tiny nod. When Cory and I had first started dating, Len was chasing Doreen all over the rodeo, and she wouldn't give him the time of day, having her sights set on Cory. But now, she was further proof that people liked a winner.

When he stepped back, Doreen wrapped herself around his arm again. Her lashes, thick with mascara, swept down, and she pursed her crimson lips. "I heard them say you won something too, Jane, but I don't pay much attention to anything outside the rodeo." Her gaze slid over me and landed solidly on

Cory. The spidery lashes fluttering down again, and her shiny lips parted in a slinky smile.

"Hi, Doreen." I said pointedly in an icy tone, sliding an arm around Cory's waist again. "Good to see you. You had a good ride tonight."

When Len looked like he was going to start more conversation, Doreen pushed him to walk. "Thanks. We've got to get moving. Time to celebrate. See you later, Cory." With one last slow, inviting blink toward Cory, she tugged Len's arm and flounced away.

I watched as she kissed Len's cheek, her rhinestones sparkling in the bright lights. I murmured, "Len is probably happy he picked up the winner's check tonight."

*CHAPTER*

# 9

I slammed the heavy door of Cory's truck and slid over the bench seat until our thighs touched. He flicked the headlights on and eased the truck over the bumpy grass of the nearly empty parking lot, heading toward the road. As I glanced out the back window, the arena lights blinked off, leaving only the dim light of a few street lamps. "See you next year, bulls and broncs," I whispered.

Once we were on the smooth macadam cruising to Cory's, he lifted his arm, letting me snuggle in under it. Leaning my head on his shoulder, I struggled to keep my eyes open. I was pretty sure if I closed them, I would be instantly asleep. "I got a taste of your life of fame tonight and I liked it," I murmured, wiggling closer to Cory's warmth, inhaling the leather and dust smell of him.

"It's not all it's cracked up to be." His arm tightened around me, his fingers stroking a slow rhythm up and down my bicep.

"I liked when people recognized me and congratulated me. No one asked for my autograph, like you, but I don't think that would bother me. Don't you like that they all think you're great?"

Cory was silent as he switched the blinker on and turned into the trailer park.

Sometimes I wondered why Cory didn't take advantage of his looks and talent. After he won the World Championship, he had had sponsorship offers and had been asked to represent equine products, but he had turned them all down. At the time, I thought it was because of his grief over losing his horse, Jet. He had even stopped riding for a while. But now, something about his

49

thoughtful look told me there might be more to it than I originally surmised.

He eased the truck into his regular parking spot between the trailer and his mom's economy car. He pushed the gear shifter to park, turned off the headlights, and shut the truck down.

I tipped my head back to look at him, not sure if he was going to answer my question.

The curtains to the tiny living room of his white mobile unit were open, and blue light from the television flashed across his features, making his serious expression spooky. He shrugged the shoulder I wasn't leaning on. "I'm not the same guy that I was when I won my medal. Things happened that changed me, and I don't want to be that guy—the one who sacrificed everything for a competition. Back then, I rode to please the fans, to get the win. Sure, I worked hard, but did I pay attention to what my horse needed? If I had, would I have been able to save Jet? The truth is I hate that medal."

I sat up, putting a hand on his cheek. "There is no way that you could have known Jet would colic. You know there was nothing you could have done. Right? You know that." He couldn't still be blaming himself after all this time.

Quietly, almost as if he didn't want me to hear him, he said, "I guess, but I'll never really know."

I cozied back into his side. "Well, I intend to make a career out of my riding."

Cory shifted so that I would sit up and face him again. "I'm just saying that maybe you should listen to your father and take the school thing more seriously."

"Are you saying quit riding?" I couldn't have heard him right.

"Maybe. Just for a few years. Time away from competition puts things in perspective. I speak from experience."

"Are you saying that I don't have things in perspective?" My hand dropped and I slid away from him, laying my head on the seat back. Where was this coming from? I thought Cory supported my riding, and now he was sitting here telling me to quit? "I know what's important," I spit out.

Cory picked up my hand. I tried to twist it out of his, but he held on to it. "I don't want to argue with you. Just think about it."

The next weekend as I was bumping down the barn driveway, I sucked in a deep, intoxicating breath of clean air, warm sunshine, and horse. In the dimming afternoon light, Windsong's black form was clearly visible from across the farm. His head lifted and he gazed at my car. I comforted myself thinking he recognized me and gave him a little finger wave. My anxiety lowered a notch.

This familiar, routine approach to my favorite place reminded me that I was doing everything I could to prepare for Regionals and protect Windsong's health. One more weekend before we went and only one more weekend of evading my parents. Because they believed I was at school, I didn't have to directly lie. I was just omitting the details of my whereabouts.

I loved the smell of fresh shavings, like newly cut lumber. As I walked down the barn aisle, I called out, "Has anybody seen Cory?" The two girls tacking up their mounts shook their heads, and I kept moving out the end of the barn.

Scanning the outdoor arenas as I jogged up the dirt path to the second barn, I looked twice at a cowboy-hatted rider in the higher ring. It wasn't Cory; the rider lacked his erect and effective posture. Besides, no horse Cory rode would be slouching along like that one was.

The barn was like a ghost town. I poked my head in each of the tack rooms full of western saddles and the tiny office between them. Blocking the glare of the sun with my hand, I stood at the other end of the aisle scanning the farm as it sloped away into more pastures and the round pen.

Hoping the dust rising in a drifting cloud of gray above the circular pen was Cory and a horse, I picked my way down the hill. The walls of the round pen were wood planks and sloped outward like a salad bowl. I peered through the slats and glimpsed Lakota, the two-year-old colt Cory had adopted from EMA Rescue the year before.

I watched for a few minutes as Cory used his body and a coiled rope to urge Lakota around the pen. Cory's firm voice offered encouragement as the colt trotted, his hooves thudding on the loosely packed footing.

Neither horse nor man could see me, and I wasn't sure how to announce myself without startling either of them. Lakota solved the problem by skidding to a stop in front of me and snorting at the crack where my face was. I poked my fingers through. "Hi, boy. How are you doing?"

Cory opened the gate with a smile. "You might as well come in here. He won't pay attention with you out there."

I slid through the opening, and Lakota came right up to me, pushing his soft nose against my ribs. I stroked his delicate little head and he licked my arm with a hot, wet tongue. I pushed his face away from my arm. "I'm not a salt lick. He looks magnificent," I said to Cory.

The colt's coppery brown coat glistened in the bright sun, no ribs showing on his rounded sides. He was starting to look more like a grown-up horse than the gangly, undernourished teenager we had loaded on the trailer months ago.

"His confidence has grown and he's smart as a whip." Cory stood, feet apart and arms crossed on his chest. He was watching me and Lakota from under his hat.

Running my hands over the colt's smoothly muscled neck and back, I marveled that he allowed my touch. "You've done so much. I remember when he wouldn't let us within ten feet of him."

"Watch this." Cory put an arm around me, drawing me away from Lakota. He lifted the coiled rope in his hand, and Lakota leapt away, bounding across the pen. He kicked his heels out and loped around the perimeter, sending chunks of dark sand flying. Cory took control, waving the rope to keep Lakota moving and using his body and arms to signal him. He soon had the colt stopping and turning on command.

When Cory allowed Lakota to come to a standstill, he turned me so we both had our backs to the snorting colt.

With our eyes connected and little smirks on our faces, Cory and I waited expectantly for the colt to come over to us on his own. He did not disappoint. Wet lips tickled my elbow, and he gave me a nudge.

A slow smile spread on Cory's face, which made my heart speed up. "He came to you instead of me." Cory's voice was full of astonishment.

I turned and rubbed Lakota's neck. "See, he trusts me."

Cory snapped the lead rope on Lakota's halter and slanted me a speculative look. "Maybe you should get on him then."

I grinned. "You saddle broke him, too?"

"I haven't, but I mean right now, bareback, just sit on him and I'll lead you around once or twice just so he gets the feel of carrying some weight. With me on the ground, he should feel comfortable. Plus, he obviously likes you."

Liquid brown eyes calmly studied me as I fiddled with his mane. "Are you sure? I don't want to scare him or anything." Lakota looked far from nervous, but my stomach was full of butterflies.

"Yep. He has to start somewhere."

All of those butterflies took off flying at the same time. I had never been the first person to get on any horse. Images of the bucking broncos Len and Cory rode floated through my mind.

"Maybe you should go first. I could hold him. After all, you have experience with bucking horses."

Cory rubbed his hand on my back. "He's not going to buck." But when I quirked an eyebrow at him, he added, "I don't think."

Swallowing, I nodded. While Cory held Lakota's head, I laid over his back on my belly, patting his side and wiggling around. Other than turning his head and nudging my leg, Lakota just stood there nibbling Cory's fingers.

With Cory's help, I carefully put my leg over and sat up, gently stroking the thick, muscular neck and talking to the colt. He cocked his head sideways and looked at me but otherwise seemed relaxed and comfortable.

I nodded to Cory. With a light tug on the halter, he clucked so Lakota would step forward. The colt resisted, pulling his head back with a small hop to the side. He continued to hop around and Cory struggled to hold him still.

"Maybe you better slide off."

"Let go of his head."

"Are you nuts? He'll dump you."

"Trust me, Cory. Let go of his head."

Cory bit his lip but eased his grip on Lakota's halter.

The colt twisted around, taking a few more sideways steps, until his neck was bent in half and he was looking me in the eye.

"Easy, Lakota. It's just me up here."

Leaning down, I held out my hand so he could reach it. He touched it with his nose, sniffing softly. The tension in his body eased. I stroked his neck and spoke in soothing tones, nodded to Cory to signal a walk. Straightening up, Lakota started forward with an awkward, slow gait.

Slowly, I let my calves touch his barrel and he stopped abruptly, cocking an eye back at me. "It's okay. I won't fall, you can move and so can I. See?"

Cory stood in the center, giving cautious signals to keep Lakota walking. After a lap or two around the small pen, I decided that was enough of an introduction and slid off. When my feet connected with the earth again, I let out a whistling breath that I didn't even know I had been holding.

Lakota immediately spun around and put his head in my arms. I tugged his ears and scratched his poll. "Good boy." I grinned at Cory.

"He is a really good boy. Won't be long before he's loping around with saddle, bridle, and rider."

I clapped my hands together and pressed them to my lips. "That almost felt as wonderful as winning a championship ribbon."

Cory's gaze met mine. "I think it's better, way better."

CHAPTER

# 10

I had been keeping a notebook with Windsong's vital signs. I had a good idea how high his heart and breathing rates would go when I worked him. And I even knew how long it took for them to return to normal.

As we pulled in the long dirt drive of the state horse park, I was hoping the three-hour trip hadn't stressed Windsong too much. I brought Windsong into his stall and took out my stethoscope to check his numbers while Kate and Cory unloaded my equipment and took the trailer to the camping area.

"Well, Windsong. You are becoming quite the good little traveler. All your numbers look perfect." I gave him a kiss on the soft part of his nose and stepped out of the stall. I was carefully packing the stethoscope back into its cushioned case when Cory and Kate came back from hooking up the utilities to the camper.

We ate dinner in front of Windsong's stall and worked together to bathe and braid him.

"Do you think we should leave him alone through the night?" I asked Kate.

"We signed up for night watch, so I think he'll be fine. He seems pretty well settled in."

With my face between the bars, I watched Windsong quietly munching his hay. "I guess you're right."

Because the secretary's office had been closed when we arrived the previous evening, I had to turn in my music disc first thing in the morning. I checked

55

my watch. If I hustled, I would have plenty of time to drop off the music, rush back to the trailer, and get dressed before tacking up and heading to the warm-up ring.

After I won the Junior Championships, Kate had suggested that I start showing Intermediate I—skipping an entire level—since Windsong was already trained for it. In only two shows, Windsong and I had scored high enough to qualify for this regional competition in the Musical Freestyle. It was the first class scheduled this morning. I wasn't riding first but still had to get my warm-up in before my assigned time.

I left Cory filling Windsong's water bucket and started the trek across the show grounds. My parents were driving down to watch my class, and they were bringing coffee and breakfast sandwiches. I gratefully marched right past the long line at the food stand, hoping they would be at the trailer by the time I got back.

A volunteer was opening the door to the office just as I came up to it. I smiled and followed her back to her table. "Jane Mitchell." I stated as I handed her my two properly labeled CDs.

"Good morning. Congratulations on the team gold this summer. Well done."

"Thanks."

A nasally voice chimed in, "She didn't do it all by herself, you know."

I spun around with an uncharacteristic squeal. "Melinda!" We hugged for real, actually letting our bodies collide and pressing our cheeks together. "How are you?" I sung, keeping a hand on her shoulder as we parted.

Her auburn hair was tightly coiled into a bun at the nape of her neck and, as usual, she looked like she had just stepped out of a premier dressage clothing catalog. But the smile on her face was genuine.

"Better and better. Belvedere and I are ready to rock the arena. Happy to see that you moved up and out of my class, allowing me to dominate again. Jealous that your horse already knows the new movements. Belvedere has some kind of learning disorder and struggles with anything new. It's taking forever for him to get the new stuff. It'll be years before I have him ready to move up."

Before I bought Windsong, Melinda and Belvedere had beaten me in every class we competed in, but I had been riding my horse Paddy back then. I used to call Melinda my nemesis, and our rivalry had been pretty fierce and sometimes mean. But when we were on the junior team together a few months ago, we had become close friends. And that snooty tone that used to be so offensive to me was just the way she talked, and it didn't bother me anymore.

"At least you know you'll probably win today." I smiled.

"Imagine if we both win, we'll both go to Finals."

Taking her hand, I gave it a firm squeeze. "That would be awesome. Good luck, kill it today."

"Jane, here's your packet," the volunteer interrupted us, holding up a manila envelope. "Good luck."

"Thank you." I plucked it from her hand and gave Melinda another quick hug. "I gotta run. Talk to you later."

My mom rubbed hair gel between her palms and smoothed down my wavy locks. She made a bun and pinned the hair net in place. She ran her hands over my shoulders, giving me an affectionate squeeze. "You always look so beautiful and elegant in your show clothes. I'm going to miss that." She kissed my cheek as I turned toward her, a wave of guilt sealing my lips.

Stepping out of the trailer, I shrugged into my shadbelly coat, shaking out the long tails and straightening the collar. I lifted one booted foot and rested it on the edge of a chair, adjusting the spur strap.

"You look lovely. Ready for your last big performance?" My father handed me my gloves.

Keeping my eyes down, I nodded. They followed me to Windsong's stall.

"Good morning, Mr. and Mrs. Mitchell. He's ready for you, Jane." Kate inspected me as she led Windsong out of the stall. "You look great. Cory, grab that bucket. I put a shine rag, a clean brush, and a water bottle for a last-minute touch-up at the ring."

"Please put my stethoscope in there, too," I added.

Windsong stopped when he stepped outside beside Kate, his head high, taking in the scents and sounds of the busy show grounds. His black coat glimmered in the sun. People and horses were bustling here and there, the paths and barns in constant motion. Windsong called out, stepping sideways and looking back in the barn.

Fiddling with my helmet strap, I reassured him from behind, "I'm coming, big guy."

Cory cupped his hands, and I kissed his cheek before putting my bent knee in them. He boosted me up. As I tucked my toes into the stirrups, I observed the activity around us. The view from on top of my tall horse gave a different perspective. People looked up to me, admiration in their eyes. I was someone to be noticed when I was partnered with Windsong. And nothing felt more natural than moving forward on the back of my horse. I was bigger, stronger, safer.

A fluffy little Pomeranian dashed to the end of his leash, barking loudly at Windsong. The twelve-hundred-pound horse leapt sideways and back, as if the ten-pound lion dog could actually eat him. I tensed the reins and gripped with my knees to hold on, making a *don't worry* face at the apologetic owner who held the other end of the leash. She scooped the dog up, her face red, and eased past us.

Maybe *safer* wasn't the word I was looking for, but people kept a respectful distance from Windsong as we jigged and swung down to the warm-up ring.

As I rode among the other competitors preparing for their classes, keeping Windsong busy with circles and figures, I tried to relax. I thought about what I wanted the outcome of this ride to be. Since I was riding up a level and in an open class with experienced adults and professionals, I probably wouldn't win. Although a tiny part of me always hoped I would earn a blue ribbon, and I would love to go to the U.S. Dressage Finals if I did, it was better to be realistic. Besides, my parents wouldn't allow me to go to Finals. Or maybe a win would convince them that I should never give up riding and showing?

I looked around the warm-up at the intense faces of the other riders. Most stared at their horses' heads, their concentration so complete they might as well have been alone in this ring. Across the show grounds, a competitor and his horse glimmered against the crystalline blue sky, the creamy white footing sparkling in the sun. It was a lovely picture and in a few moments, that would be me.

I had prepared the best that I could, and there was no sense worrying about what my score would be. I was going to enjoy my ride and this beautiful day. I patted Windsong's neck and pointed him at the gate.

It was time.

# 11

Kate held the stethoscope against Windsong's side behind his leg, her eyes on her cell phone screen. "Fifty-seven beats."

"Wow, that's great," I answered, holding my boot out so Cory could polish off the dust. "That's a lower heart rate than at the end of my workouts at home. He's such a pro anymore."

The competitor in the ring came to a final halt.

Kate stepped back. "Have fun."

I rode through the gate and pressed Windsong into a trot. Putting the reins in one hand, I waved to my parents. The judge's bell tinkled, so I halted Windsong on our starting mark.

Cory stood by the entrance gate. He lifted his hat, ran his hand through his curls, and set the hat back on just right. Blowing out a big breath, he pointed at me, then down to Windsong, and then crossed his hands over his heart. I nodded, smiled, and raised my arm to signal my music.

Windsong swelled when he heard the notes and, with the lightest brush of my boot, he lifted gracefully into a collected canter. We turned down the center line and he slowed infinitesimally one beat before the music stopped. One more stride and I braced my shoulders; he halted square and motionless on the last note. Dropping my hand, I saluted, and the judge seated herself.

Windsong knew the music and the moves as well as I did. We worked together effortlessly and somehow Erica's face popped into my mind. When I had watched her ride Santos, it was impossible to see her aids. Santos responded to every invisible shift of her weight or tightening of her muscles. The result was a powerful, emotional display of the discipline and beauty of the sport. That's what I was going for today. *Let them see us dance, Windsong.*

I laughed out loud as we trotted to our final halt and saluted with a flourish. The judge stood and grinned back. "Thank you," she emphasized, like I was doing her a favor.

As we strolled out of the ring, a wave of applause followed us. I couldn't stop grinning. What fun. Give this up for four years? No way.

Windsong was all settled in his stall. I had rinsed the sweat off, thrown a light cooler over his damp back, and put fresh hay and water out for him.

My parents entered the barn and Mom asked, "When will we get the results?"

I glanced at my watch. "The class ended about fifteen minutes ago. Maybe in an hour or so. Let's go get lunch. I'm starving."

Kate, Cory, and my parents all walked to the secretary stand with me after we ate. The volunteer who had signed me in called my name as soon as I stepped through the door.

Turning my shoulders sideways and ducking elbows, I made my way over to her table through the packed room. I dragged Cory behind me, assuming the others would also follow.

"I have your test. Congratulations." She handed me the folded paper, delight on her face.

I looked at the front of the test and smiled at my score. But what made me freeze in place was the number one written next to it and circled. My score was in the high sixties, a really good score for this level, but did that little number mean what I thought it meant? I looked up at the volunteer.

She nodded. "You won the class."

Everything went dark as Cory grabbed me up in a bear hug and my parents and Kate patted my back, my arms, whatever wasn't enveloped by Cory's body.

I had no words, but laughter bubbled out every few seconds.

"You know what this means?" Kate shouted.

I nodded, still giggling.

"Great note to end on, baby." My father kissed my cheek, and my heart dropped to my toes.

Kate's mouth dropped open. "Do you want me to tell them?" she whispered.

An elbow bumped my back, sending me into Cory's chest. I tried to step forward, but there was no room. I pointed to the door. "Let's go back to the trailer and we can explain."

On the ruse of helping me get dressed for the awards ceremony, Kate closed the trailer door behind us.

"You haven't told them that this could qualify you for Finals?" she immediately demanded.

Tugging my white breeches back on, I explained, "I really didn't think I was going to make it. It's an open class, for goodness sakes."

Kate shook her head and rolled her eyes. "When are you going to learn to trust me when I say that you can do it? I keep an eye on the scores from the shows. I knew you were scoring as high as the other qualifiers. What are we going to do now?"

I snapped my collar closed and threaded my stock tie through the loop on the back. "*We* are going to go out there and *you* are going to tell my father that this is important and that I can't not go."

Kate stopped pacing in front of the tiny couch. "You want this, right, Jane?"

I looked at her reflection in the mirror behind me. Her eyes were intense. Pausing a moment, I arranged my tie. I turned, meeting her gaze with equal intensity. "Yes, I do."

"You understand what it means—more riding, hard work, focus."

I turned, dipping my chin. "Yep."

She grinned. "Then that's what we'll tell them."

My father's arms were crossed, his face stern. "You are not taking a whole week off from school for another ribbon. I said this was your last show and I meant it."

"It's not just another ribbon, it's a national championship." I hated the whine in my voice, but my father's shuttered face seemed impenetrable to plain reasoning. When that look appeared, I reverted back to his little girl, tears making my voice tremble.

Kate tried to interject in a neutral voice. "It is probably the last time Windsong can do something like this due to his age—"

My father interrupted her, holding up a hand to stop the flow of words. "I respect your opinion, Kate. But Jane is a college student now, and college and her future need to be her priorities. She's not going to go."

I wanted to shake him, I wanted to poke him in the chest, stomp on his foot, do something to change that hard expression. I didn't bother looking to Cory for backup, and my dad had already shut Kate down.

I locked eyes with him, clenching my teeth, trying to keep my voice steady. "But I want to go. This is Windsong's last chance, Dad." I wrapped my arms around my chest, my muscles hard with the effort of keeping my chin up and holding his gaze.

His eyes narrowed, and he pointed his index finger at me. "No. More. I won't give you the check for the nomination, and if you keep badgering me about it, I'll sell the horse. You are not going." He turned on his heel and stalked to his car.

"Mom?"

She was unsympathetic. "Your father's right. The only reason you can afford to do all of these shows is because your father and I have excellent careers. We have supported your riding, now we will support you in college. That's the way it's going to be. You need to stop this arguing and think about your priorities." With a last meaningful look over her shoulder, she turned toward the car.

"So that's it. You're not even staying for the awards ceremony?" I called after her.

She glanced at the car. My father waved angrily through the windshield. "No, we've been to all the others. What's one more when the rest of your life is at stake? Finish up here, and I expect you home for dinner."

After they pulled away, I slumped into a chair. "This is unbelievable." They had acted like this was a local show and I won a measly blue ribbon. I won *Regionals*, for goodness sakes. I had a chance to compete at the National Finals. Only a couple hundred people in the whole country qualified to do that. This was *big*.

Cory, who had been leaning against the trailer hiding behind his hat brim throughout the whole argument, sunk in the chair next to me.

"They have a point, about paying for the horse shows."

The lump in my throat expanded. "Seriously? You're on their side?" I rasped.

"I'm just saying. When you're paying the bills yourself, you can do whatever you want." He handed me my boots.

I glared at him, then snatched the boots and started tugging them on. Apparently, I had been living in a cushiony fantasy world all through high school. My parents gave me everything I wanted, acted so proud of me as I competed in horse shows, and had bought Windsong for me with no hint that it was all temporary. I had invested my heart and soul in riding. Cory had been my only distraction from the intensity with which I trained. And now, he pulled his support out from under me when I needed him most. None of them understood.

Kate lifted my shadbelly coat from the back of the chair, smoothing the fabric like she was petting a cat. She shook it out and held it for me to slip my arms into the sleeves. Our eyes met, and I was surprised to see hers glistening. I paused, ducking my chin to swallow.

She stepped forward, wrapping her arms around me as she helped me on with the coat. Holding me tight for a moment, she whispered, "They're angry, but maybe we can talk to them later, when they calm down."

I closed my eyes and leaned into her small, strong frame.

Before dinner, I trudged up the stairs to my room, but my father stopped me.

"I'm sorry we argued, honey. I know this is all really exciting to you right now. I'm telling you, it's just a small blip in your life. When you're older and have kids of your own, you're going to look back and thank me for looking out for you."

I came down a few steps to be eye level with him. "What if I told you that I wanted a career with the horses? I'm really good at it, Dad. It feels right to me."

"I'm not saying you aren't good, but it's not a real career." He patted my shoulder. "You'll see when you get back to your dorm tonight. You'll get right back into the routine of school and you will barely have time to think about your horse."

On the hour-and-a-half drive back to school, I had a lot of time to think about my father's words. Windsong was fourteen years old, and he had a heart condition. Finals this year would probably be his one and only shot at a national title. And if I wanted my riding career to continue, I would have to get myself noticed now, before it was over for him. Especially if my father refused to pay my bills, I would need an owner or sponsor to get the ride on another horse of Windsong's caliber. Otherwise, I would have to wait until I got my degree, found a great job, worked my way up the pay scale, and then, maybe, I would be able to afford a horse that had the talent that Windsong had. I didn't want to wait twenty years before I could do this again. When I told my father that it felt right, I meant that the only place where I felt focused and driven was in the saddle. No. I had to do this now.

My father's shuttered expression and patronizing pat on my shoulder halted my thoughts. There would be no convincing him to change his mind. I needed to get the money another way. I had no doubt I could continue to train and go to Kentucky without my parents knowing. I would just pretend I was still at school. Maybe I should get a job? I didn't think I could find one that would make enough money quickly. The nomination fee was due immediately and the entry fees pretty soon thereafter.

Flicking on my blinker, I shot a quick look over my shoulder to check for oncoming cars before easing into the right lane. As I turned forward, my eye fell on a crumpled paper on the passenger seat. The letter from EMA Rescue. After I had pulled it out of my pocket for the last time a couple of weeks ago, I had tossed it there and forgotten about it. EMA Rescue. A job. I grinned and pulled into the next parking lot.

Scrolling through my phone, I found Michelle's number and pressed it. "Hi, Michelle. It's Jane. Is that offer for me still open?"

Carly wasn't in our room when I keyed open the door. I tossed my bag next to the bed and flopped down, eyes snagging on Erica's picture. Grinning, I told her about my win. I sat up and looked in her eyes. "I'm not you yet, but I'm trying. I'll do my best to make EMA look good. I won't let you or the organization down."

I rolled over onto my stomach and called Cory. "You won't believe what I just did. I called Michelle and told her I would take the spokesperson position if she would pay my way to Finals!"

"Wait a minute. Your father let you do that?"

"Oh, no, I don't plan on telling him until it's all over. It's only three weeks away." My legs bounced off the bed as I lifted them up and down. I squirmed deeper into the comforter. I was so clever.

"You plan on more lying to your parents."

My legs dropped with a thump. "It's not lying. I just won't tell them."

Cory's voice was quiet but still forceful. "It's lying."

I was glad I was eighty miles away and didn't have to look into those piercing blue eyes. "Look, I have to do this. It's Windsong's last shot and I need to do well."

"What if it's too much for Windsong?"

"He was awesome at Regionals. I'll monitor his heart rate and he'll be fine."

"What about your college classes?"

Geez. Was my father rubbing off on him? "I'll alert my professors and make up the work. Again, I can handle it." Where was my support? He usually was the one to lift my mood, not crush it.

"I don't like it."

"You don't have to. It's my life, my decision." The lock in the door clicked open, and I sat up. "Carly just came in, I gotta go." I hit end without waiting for him to reply.

I spoke to Michelle again after classes that day. She promised to send in my nomination with a check from EMA if I faxed the signed form to her. I skipped the blank line that said Parent/Guardian If Rider Is Under the Age of Eighteen and firmly wrote my name on the line for the rider's signature. My life, my decision. I scanned it into my computer and faxed it to Michelle online. Easy, peasy. Who can't handle a riding career and getting a degree? I flipped open my textbook and got down to studying.

Kate nearly damaged my eardrums when I called to tell her that we were going to Kentucky. When she finished shrieking, I told her EMA gave me a budget and would pay for me to continue my lessons. And that's what we did.

My car smelled like leather and barn from my boots and coat that had been sitting on the back seat for three weeks. I wasn't complaining; I loved that smell. Next to them was a stack of books and binders. I had assignments due and exams when I returned to school. I planned to study during down times at the show.

I was turning into the barn drive when my mother's ringtone sounded. "Hi, Mom," I answered cheerfully.

"Hi, Jane. I hoped to catch you before your Wednesday evening class. Is this a good time? Are you studying?"

"Yep, studying." I pressed the brake and steered with one hand.

"Do you want to come home for dinner Sunday? Uncle Rob and Aunt Deb will be here."

I rolled slowly over the ruts, bouncing off the seat, racking my brain for a viable excuse to refuse. My championship class was on Saturday, and we were planning on arriving at the show grounds Thursday afternoon. I would ride a warm-up class on Friday and do some activities for EMA promotion. And then we would drive the ten hours back home on Sunday. We probably wouldn't make it in time for dinner. What could I say? "Carly invited me to her house.

Her dad's a doctor," I blurted out.

"Really. I wouldn't have guessed that when we met him. That's nice of them. We'll miss you though." I frowned because she sounded sad, but then her voice perked up. "Maybe next weekend? I know you must be missing home-cooked food. You haven't been back for a month."

I cringed again, because I had been coming home every weekend and had stayed at Cory's. "Definitely next weekend."

I got off the phone quickly as if my mother could somehow know I was pulling up to the barn. Kate had the trailer hitched up and parked in front so I could easily load my tack. The ramp was down and I peeked in at bare floor mats. I guess I needed to add "spread shavings in trailer" to my to-do list.

Cory strode up the aisle, cowboy hat silhouetted against the setting sun that glowed through the opposite barn door. Grinning, he opened his arms and enveloped me in a bear hug. "Missed you."

I pressed into his warmth. "It's only been two days. I just left on Monday morn—" His lips covered mine and I stopped talking.

When he released me, I wondered how I had the strength to drive away from him each week.

"We have a lot of work to do, so we best get started. Kate wants to leave early tomorrow morning to beat the rush-hour traffic." After taking a step back, he corrected the tilt of his hat.

"Right. Let's go." I headed to the tack room. "My mom called right before I pulled in the driveway. She asked us over for dinner Sunday, and I had to think quick. I told her I was going to Carly's for the weekend."

Cory's lip curled, and I bit my tongue, regretting my easy habit of telling him everything. But I was no liar, and the only reason I could tell my mother something untrue like that was because she couldn't actually see my cheeks turn red and my palms get all sweaty. It was impossible to keep things from Cory when he was standing right in front of me.

Cory shook his head. "I hate that your parents don't know about this. You're disrespecting your father."

"Was he respecting me when he told me I couldn't do this even though it was important to me?" I snapped in a belligerent tone. I wiped my palms on my pants.

Cory sighed. "He is just trying to look out for you. You don't realize how lucky you are."

I swung around and stopped him with my hand on his chest. "It doesn't feel lucky when he orders me to quit the most important thing in my life."

"Don't be a drama queen. College is important too."

"Is it? A diploma is just a piece of paper," I spit out. Cory's ability to cut to the heart of the matter was helpful when he was bolstering my confidence, but this time his directness was condescending.

"A championship ribbon is just a piece of material." He echoed my words.

My eyes narrowed to slits, and I turned around. I pushed through the door into the tack room and proceeded to check the locks on my trunk. I had cleaned and packed everything over the weekend. I waited for Cory to get a grip on the opposite handle. "I thought you understood. I thought you were a horseman above everything else."

He lifted his side of the trunk and started moving backward out the door. "I am because I have to be. I would go to college if someone gave me the chance. If I had a father who cared enough to help me."

He set the end of the trunk in the trailer tack room, walked around to my side, and shoved it in. Climbing in after it, he dragged it into the corner.

"Then *you* go. They have all kinds of scholarship programs and online schools. Get your own degree. You don't need anyone else to do it."

He paused on the edge of the running board and stared at me. I lifted my eyebrows. He jumped off, causing me to take a step back. "Maybe I will. But that doesn't change the fact that you're lying to your parents."

I slammed the door back. Why didn't he see that I needed this show? He was reminding me of my dad when he talked about how important college was. I knew that I should get a degree, but this opportunity was happening now. I had to grab it. Like I had said to him, there were other ways to get a degree. And anyone could do it at any time.

Clenching my fists, I spit out, "I'm not lying. I am an adult; I am making choices for myself. Because you don't have a father, you think anything my dad says is golden. Believe me, if you had a dad, you wouldn't agree with everything he told you to do."

Cory's mouth tightened and his eyes turned steely. "Maybe not, but I sure would appreciate him caring enough to give me good advice." He stalked into the barn.

Biting my fingernail, I whispered at Cory's stiff back, "What was good about it?" I was used to Cory being right about most things, but this once, I believed he was dead wrong.

*CHAPTER*

# 13

After two hours on the road the sun was high and the sky clear. The highway was full of tractor trailers that kept a polite distance from the horse trailer. Occasionally, one would pass us, rolling forward steadily in the lane on our left. I sat in the middle between Cory and Kate. Cory's hat was tossed on the seat behind him, and I marveled at the difference in his appearance without it. If he changed his boots for sneakers, I could picture him on a college campus. The college girls would love him. I frowned; maybe he should just do online courses.

He glanced down at me, still acting cool after our argument while we were packing the trailer.

I had gone too far. Cory had always been sensitive about his family, or lack of one. I picked up his limp hand, holding it between mine like I was trying to warm it to get the ice to melt in his eyes. "You know, maybe we can look into online courses or something for you, after this."

He rolled his eyes and snapped his tongue against the roof of his mouth. "Right, because I'm college material."

I nodded. Still speaking gently, "Why not? You're smart, you're driven, and you want it. I think you would be a great student."

"I wasn't in high school. I was busy doing rodeo and training Jet. My grades sucked, so I wouldn't be accepted anywhere." He turned to face me more fully. "That's why you need to think about what you're doing. I blew my chances at college for the horse. I regret that now."

70

"I still think we should look into it if you really want it." I kissed the back of his hand. He searched my face, but I meant it, and I lifted my chin holding his gaze.

After a moment, he kissed me lightly and lifted an arm, inviting me to snuggle in next to him.

"Next rest stop in fifteen miles. We'll stop there," Kate announced.

Kate went into the building first to hit the restrooms and buy some breakfast. I dropped the window in front of Windsong and hopped off the running board, covering my ears. His whinny was not so piercing; he sounded puzzled.

"The only horses here, big guy, are under metal hoods," I told him. I unzipped the stethoscope bag and climbed into the trailer.

It was too dangerous to unload Windsong in a parking lot, so I took his vitals inside. I determined that his numbers were barely elevated. I offered him a drink by holding a bucket up to his head. He splashed around a bit, and then gave it a shove, almost dumping it all over me.

When Kate returned, Cory and I headed in to the visitor center. I held my coffee cup under my nose, savoring the wonderful, warm aroma as we walked back to the truck. Kate closed Windsong up and climbed in the passenger seat. Cory was going to take a turn driving until our next stop.

A couple hours and many miles later, we went through the same routine. Once again, I was pleased with Windsong's heart rate. The smooth, monotonous ride seemed to be soothing his nerves.

The effects of the caffeine wore off and my eyelids started to droop. Fighting the drowsiness, I tried changing the radio station to stay awake.

Cory laughed when my chin dipped down and my head jerked. "Go to sleep. We don't mind."

Grinning, I laid my head on his shoulder and gave in.

The crunch of gravel woke me up. I opened my eyes to the late afternoon sun. The truck rolled past the sign for the Kentucky Horse Park and my heart started thumping. At this rate, I would need that stethoscope for myself.

This was it—national competition. Only the best in the country would be competing this weekend. I sat on my trembling fingers, determined to push that numbing thought way into the back of my mind.

We drove past a covered arena dotted with riders. Each horse was beautiful, moving gracefully through its exercises. The riders were in casual schooling attire: spotless, collared shirts and classy, well-fitted breeches. I unglued my eyes from their highly skilled work as Kate stopped the truck. A pair of placid, blond Belgian horses ambled in front of us drawing a carriage full of happy-faced visitors. I grinned and didn't stop as we passed clean, gabled buildings and finally parked beside a long, narrow barn, one clustered in a group of four.

"Our stall is in barn nine," Kate informed us.

My head snapped left and right, trying not to miss anything, as I climbed out behind Cory. "Is this what the World Games was like?" I whispered in awed respect.

Cory shrugged. "Pretty much."

My knees were shaky as I dropped Windsong's window. "Shhh," I hissed, but that didn't stop him from screaming. Surprisingly, faint answering whinnies floated out of the barns. Stroking his head, I reminded myself that it was just a horse show.

Cory, Kate, and I made quick work unloading. Cory held Windsong still while I went through my routine with the stethoscope. All of his numbers were in normal range, and we released him so he could do his stall pacing and ignore his hay.

Keeping the stall door open for a few minutes, I let him hang his head out and look up and down the aisle. He nickered to each passing horse but seemed sad that he didn't recognize any of them. Finally, he backed into the stall, spread his legs, and peed. The poor guy probably had been holding it for hours.

When he finished and moved over to munch hay, I removed the wet shavings so he would have a nice dry bed to lie down in and take a nap.

My stomach grumbled in instant answer to Kate's suggestion that we go find some food. I called Michelle as we were walking, and she suggested we meet her at one of the restaurants, dinner on EMA.

Michelle gave me a hug, and then laughed and hugged Kate and Cory, too. "Jane, I can't thank you enough for what you will be doing for EMA. Already the feedback from supporters is pouring in, and they all are very excited about you."

As we followed Michelle through the restaurant to our table, I recognized many faces from photos in dressage magazines and dressage videos. She stopped here and there when someone called out to her. Introducing us, she briefly explained that EMA Rescue was sponsoring me. Each time, the person responded with a polite smile, saying that was wonderful.

As we pulled out our chairs and sat, Michelle enthused, "See, everyone is excited about you!"

I crinkled my brow at Cory but kept my mouth shut.

I ate but barely noticed the taste. My head whirled left and right. The electric buzz of anticipation in the restaurant was palpable. High hopes were prominent in the loud, happy voices. The sound of people calling out and chairs scraping back as people jumped up to hug fellow riders they hadn't seen in a long while punctuated the steady hum.

Every time the door opened, I looked to see who came in. I surprised myself and Cory by scraping my own chair back in excitement when Melinda and her parents arrived. I waved until Melinda spotted me.

Her parents went to find a table while she made her way over to us.

"Really, Jane?" she said, pinching at a green smudge on my polo. "You could have changed your shirt for dinner, at least. What is that smear, horse slime?" In the past, her comment said in that nasally, upper-crust tone would have made me feel two inches tall. But now that I knew her better, and considered her a friend, I realized it was just her way of caring to inspect my appearance for flaws.

I put my arms around her, pretending to wipe the green gunk on her. She squealed and jumped back, equally pretending to be horrified. She hugged Cory with good-natured complaints about my lack of consideration.

Robert Peterson, Kate's old trainer, entered through the double doors with a small group of people. Beside me, Kate rose, adding her scraping chair to the din and grinning widely. He saw her wave, but it took him a few minutes to reach our table because others were stopping him on the way.

I rubbed my sweaty hands on my jeans, watching his tall, slender frame hug Kate. His dark hair was combed back severely and gelled into place, but instead of making him look stern, it made him look like an old-time movie star. Intending to shake his hand, I wound up smacking him in the stomach as he leaned forward to hug me. I stepped back awkwardly and mumbled an apology. He gave Melinda a quick hug and leaned across me to shake Cory's hand.

I jumped when he said my name. It always surprised me that he knew it. "Jane, I saw that you qualified in Intermediate I. Congratulations." His perfect white teeth glowed as he smiled widely. "I qualified one of my client's horses in that division, so we'll be showing in the same class."

I twisted my lips, trying to turn an instinctive grimace into a polite smile. I groaned, "Great. There go my chances."

Robert squeezed my shoulders, teasing, "Ahh, no worries. This horse I'm riding is an imported Dutch Warmblood that is syndicated for a couple hundred thousand. He may be my next Olympic mount."

I nodded, finally making my dropped jaw form the words, "He sounds perfect."

"I have high hopes for him. Listen, I'll see you around."

After he moved on to his own table, I asked Kate, "Was he serious? About the horse being Olympic caliber?"

She nodded. "Probably." Seeing my face fall, she put a hand on my arm. "Really, no worries, like he said. This is your first national competition against professionals. A good ride is what you need to focus on. It's not always about first place, but about how well you showed your horse."

Melinda snorted, patting her perfect, auburn bun. "I'm glad he's not in my division. I'm glad you're not either," she said, leaning into me. "Gives a girl a chance."

With a promise to catch up later, Melinda left us to join her parents.

I was wishing he wasn't in my division either. I pushed the food around on my plate until everyone else was finished eating. Cory's arm around my waist propelled my leaden bones forward, and we walked out of the cafe.

Later, after one last check on Windsong, I pulled the covers up to my chin. I thought about what Kate had said earlier. How quickly I had become accustomed to winning, to placing first. Melinda even seemed to expect it. But I had been competing against young riders and amateurs, not professionals. The idea of not having a chance at the first-place ribbon and the championship put a chink in that secret hope I held of winning and getting a big break toward my career. As a Finals champion, I would be someone whom fans would recognize. People remembered champions, not runners-up.

# 14

Kate and I had decided to do Fourth Level Test 2 as my warm-up class, and it was conveniently scheduled around lunchtime on Friday. The easier test would give Windsong a chance to perform in the arena without challenging or tiring him too much. And Melinda, after placing first in her division at Regionals, was supposed to be showing in the third test of this level, too. Her class was scheduled after mine.

Windsong was bathed and braided after his breakfast and was relaxed before we entered the arena if his heart rate was anything to go by.

When I dropped my hand for my final salute, I remembered how relieved I used to be to make it to the end of a test still on top of Windsong's back, not lying in the dust somewhere. This time it occurred to me that this performance was on the easy side, nothing to worry or be nervous about.

As I rode out of the ring, Michelle waved me over. "This is Chris Redicci. He's the photographer we are using to get the promo pics. He took some in the ring but has a few more he wants to do in front of some of the sights in the park."

"Shouldn't she cool Windsong off first?" Cory asked. "He's damp and it's not exactly a warm day."

Chris Redicci slid dark brown eyes over Cory's attire, his eyes narrowing. "I want the sun to glisten on the horse's wet coat and the raised veins for the photograph. It will show the strain and the effort he has put forth."

I blinked. The snooty English accent didn't match the burly, baseball-capped, bearded man.

Cory cocked his chin at me. "Jane, don't you want to check on Windsong?" He lifted the leather stethoscope pouch.

I looked from his annoyed face to Michelle's hopeful one and then to the photographer, who shifted his weight and pursed his lips in impatience.

"He feels fine. Let's just get the pictures done." I tapped my legs, walking Windsong behind Chris.

A ridiculous amount of shots and angles later, Chris finally pronounced that he may have caught a few good ones. He disappeared without another word and I slid down from the saddle. My mouth was dry and I reached for the bucket Cory held with ringside supplies in it. I patted Windsong, his coat stiff from dried sweat. He head-butted me with impatience, trying to tip the bucket from Cory's hands, looking for a drink.

Cory's brow wrinkled as he took the reins from me. "This is what you have to do that is more important than college and worth lying to your parents about?" he hissed in my ear. He turned and walked Windsong back toward his stall, not waiting for me.

I tipped the water bottle up, draining half of it in one gulp. Kate held my gaze for a moment, and then turned and silently followed Cory.

Michelle clapped me on the shoulder. "That went well." She smiled and strolled off in the direction of the offices.

Wiping the water from my chin, I mumbled to myself, "Is this what models go through? Because that was the most boring yet grueling hour of my life. I hope he got his perfect picture." I glanced at my watch. If I rushed straight to her arena, I would be just in time to catch Melinda's ride.

Cory stalked next to Windsong without looking back, and Kate following purposefully behind them. They would take care of Windsong. I speed-walked in the opposite direction.

Melinda rode a nice test, but the competition in her level was fierce. Only time would tell whether hers was a winning ride. We clasped hands and I said I would be rooting for her.

When I stopped by Windsong's stall, he was quietly munching hay, wearing his clean sheet, and fresh water and shavings had been put in his stall. Nodding to myself, I continued on to the trailer to change.

"Where were you?" Kate demanded when she spotted me.

I plopped into a chair. "I went to watch Melinda's ride. I told you I wanted to support my teammate."

"Did you forget that Windsong needed to be taken care of?"

"No, but I knew you and Cory would be fine."

Kate squared off in front of me. "It should have been you. We're not your grooms. He's your horse and he got you here and he deserves your attention."

"Geez, this once I try to support someone I care about. Give me a break."

She shook her finger in my face. "I don't know what is going on with you, but your horse comes first. Do you understand? I don't care how famous you think you are, but I taught you that you take care of your horse, your partner, before anything else. That includes publicity, friends, and whatever else you think you have to do. Are we clear?"

I curled my fingers, resisting the urge to cover my flaming cheeks with my hands. I glanced toward Cory. He dropped his chin, hiding behind the brim of his hat.

Lips pressed tightly together, I inclined my head. "Of course." I stood, leaned sideways to pass Kate, throwing a glare at the top of Cory's hat, and stomped into the trailer.

What did a girl have to do to get a break? If I did what Michelle wanted, Cory and Kate were annoyed. If I supported a friend, I was neglecting my horse. If I chose riding over school, my parents were angry. It's not like I was off playing video games or something.

Besides, Michelle was supplying the funds for Windsong and me to be here at this show. Didn't they understand that? I owed her a little consideration. If she wanted me to stand around for an hour posing like a Barbie Doll, then that's what I would do. It's not like the photographer made me gallop Windsong or anything. And Melinda had stood by me when I was almost thrown off the team last summer, so I needed to be there for her, too. Windsong wasn't neglected—Cory took care of him like I knew he would. Really, weren't they here to help me?

Dinner with Kate and Cory wasn't as fun as the first night's. One day down and results were in. Riders were more business-like, discussing performances and plans for the next day, or year. My little group was tense. I had fielded a call from my mother while we were walking to the small dining area. Cory gritted his teeth as he heard me blatantly lie, pretending that I was with Carly and her parents. It was one small sentence and I quickly changed the subject and ended the conversation.

When I put the phone back in my pocket, no one said anything, but the disapproval emanating from the two of them was a physical thing. I dropped back a few steps out of the force field that shimmered between them. We avoided the subject all through dinner. We actually avoided all subjects through dinner, barely speaking to each other.

I said I would check on Windsong one more time by myself to escape the tense silence, and as soon as I finished, I jumped between the covers of my bunk and shut my eyes.

The translucent shade over the camper window was still dark when my eyes flew open. No sounds other than steady breathing came from Cory and Kate, but there was no use staying in bed. My nerves were jumping, making me unable to lie still another moment. Noiselessly, I pulled on some sweats and a hoodie and slipped out of the trailer. The show grounds were quiet in the near darkness, with only a few sleepy grooms moving groggily toward the barns. I wasn't exactly running myself. The beauty of the early morning scene was worth the loss of a few winks of sleep.

The orange rim of the sun was just visible over the distant treetops. The arenas were empty; the sand perfectly smooth, all footprints erased as if no horse had ever stepped there.

With the lights off, I had a hard time seeing in the barn aisle. I was reluctant to flip the switch and disturb the final peace the horses would have before a hectic show day. I slowly made my way, weaving between the trunks and chairs by the light of my phone screen.

I looked in on Windsong. In the dim light, he looked like a cuddly kitten, lying down with his neck curled on his knees and his nose tucked into his belly. His sides rose and fell rhythmically with the faintest whistling breath. I rested my chin between the bars and watched, the tranquil scene washing over me and calming my anxiety.

"Good morning, Windsong," I called softly.

His head rose and he whickered back to me. Putting his front legs out, he stretched his neck and rolled his eyes up until they disappeared and all that showed was veiny white. With a groan and a mighty shake, he pulled himself up to his feet. He shuffled over and blew hot, horsey breath gently into my face. I kissed that mushy velvety part of his nose but ducked when his tongue came out. I let him lick the palm of my hand instead.

The lights flickered on and we blinked, temporarily blinded. The bright-eyed girl with her finger on the switch tugged at her baseball cap and gave us a jaunty wave.

"Time to make the donuts," I mumbled as horses started nickering for their breakfasts.

I slid the door open and removed the water bucket, giving Windsong a pat as I stepped out. Ever since Alison had contaminated Windsong's water at the Junior Championships, it was the first chore I did. While the bucket was nearly empty, the water in the bottom was clear. I refilled it, lugged it back up the aisle, and hung it. Windsong looked in it and, disappointed, he pawed the shavings.

"I'm coming with your grain. Here, chew on this while I get it ready." I tossed in a few sections of hay. I opened my trunk in front of the stall and lifted out portioned bags of grain with measured supplements already added. I dumped a whole bag into a rubber feed tub and gave it to Windsong. He took a mighty bite and looked down the aisle as he chewed.

Checking under his stable sheet, I determined that Windsong had stayed perfectly clean. I would only have to dust off the shavings and comb out his tail. I cleaned up his stall, spreading another half bag of shavings, while he ate. When I returned to the stall after dumping the manure, Cory was standing in front of it holding two steaming mugs.

I reached for one. "I love you. I love you." Inhaling the aroma, I took a noisy sip. Sweet and creamy, just how I liked it.

"I'm sorry about yesterday," I murmured. "Thanks for taking care of Windsong. I can always count on you to help me."

Hitching one shoulder, "Sure," he said and sipped from his cup.

Glancing at my watch, I made a quick calculation. "I don't have to braid and get dressed until noon. Let's go explore the attractions." I cocked my head hopefully.

"What about your books? I thought you said you had work to do." Cory fell into step beside me.

"I'll do it later, or in the car on the ride home. I'm too excited to concentrate anyway."

Another shrug. I took his warm hand, swinging it between us, smiling until he quirked his lips, too.

C ory straightened my jacket collar, sliding his fingers down the lapels, smoothing out the wrinkles. He adjusted my helmet and leaned under the brim to give me a kiss on the tip of my nose.

"Good luck. Focus on the moment and enjoy your ride."

"Thanks, coach." I smiled rubbing on some tinted lip gloss. With a deep breath, I took the reins from Cory and led Windsong to the mounting block at the end of the barn. As I pulled down my stirrups and passed the reins over his head, Windsong nickered and jigged away from the steps. I slid off the block and tugged the reins to still him. That's when I noticed the unusually large number of people milling about. I wondered what they were waiting for.

Cory stepped up to Windsong's head as I heard Michelle's voice. "Hi, Jane. Nice crowd you've got here." An EMA baseball cap rested on her fluffy brown curls, and she wore sleek designer breeches with a stylish polo shirt also sporting the EMA logo.

"Good afternoon, Michelle. I don't know what all these people are waiting for, but they're making Windsong a nervous wreck." As I spoke, Windsong swung his hind end away from me again. Cory went on his other side and pushed him back into position. I stepped aboard and lowered myself gracefully into the saddle before he could move again.

"You, Jane. They're here to see you and Windsong."

"What are you talking about?" I checked Windsong back as he did a little Fred Astaire dance step to the side, heading right for a woman holding the hand of a toddler. Cory put a hand on Windsong's neck and slipped him a treat. I nodded, and we moved Windsong forward, hoping the crowd would back off.

I gritted my teeth in irritation, encouraging a jittery Windsong to walk through the crowd. Out of the corner of my eye I caught a glimpse of Michelle's huge smile and wave for the crowd.

She turned to me and nodded. "Social media is amazing! I posted your ride time and when you planned on beginning your warm-up. These are your fans. They've come to watch."

I looked back over my shoulder. They were following us, but Kate had arrived and was walking backward with her arms out, asking people to keep their distance. Windsong pranced and blasted air through his nose every few steps.

My fans? A slender little girl, about twelve or thirteen years old, who walked next to an adult caught my eye, and I automatically smiled. She grinned and tugged her mother's arm. The woman also smiled at me and gave me a thumbs up. The girl reminded me of Mandy, and my mind darkened for a minute.

I faced forward, but I was seeing twelve-year-old Mandy, not the path in front of me. Mandy was sitting on the top rail of the fence with Shawn beside her, holding her steady. She used her fingers to push the corners of her mouth up, telling me to smile, just like her mother, Erica, had.

I missed them.

I swallowed the hollow ball clogging my throat and let my gaze fall on Cory's cowboy hat as it bobbed along next to Windsong's head. As if he felt my gaze, Cory turned, and his calm, confident blue eyes latched on to mine.

If he heard my thoughts, he would say, "Just you and Windsong. None of the rest matters."

I stroked my nervous horse's neck, sure that this time the rest *did* matter. EMA expected me to shine, to get noticed. They would be comparing my results with Erica's, and I couldn't disappoint them. I needed to do well to prove to my parents that this was a viable career option for me—and to make it worth being so deceptive. And somehow I needed to compete with Robert and his international horse.

No pressure, I thought, as I bounced on Windsong, doing my best to keep him from dancing into anyone on the path to the warm-up.

In the warm-up ring, there were more land mines than usual. We dodged left and right as people crowded the fence. Flapping arms and surging bodies startled Windsong, and he wouldn't concentrate on my aids. I kept to the middle but didn't make much progress toward relaxing him.

We made our way from the warm-up to the show ring with Cory right next to Windsong's head again. When we stopped, I nodded, and Cory listened to Windsong's heart. "Fifty-eight."

That was a bit high. The crowd was making him more nervous than usual. I could only hope that when we entered the show ring and got away from the people he would calm. I closed my eyes and leaned down over his neck. "Easy, boy. Just doing our thing. Such a good boy," I crooned, wondering if my shaky voice was soothing in any way.

Robert passed us to enter the ring. "Good luck!" Kate called.

I groaned, not sure I wanted to watch him and discourage myself. Melinda jogged up and leaned on the fence next to Cory. "That horse is magnificent," she breathed, sending me a wry look.

An older couple, the man in a three-piece suit and the woman wearing a floppy, fashionable hat, stopped next to Kate. "Do you know Robert?" the woman asked. "He's riding our baby." The pride in her voice was obvious.

"Your horse is beautiful. I trained with Robert when I was younger. I train Jane and Windsong now." She patted Windsong's neck. "They're in next."

The women's eyes clouded. "In the same class?"

Kate nodded.

"Oh, well, good luck." Her tone clearly implied that she thought I had no chance of beating her precious baby. She probably was right.

I couldn't look away from Robert. His back was straight and shoulders square, but he still exuded suppleness and an elegance I hoped I would one day achieve. Their transitions between movements were so oily smooth I imagined that the horse's hooves didn't leave marks on the sand. Despite my trepidation in competing against him, I had to smile. That was the way this freestyle should be ridden, and we were all lucky enough to witness it.

The crowd enthusiastically roared and applauded as he donned his top hat and saluted the judge.

The phrase from grade school when we were square dancing in gym class, *Bow to your partner,* drifted through my mind as I rode a stiff, tense Windsong past Robert and into the arena. He inclined his head and I returned the nod.

As I used my hands and legs to control Windsong's zig-zagging path, an amazing hush fell over the crowd. The spectators stilled, respecting the tradition of silence when a competitor entered the ring. I easily heard the judge's bell and, with shaking hands, halted Windsong on our starting mark. My gaze strayed to the expectant crowd hanging on the wooden fence. My fingers turned icy, yet a trickle of sweat slithered down my ribs.

I shifted in the saddle, causing Windsong to sidle forward a few steps. Not meaning to, but my numb hands jerked Windsong's mouth as I tried to hold him still, and with horror, I felt his hind end begin to spin sideways.

Out of the corner of my eye, something white moved, snagging my attention. From where he stood by the gate, Cory waved his hat gently. His blue eyes locked on mine as he replaced it on his head. He circled his fingers around his eyes like binoculars. Focus. Melinda held up her thumb, a big encouraging smile on her face. Support.

Just me and Windsong—not a thousand eyes watching. Just the horse and this freestyle—not my entire future. Just the music and my joy floating across the arena—not my lies to my parents. Pulling in a restoring breath of oxygen, I lifted my chin and raised my hand to signal the start of the music.

Not a thing disturbed our concentration. Windsong, soothed by the familiar work, focused his energy on my aids. His heart murmur, his nerves, even his age had no bearing. He performed like the champion he was bred to be. And I strove to ride him as he deserved to be ridden, tamping down my nerves and letting the rhythm flow through me.

I swallowed a lump of pride as we floated down the centerline. Windsong could not have given me more than he did in this test. I blinked back tears of gratitude when his feet settled into the dirt perfectly square, his neck softly rounded, and his lips wiggling the bits.

As I dropped my hand and my chin for the final salute, the spectators erupted with noise. Windsong bolted forward, and I laughed with the judge. Poor thing, he did not appreciate the love of a crowd, but I hoped the applause meant I didn't look half bad compared to Robert.

With big pats on his neck, I turned Windsong to exit the ring, nodding and waving. Again, I spiraled into the past, recalling Erica on Santos leaving the arena after an electrifying performance, interacting with her fans the same way.

Is this how she felt? Grateful but a little overwhelmed by their expectations?

Cory, Kate, Melinda, and Michelle were waiting for me at the gate. After the ring steward checked the legality of my equipment by poking a rubber-gloved finger into Windsong's mouth, Kate patted Windsong's neck. "Lovely ride, a few tense transitions, but overall quite nice."

"Nice ride. You've come a long way since I saw you over the summer." Michelle held her hand up for a high five. "Don't forget after you untack to meet me at the EMA vendor booth. We're doing one more prize drawing today and I want you there for it." She gave Windsong a scratch and then turned to leave.

Determined to make up for yesterday, I nodded. "After I'm done taking care of Windsong." Slouching like a trail rider, I was glad I didn't have to walk all the way to the barn myself. A tiny spear of guilt flashed when Windsong tripped wearily on some loose stones, and I decided to dismount anyway. Cory caught my waist as I slid off, and I leaned into him.

"Tired?" he asked.

"Tired and hungry," I replied. I straightened up and pulled the reins over Windsong's head. He shoved me with his nose, and I tickled his muzzle.

"I can take him," Cory offered, holding out his hand for the reins.

"No, I'll do it." I shuffled toward the barn.

Taking the reins anyway, Cory patted my shoulder. "It's okay."

Like yesterday, he began to lead Windsong away with Kate following behind, except this time, I followed too.

Cory led Windsong right into his stall and immediately pulled the bridle off. The black, sweaty horse plunged his nose into the water bucket and sucked down half of the water. The long walk back to the barn had cooled him and his breathing was normal, so I didn't take out the stethoscope. He was doing just fine.

After getting the sweat off his coat and covering him with his wool sheet, I was ready to collapse in the trailer. My phone buzzed with a text.

Michelle was sending a golf cart to pick me up. I had forgotten about the promo booth. She wanted me in my formal black and whites, so I couldn't even change.

"See you later." With envy, I watched Kate and Cory head back to the trailer. I climbed on the golf cart.

CHAPTER

# 16

It wouldn't have been so bad if I was able to sit through it. But Michelle had me standing and greeting people who came up to the booth. I was supposed to encourage them to enter the contest by pledging a donation, large or small. The sides of the U-shaped cubicle were covered in photos of rescued horses. Some included volunteers at rescue operations. Erica was prominent in many of them, and the famous poster of her with the tiny pony, Lucky, held a place of honor in the middle of the back wall.

Someone handed me a steaming cup of coffee, and I sipped it gratefully. Kate came up, and I wanted to whine at her to rescue me but rubbed my aching back instead. I took a second look at her. She had that grin on her face, the one that said I won, and she was carrying a test. Had I won? That was impossible—but did I? My knees sagged.

"No one can say you're inconsistent anymore. You got the same exact score you had at Regionals." She hugged me tightly before handing me the test.

My heart thudding, I wished I had a chair. With a deep breath, I turned the paper over. There was a three in the upper corner. Third. My shoulders slumped.

"What is it?" Michelle asked, holding out her hand. "Third? Excellent! Let me take a picture so I can post it online." She laid it on the table as she pulled out her phone. She didn't seem disappointed.

I frowned. "I didn't win."

Kate was still smiling. "Nope, Robert and Samantha Deciliano beat you. Robert's score was only two points higher than yours, though. Congratulations." She hugged me again, bubbling with excitement.

Samantha was a well-known rider who had won several world and national titles. "Only two points?" Could that be good enough?

I finished helping Michelle with the drawing, and then we met Robert for dinner. He praised me, saying that he had stayed to watch my ride and that I had improved greatly from the team championships.

Samantha also stopped by our table and chatted with Robert about his horse and his plans for the Olympics. Her disheveled dirty-blond bun and soiled white polo were in sharp contrast to Robert's always fastidious appearance. But she spoke clearly and confidently as if the Olympics were just another horse show to qualify for. Robert treated her respectfully, without the casual teasing he did with Kate. A good half foot shorter than me, she raised her head to look at me when Robert introduced us.

"Good job today," she said politely. Her eyes shifted back to Robert. "I better watch my back with this one, Robert. She's nipping at my heels." When she turned back to me, her expression was flat and hard to read. "I'll see you around, Jane."

Was that a challenge? Or a threat? My ears burned as she walked away.

"Is it that simple to qualify for the Olympics?" I asked Robert, staring after her.

He picked up his napkin and spread it on his lap and then looked up at me. "Simple?" He shrugged. "There are no breaks at that level. No, I wouldn't say simple. But with hard work, a strong and talented horse, and determination, absolutely doable." He smiled. He would know; he had already done it six times.

I slept most of the way home, abandoning Cory and Kate and lying down on the back seat with a pillow under my head. It was dark when we finally pulled in to the barn driveway, and I plodded into the barn with my arms full, keeping my eyes half closed, as if that would keep me from waking up all the way. Heading to school and studying were not going to happen. "Cory, can I crash with you tonight? I'm too tired. I'll drive back in the morning."

I tossed my books—never touched the whole weekend—on the back seat of my car.

The next morning in the lecture hall, I sipped a cappuccino and flipped through my notebook. One seat separated me from Carly. Students were arranged every other seat for the exam so there would be no cheating. I read the words on the page, trying to cram in a few more facts, but my brain wasn't absorbing much. Visions of victory gallops and cheering fans still danced in my head. How important was this one history test when my future was shining so bright?

The professor passed out the exam booklets and gave us instructions. As he said the words "You may begin" a silence fell over the room similar to the hush of the crowd as I had prepared to start my freestyle. I closed my eyes and relived that moment. I had lifted my arm to signal and then the music had taken over my body. Windsong had lightly cantered down the centerline.

The sound of Carly turning the page, her pen scratching furiously over the paper, brought me back to this test. Sighing, I opened the book and started.

Carly waited for me outside the lecture hall. I trudged out, dragging my book bag behind me.

"How did you do?" she asked, humming with pleasure.

"Bad. I forgot most of the dates. How about you?"

Her face fell. "Really? I thought it was easy. I think I did great. I'm sorry."

"Don't be. You studied hard. You probably aced it."

"You've been distracted, I know. I'll help you study for tomorrow's Statistics exam. Let's pick up some munchies and get right to work."

"Really?" I hugged her. "Thanks. My treat."

Propped up in bed with pillows tucked all around me, I flipped pages in my notebook. "Did I ever tell you that I hate Statistics?" I groaned.

Carly, who was sitting on her bed in a similar pose, laughed. "At least twenty times a day. Did I ever tell you I love it? And science, and writing. Good thing, if I want to be a vet, huh?"

"Oh, shush. I'm studying." I threw my eraser at her. For all her partying, Carly kept a flawless grade point average. I had no doubt that she would be at the top of the class at the end of four years and get into vet school no problem.

Missing all of those classes made it hard for me to learn the information I needed for the exam. I regretted not opening a book all weekend. The good thing about college? They expected you to be responsible for yourself, so there was no way for my parents to know what was going on, including with grades, unless I told them.

Just as well, since we seemed to be on opposite sides of the fence these days. I was so proud of what I had accomplished with Windsong, and I didn't understand how they couldn't see what a great thing that was. School was still here after it was all over, and here I was studying.

Now that I was back, my deception seemed silly. I should have had an adult conversation with them and simply informed them of my plans.

"Stop staring into space and get to work," Carly ordered without lifting her gaze from her book.

"I am. I am." I was going to ace this Statistics exam. And then my English literature test at the end of the week. And my parents wouldn't be able to say a thing about me going to Kentucky without telling them. They would see that I had it all under control and that I was right.

Friday evening, when I was standing in front of the Statistics professor's office where exam results were taped to the wall, with my finger on my name, I realized I was so wrong. *F*. I had failed the exam. I stepped back to let the others check their grades. I had failed my history exam as well and was hoping for a D on my English lit. I slumped down on a hard wooden bench in the entrance of the building. The only decent grade I had in my history class was the first paper I wrote way back in September. From there on, my quiz grades and make-up work never received anything higher than a C. I won't even go into Statistics. I was so sure it would all work out and my final grades would be passing though not on the Dean's list.

If this was a horse show and that was a dressage test score, Kate would just raise her eyebrows at me and say, "What did you expect? You didn't do the work to prepare. Nothing just happens on its own."

The truth is, I knew that. That's why I spent so much time going home to ride Windsong. But for school, Statistics especially, I was unmotivated and struggling to convince myself that this grade was just as important as my score on my dressage test.

Was that an immature attitude? I expected to graduate, to get a degree eventually. I expected to look for employment. But that seemed far in the future and my success in the show ring was happening right now. I only placed third in the Finals, but Robert praised me. He had noticed how much I had improved, and if he thought I was good, I was going somewhere. People valued his opinion and he would tell them that I was a promising competitor. I would be asked to ride talented horses, I would help EMA stay in business, and I would inspire other riders by my great accomplishments. It was clear how important my success at Finals was.

Failing my courses was going to make my father mad and that was bad. I promised him that I could do both. But give me a break, I had a lot to manage and I didn't do it that well. It was my first semester, though; I just needed time to get myself organized. I would have no problem next semester. I learned my lesson, I won't push the books aside, I won't skip classes. I'll sign up for better class times so I could go home to ride Windsong without missing them. I would manage it all so much better now that I knew what I need to do.

I rose from the bench, hefted my backpack onto my shoulder, and headed back to my dorm without bothering to check on my final grade for English literature.

*CHAPTER*

# 17

Holding the front door open with my back side, I put the strap of my smaller bag in my teeth and lifted my suitcase over the threshold. My mother rushed up the hall, drying her hands on her apron. "Let me help." She took the bag from my mouth and closed the door. "Is there more out there?"

Sticking my chin out, I air-kissed her cheek. "Hi, Mom. This is everything."

She one-arm-hugged me. "How did exams go? I made a great roast and veggies for your first dinner home."

The aroma was making my mouth water; the school dining hall never smelled that good. "I can't wait to eat it. Let me drag these bags upstairs and hit the bathroom. I'll be right back."

"Sure, sweetie. Your father will be home any minute, too. You can fill us in on your exams over dinner."

I started up the stairs, inwardly groaning. Give it up, already, with the exams.

Through dinner, I successfully steered the topic of conversation clear of academics until I was on my third helping of mashed potatoes and gravy. Humming in appreciation, I complimented my mother again. "I don't know how it is possible to screw up smashing potatoes, but the dining hall somehow manages it. Their mashed potatoes taste like cardboard. These are amazing, Mom."

My luck ran out right after she smiled.

My father wiped his mouth with a napkin and turned a direct gaze on me. "Tell us how exams went. Do you think you did well? Statistics was my worst class in school. But you always do well in math. Did you ace it?"

Shoving a mounded spoonful of potatoes in my mouth, I bought myself a few seconds to think. Unfortunately, the creamy smooth potatoes didn't need much chewing. Sighing dramatically, I went for evasion and misdirection. "I am so glad to be home and done with exams. I am sick of cinder block walls and immature kids. I'm looking forward to just hanging out with you guys."

My father's keen business mind wasn't buying my obfuscation. "I was always glad when exam week was over, too. Did you check you grades before you left?"

"They weren't all up yet, but I left anyway. I couldn't wait to be on my way home." Not exactly a lie, since I didn't go check my English lit. With another noisy sigh, "I am glad I don't have to think about exams or studying or anything about school for a whole month. Let's talk about Christmas. I have shopping to do. When can we get the tree out to decorate?"

My mother started gathering dinner plates. "We can go get it right now. I've been so busy at work, I haven't had a chance to start decorating. I'm glad you're here to help."

I pushed back my chair and jumped up to help with the dishes, making plans to go shopping over the weekend and keeping my eyes averted from my father.

Ten busy, festive days passed without another question about my grades. I followed my mother into the house, our arms full of shopping bags.

"Don't look, Dad! I have one of your presents in here." I laughed. I was so unprepared for my father's wrath.

He was standing in the foyer, arms crossed. The force of his stare stopped me short.

"What's the matter, Warren?" My mother set down her bags, concern in her voice.

He held up an envelope. "This came in today's mail. It had Jane's name on it, but it was from the university, so I figured it was her grades. I opened it."

I rushed to speak over his voice. "Wait, Dad. I can explain."

"Two Fs!" he shouted. I flinched like his words would hit me on the way past. "And a D and a C. Seriously, Jane, did you even try?"

My mother's mouth dropped open and the look she gave me brought an instant sting to my eyes. Before she spoke, I dropped the bags and held up my hand. "It looks bad, but I can retake the courses next fall. I already checked.

This was my first semester. It was different from high school, you know. With Regionals and Fi—. I mean, it was busy, but I get it now. I'll be more organized, do better from now on," I tried to explain.

My father threw up his hands. "You're blaming the horse! I told you that you couldn't handle both. That's it. It needs to go. I'm selling it. These grades are atrocious. I told you the horse was distracting you." He tossed my report card on the hall table, spun on his heel, and stalked into the living room. "Get out of my sight. I am so angry with you right now."

My mouth fell open and I ducked, his words hitting me like a slap in the face this time. I couldn't tear my eyes from the back of his head.

"You have never gotten an F in your life. What is going on with you?" my mother said quietly, the puzzlement and hurt in her tone more damaging than any punishment she could have doled out.

I closed my eyes; my arms lead weights hanging from my shoulders. "I'll do better. I promise."

"Your father told you this would happen. Why can't you ever listen?" All the joy and camaraderie of our shopping trip had vanished. She left me in the foyer. The springs of the couch squeaked as she sank down next to my father. Their low tones were indecipherable.

I stood alone, staring at my shoes. Were they talking about me? Of course they were. When had they become so mean? Not mean, I guess, just wanting something different from me than I ever expected. All right, I didn't expect to fail college courses, but now that I had, it wasn't the end of the world. I would just retake them. My parents just needed time to cool off, and then I would talk to them. I would promise to be more focused and work hard and get As. I dropped the shopping bags next to my mom's and slipped out the front door.

Cory made hot chocolate in his tiny kitchen and set the mug in front of me as I explained the scene at my house.

"I told you all of that sneaking around wasn't going to do you any good. How could you just dump your studying?"

"I didn't dump it. I had a lot going on. I didn't realize how hard the exams would be."

Cory shook his head, rolling his eyeballs. "I don't get you. You have the opportunity to go to college and you're screwing it up."

"It's like, I know that I have to get a degree and all, but I am doing so well on Windsong. I don't want to give that up just for a few grades."

Cory gave his mug a last stir as he sat down across from me. "Those grades add up to your future."

I rubbed my eyes with the heels of my hands and rested my forehead on them. Without looking at him, I sighed. "You and I both know this is probably Windsong's last chance. If I wait, he will be too old to compete at these levels. And if I take a break from training him, his heart may not allow me to bring him back to this level of fitness."

I raised the mug to my lips and took a long, slow sip. "If I keep going, I can show at Grand Prix this spring. It could be years before I have a Grand Prix horse again. If I keep going with Windsong and get my scores for my Gold Rider Achievement Award—the highest award a rider can earn!—my reputation will be made and people will recognize me as a professional rider."

"So? You'll be a professional rider with no degree, and no means of financing your next horse, anyway, let alone all of those horse shows." He quickly dismissed my argument.

Cory had lost his talented performance horse, but that was after he had been able to take Jet all the way to a world championship. Now he didn't have a horse to show, but Lakota had the potential. Cory worked with him every day, training him for the very thing he was telling me not to focus on. He was holding himself back from earning good money training because he certainly didn't lack the skills or the knowledge. Did he—like my father—believe that if you weren't wearing a suit and making a living in an office, you weren't really a success? I didn't believe that.

I drained my cup and stood. "I'm going to head home. I need to come up with a way to clear this up with my dad."

On the way home, I pulled into the parking lot of the supermarket, parked, and sat in the warm car, thinking. I needed the opinion of another college kid. I called Carly.

She answered with a cheerful hello.

"Did you get your grades?"

"Yep. All As. How about you?"

"I failed Statistics and History." Cringing, I waited for her criticism.

"That sucks, but, really, I didn't think you could pull your grades up even if you studied for your exams." Her tone was even; I couldn't detect an ounce of judgment. "Realistically, you should have withdrawn or something; you had a lot going on. You'll just have to retake the classes. People do it all the time, you know. It's not like you were slacking off partying. You did some big things."

A lump formed in my throat. She didn't think I was stupid or the scum of the earth because I failed my courses. "Thank you for saying that. My father went through the roof."

She laughed. "I could imagine. It's not the end of the world. You'll do better when you can concentrate. And I promise to make sure you study before I drag you out to parties next semester."

Next semester, when I was supposed to just study and not go home to ride every weekend. A semester of sitting at my desk staring at books and writing essays. A semester without the feel of Windsong's soft coat and warm breath.

"It feels like the end of the world. They are trying to get me to quit riding while I am in school."

"That's crazy! You *need* to ride like a duck needs to swim. It is vital for you to thrive."

"I know! I can't imagine not preparing for my next show. What would my goals be? What would I do on the weekends if I didn't ride?"

"And after getting all the way to Nationals, why would you stop there? They're not making sense. Give them a few days, be the perfect daughter, then talk to them again. Sometimes I cook dinner for my mom or clean the bathroom when I want to ask for something. That always softens her up."

Snowflakes dotted my windshield, and I unclicked my seat belt. "That's a great idea. You're the best. Talk to you soon."

My parents *weren't* making sense. They were overreacting. People got Fs, just like people got low scores at horse shows, for making mistakes. They learned from it, went back, practiced—or, in this case, studied more—and came back stronger, readier, and tried again.

That's what I would do.

I stepped out of the car and held up my hand. Taking a deep breath, I looked straight up, letting the tiny icy particles melt on my skin. We were going to have a white Christmas.

I slid back into the car and started it up, thinking about what Carly said.

I parked on the street in front of my house and stepped onto the curb, stopping to admire our decorations. Twinkle lights lined the gutters and the porch, wreaths with red velvet bows hung in all the windows and on the door, and glittering wire reindeer grazed on the lawn. Grinning, I let the holiday anticipation turn my mood festive and hopeful. I quietly let myself in the house and tiptoed up to my room. Tomorrow there would be time enough to smooth things over with everyone.

CHAPTER

# 18

Both of my parents had Christmas Eve off from work, and I spent the morning helping my mother prepare an elaborate dinner. My aunt and uncle with their two kids, as well as my grandparents, were coming for the feast and gift giving. Cory was coming, too, since his mother had to work. We planned on having dinner with her after her lunch shift on Christmas Day.

I placed the last piece of my mother's silverware on the table and stepped back to make sure I hadn't forgotten anything. Smiling, I pulled out my phone and took a picture. It looked as beautiful as any magazine spread.

My mom slid an arm around my shoulders. "It looks fantastic."

Taking Carly's advice, I was helping my mother get things ready for our guests. "Thanks. Is there anything else you need? I am going to meet Cory at the barn to give Windsong his holiday carrots and apples, and then we'll come back here."

"Nope." She kissed my cheek. "Don't be late."

By tacit agreement, no one had brought up the subject of school or my grades all day. As I set Cory's small, carefully wrapped present on the passenger seat, I wiggled and shimmied. I loved this season, and I couldn't wait for Cory to open that box.

I brought Windsong into the barn and slipped off his waterproof blanket. "What do you think of this snow? You feel all snuggly in your blankie." I groomed and sprayed his sleek black coat and cleaned his feet. He didn't protest when, instead of his saddle, I tossed his blanket over his back and began fastening the buckles. "Even hard-working superstars like you get the holidays off."

Cory came in as I was mixing the chopped treats with some warm water and bran mash for Windsong's Christmas dinner.

Windsong nodded as the yummy scent hit his nostrils. He pawed at his bucket, using his nose to fling it to the side and make as much noise as he could.

"I can't dump it in if you're knocking the bucket around, silly." Tipping the container up, the gooey, lumpy mixture plopped into his feed tub. He plunged his muzzle deep into the warm food and slurped some up. Before I could get out of the way, he nudged me with his dripping nose and left a long smear on my coat sleeve.

After latching the door, Cory and I watched him enjoy his special treat. I grabbed Cory's arm. "Come on. I am dying for you to open your present."

We climbed to the hay loft with our gifts. Cory arranged the bales so we would be comfortable, and then set down a large, rectangular box covered in bright red paper with a big gold bow. It was so perfectly done, he must have had it wrapped by the store. The eight-inch-square box that I brought looked less than spectacular next to that fancy gift, but I didn't care. I knew Cory would love what I had got him.

"Ladies first." Cory set his hat down on the hay bale next to him.

Grinning, I tore off the gorgeous paper, ripping it to shreds. I lifted the lid off the box and then leapt up, gasping, as I pulled the green, stylish barn coat out. Immediately, I unbuttoned my old one and shrugged out of it.

Cory stood and helped me put the new coat on and leaned down to kiss my neck. "I thought if my arms can't keep you warm up at school, then the jacket I gave you will and you won't forget about me," he explained.

How thoughtful and romantic! I turned in his arms and gave him a smacking kiss on the lips. "I love it! I will imagine it is your arms every time I put it on. Now, do yours." I pushed the small box into his hands.

With gentle fingers, Cory untaped the paper and opened the lid. He lifted the delicate ceramic figurine from the soft tissue paper. It was a bay horse executing a sliding stop. Dirt spit up from around his legs, his nostrils were flared, and sweat darkened his coat. The cowboy's white Stetson sat low on his brow, and he had one hand on the reins and the other positioned precisely over the little horse's withers. The statue was so detailed you could see the steely determination in the cowboy's blue eyes.

Cory turned and twisted the figure, closely examining it. "It almost looks like me and Jet," he said with wonder.

"It is. I had it made for you."

Tears glistened at the edges of Cory's eyes, and the look of warmth and love he gave me was exactly why I didn't want him to open this gift in front of everyone. He carefully wrapped the statue in the paper, put it in the box, and set it aside. He placed my palm over his thumping heart. "That gift is so thoughtful, *you* are so thoughtful. Sometimes I can't believe you are with me. Feel that? You own that, forever." And he kissed me, sliding his hands under the coat and pushing it off my shoulders.

Conditioned for twelve years to return to school right after New Year's Day, I felt funny sleeping late, treating every day like Saturday for the next few weeks before I had to return to college. Winter break—I wished it would last forever. Even with my new determination to do well in my courses, I still wasn't looking forward to it.

On the last weekend, my father turned serious as he handed me his empty dinner plate. "Before we turn on the movie, I would like to have a family meeting."

Noisily stacking dishes in my arms, I tried to stall. "Can we do it another day, please? I am supposed to meet my friends at the bowling alley tonight. It's our last Friday out before we all go back to school," I pleaded.

I knew what was on his mind and was hoping to head off that conversation. If I could just get back to school and bring home some good grades, maybe my father would forget about his new rules for the semester.

"No. Sit down."

His face brooked no argument, and I lowered the plates to the table. Sinking onto my chair, I crossed my arms and pressed my lips tight together.

"You'll be going to school on Sunday. As I said last semester, you will only be allowed to come home once per month. This time, though, I expect emails that include all test scores and other grades with copies of the actual papers attached. If you get any grades lower than As and Bs, I will call Kate and tell her to sell the horse."

His calm, matter-of-fact tone didn't prepare me for the severity of his threat.

I sat up, leaning on my elbows. He gazed at me. Just a glimmer of smugness that he tried hard to hide settled on his face.

So, this was what it felt like to be threatened, this hollow coldness in my gut and this ringing in my ears. Shaking my head, I returned his stare. "Windsong is mine. You can't sell him. And I already told you that I learned my lesson. I will be more diligent with my studies."

"Then you have nothing to worry about, do you?" One eyebrow lifted.

Searching my memory, I couldn't come up with a time when he had had to threaten me before. I was a good child and did as I was told. I freely admitted that I was spoiled, that I got everything I wanted from my parents. My father had always been affectionate and supportive.

He had bought Windsong for me, or at least he approved of the purchase. He had taught me to be thorough and conscientious in everything I did. He had comforted me when life got rough. He had consoled me when I did badly at a horse show, telling me to buck up, work a little harder, and try again.

Where was this menacing demeanor coming from? This strong-arm tactic? I had made a mistake, but was it so grave that my own father thought he needed to bully me into proper behavior as if I were caught using drugs and needed an intervention?

"I'm not on drugs."

"I didn't think you were. This is about making sure you work this semester."

"I promised to work. You don't have to threaten me!"

"I'm not threatening you. I am making you a promise. This is just insurance that you will make an effort. Because if you don't, I will know about it. And I will not have any trouble keeping my promise." If this were a western movie, he would lay a revolver on the table to underline his meaning.

He didn't need a gun. I got the message. "You're treating me like a child. Like you don't trust me."

"It's not about trust. Think of it as an incentive."

"It feels more like intimidation." I stood up abruptly, banging the platters into a pile with a satisfying clatter. "Don't expect me home tonight."

I dumped the dishes in the sink, plucked my coat from the hook, grabbed my purse, and slammed the door as hard as I could when I left.

CHAPTER

# 19

I spent Saturday at the barn with Windsong and Cory, avoiding both of my parents and not answering my phone when my mother called.

I didn't deserve to be threatened. And using Windsong like he was a toy to be taken away because I was being a naughty child was downright wrong. I was an adult and deserved to be treated like one. I had admitted my mistakes and promised to do better. That should have been enough.

If they ever actually sold Windsong, they might as well forget about having a relationship with me. I would rather be with my horse than with parents who treated me that way.

After dinner out with Cory, I slipped back in the house. I planned on avoiding both parents and leaving for school the next morning while continuing the silent treatment. I hung my coat on the coat rack in the hall and turned to go upstairs.

My father stood in the foyer, his body stiff and rigid, his face a cold mask of rage. My hand dropped off the banister and I swallowed loudly.

He threw an opened envelope at my feet. "Trust you to keep your promise? Believe what you tell me? After this, I can't do that. You don't even deserve my respect." He whirled and stomped down the hall.

I looked at my mother, who stood in the doorway with her arms crossed tightly over her chest, but she just shook her head. "I can't believe you would go and do something like this."

My face heated under her glare. Which "this" was she talking about?

She held up her hand when my mouth opened to ask. "Save it," she said coldly. "We're done listening to your lies." She turned and, with slumped shoulders, followed my father.

I stuck my thumbnail between my teeth and ripped. Shaking off the pain, I stooped to pick up the envelope. The United States Dressage Federation logo was on the top left corner. My hands shook. Could I be disqualified for riding without my parents' consent? No, that was ridiculous; legally, I was an adult. But what bad news in this letter had my parents livid?

Swallowing, I slid the letter out. I took a deep breath and, before my knees gave out, sat on the bottom step. I started to read.

My heart beat faster and faster as I scanned the words. The USDF *didn't* want my ribbon back. This was unreal. Slowly, my quivering lips spread in a shaky grin, and by the time I reached the end of the page, I wanted to leap in the air for joy. This was good news, excellent news! My parents' reaction was baffling to me.

My heart lightened, and I stood, holding the letter to my chest. I had done it. It had all been worth it.

The USDF was inviting me to participate in the Festival of Champions in April! Only the top fifteen nationally ranked riders—out of the thousands and thousands who competed—were invited, and I was number nine in the Open Intermediate I division. I hugged the paper to my cheek. I couldn't wait to tell Kate. She was going to scream.

Last year, Kate had taken me to the Festival to see Robert and Erica, along with many other well-known riders, perform. The show was held in New Jersey, and we had stayed overnight, without my parents. Watching the best riders in the country had inspired me. Erica and Santos's performance had captivated me, and Robert was so cool and professional.

And, now, spectators were going to watch *me* ride. I straightened my spine. I had a lot of work to do. I was determined to be just as noble and fantastic as those two were. Erica had said I could do it. I rolled my eyes skyward. *Thank you for believing in me. I promise to work hard to make you proud.* I bounced on my toes, looking around for my jacket. I had to call Kate.

"Jane, get in here!" my father yelled from the kitchen.

The grin dropped off my face. His voice was loud and sounded weird, not like his usual executive voice at all. He sounded a little wild—crazy, in fact. I glanced at the letter again, cocking my head. His fury did not match what I thought was the best news I had ever gotten. Maybe he didn't understand the honor and prestige that came with this invitation. When I explained what this meant, he would calm down. He had to. He would realize how good I was and how important it was for me to keep riding. He would be proud of me.

I leaned forward, forming an explanation in my head, seeking the right, powerful words that would have my parents melting at my feet. See, I was learning some things in college.

I pushed open the swinging door to the kitchen and jumped when my father slammed a glass on the counter with a loud crack. My eyes leapt from the glass to the open bottle of whiskey to his red face.

"Warren, take it easy. We are going to talk about this calmly, okay?" my mother cajoled as she pulled out a chair. Her tone hardening, she commanded me, "Sit down, young lady."

With two hands on the counter and his back to me, my father asked, "Tell me why that letter says you rode in the Dressage Finals? Tell me why it says you took off from school to be in Kentucky? And you better tell me it's a mistake. That you wouldn't have lied to me to do it." He turned, crossing his arms and leaning back against the edge of the counter.

"It's not a mistake, but I did so well." I got up and stood right in front of him. "You would be so proud, Daddy. I placed third, and now they want me to ride in the Festival. It's really a big deal!"

"Proud of you? You've got to be kidding. You lied to me. To your mother," he said, swinging an arm toward my mom. "We specifically told you no, and you went behind our backs anyway."

His angry eyes bore burning holes in my face, and I turned away to protect myself from their awful power. "I didn't exactly lie. But EMA was willing to back me, and it didn't cost you anything, and they'll pay for this too. I've got it all taken care of."

"What about school?"

"I'll do school. I'll be good. I'll really buckle down. I swear."

"I don't believe you."

"Daddy! I promise." I swallowed the rock scratching at the back of my throat.

"It's over, Jane. You're a college student and the horse shows are interfering with that. The horse will be sold. Give me your car keys." He held out his hand.

I reached in my pocket and then dropped the keys in his palm. "Why?"

"Because I'm taking you to school myself, and you won't have a car to sneak to the barn with. You want to come home, you'll have to call me first."

My muscles wobbled and I sank into the kitchen chair. "Daddy, please. Listen to me."

"Listen to more lies? No, I won't." His voice caught, and he rubbed the wrinkle between his brows. "Go to your room." Defeat weakened the order.

I stared at him, but he wouldn't look at me.

"Go," my mother repeated.

As I left the room, I was still thinking of arguments, the perfect words to convince him that it was all okay. Once he calmed down, I would be able to make him listen to my plan, to understand that I really could do this. The invitation was, in fact, proof that I could do this, and do it well. I would just have to wait for him to calm down.

My foot on the bottom step, I paused in my musings when I heard my father pick up the house phone and dial. After a moment, he said, "Hi, Kate." My stomach flipped. What was he doing?

I turned and tiptoed back to listen through the swinging door, breathing shallowly and straining to hear over the buzzing in my ears.

He spoke in such a reasonable tone, not at all the haggard, raspy croak he had used with me. Businesslike. He talked as if he was asking her to sell off an old dresser. When I heard the words "sell Jane's horse" I slapped a hand over my mouth. Holding in the panic, the sobs, I reached up to slam open the kitchen door but stopped myself when he said, "We know what you did."

Wait. Kate couldn't get in trouble for taking me to Finals, could she? I was eighteen, an adult, but technically, Windsong belonged to my father. Would he do something to hurt Kate if she didn't listen to him? What had I done, involving her in my deception?

I fled to my room, pounding up the stairs, not caring if they knew I had overheard. I threw myself face down on the bed and let hot tears soak my pillow case.

My phone vibrated under my hip. Swiping it on, I rolled onto my back.

"I just talked to your father. He told me you had decided to sell Windsong,"

Kate reported.

"I didn't decide that. He is trying to get me to quit riding."

"So you said before. He found out about Finals." Her tone was grim.

"I'm sorry. He read my mail. He opened an invitation to the Festival of Champions before I got home. He was furious that I went to Finals without telling them. So he threatened to sell Windsong. He said I needed to be a college student."

"Wait a minute. You were invited to compete at the Festival?" Kate said. "That's incredible, fantastic!" Her joy was exactly the way I had imagined it would be. She knew what this meant, and she was thrilled.

I grinned. "I know, right?" But then my throat clogged, and I pressed the heel of my hand between my eyes. "But I can't go. He took my car keys. He's going to take me everywhere and never to the barn. But I can't let him sell Windsong! I have to do what he says now."

"I think he's going to sell him no matter what. He told me he wouldn't pay another cent for board or lessons, so I better get the horse sold before the next bill is due or pay for him myself. Jane, the next board payment is due on the first, in ten days."

I sprang up. "He can't do that."

"His name is on the papers, he pays the bills. I have to do what he says."

Pressing my forehead harder into my hand, I murmured, "What am I going to do?"

"You need someone else to pay the bills. When I asked how much money he wanted me to ask for Windsong, your father said any price would do, as long as the sale was final in the next few days."

"A few days!" Now I pressed my hand over my mouth to keep from throwing up. "I gotta figure something out. Kate, please, don't do anything yet. Just give me a little time. Please."

"I will try, honey. Okay? I'll try to think of something too."

In the bathroom I rinsed my mouth and swallowed some cool water. With a sigh, I sat at my vanity table and scrolled to Cory's number.

"I need your help." I told him what had happened. "I barely even care about the Festival, I have to save Windsong. He can't be sold! No one would know how to ride him, he's so quirky and he's not that healthy. I mean, no one would buy him with his condition. Oh my God, he can't go to some bad trainer like the guy we got him from. What can we do, Cory?"

"Find a good home for him and get back to school. Your dad just wants you to do well in college."

"What?" I rubbed my temple, shaking my head. I couldn't have heard him right. "Windsong's life is on the line and you are agreeing with my father?" I stood, leaning a hand on the table.

"Windsong is a valuable horse; you've done well on him. It will be easy to find someone for him. He will get a good home. It's time to choose."

I stood eyes level with the poster of Erica and Santos. "I have been invited to the Festival of Champions, I am a nationally ranked rider, and I have a chance to compete with the best in the country. And all you and my father can think about are a couple of Fs on some tests that I can retake?"

"We are thinking of the future, of giving you a chance for a happy life," Cory drawled.

"No, you are thinking of a future that would make both of you happy. Not me." I started to pace, throwing my hand out at each sentence. "I do have to make a choice. I choose Windsong. I can't imagine not having him in my life. I will fight for him."

"And if I tell you I think you are making a mistake? That you are destroying your relationship with your father over a horse? What is your choice then?"

"My father picked this fight! I would have compromised to keep Windsong."

"You didn't compromise, you lied and did what you wanted to." Cory's voice rose.

"Because he wouldn't listen to me!" I pounded the door frame with my fist. "I can't believe you're siding with him."

"I told you I didn't like the lying, especially to a respectable man like your father. But you seem to think a crazy horse deserves more respect than a man that has done everything for you. I won't be a part of that."

"You are seriously saying that I should just cave and let him sell Windsong to some stranger?"

"That's right. What's fighting with your father over this going to cost you? Your relationship with your parents? Your degree? Me? Is it worth it? Figure it out." He hung up.

I looked at the screen until it went blank. I threw the phone down on the bed and pounded my pillow with both fists.

# 20

F*igure it out?*

What? That I wanted riding success more than anything else in my life? No, that wasn't true. I wanted it along with everything else important in my life. I knew what was important. What I didn't know was why it had to be a choice.

My phone jingled and I lunged for the bed, hoping it was Cory.

"Hi, girl. It's Carly."

"Boy, did you call at a bad time." Flopping on the bed, I kicked my shoes off.

"I was just going to ask you what time you were getting to school. Why? What's happening?"

Starting with the invitation, I told her my predicament. Like Kate, she actually was happy for me.

"I'm proud of you, Jane. You never really talk about it, but you must be a really, really good rider."

My eyes fell again on the poster of Erica and Santos. It was starting to show wear and tear from its travels back and forth to my dorm. But Erica's charisma and Santos's beauty still radiated strongly from the paper.

"I'm not as good as Erica was, but Windsong is so talented."

"So, you compare yourself to an Olympian and give the credit to your horse. Maybe you need to toot your own horn. Maybe your dad doesn't get how good you are."

"I'm not sure he would care if he knew." My feet waved in the air as I tucked the phone between my shoulder and cheek and massaged my stiff neck.

"I'm sure he would. It's a shame you can't hire a tutor or something, like child actors or young sport pros do. Then you can study in the down times as you traipse around showing Windsong."

"Like my dad would ever pay for that! He told Kate to sell Windsong. I don't know what I have to do to convince him I learned my lesson, but I have to think of something."

"Let me know if I can help. I guess I'll see you sometime tomorrow."

I rolled up to the edge of the bed. Erica would have liked the tutor idea. And she would have been proud of me. She was a top-level rider, one of the world's best, but she was more than just a trophy winner. Of course, she created the rescue that helped so many abused and neglected horses. She also was extremely influential in the highest echelons of the governing bodies of our sport. In person, she was all encouragement, inspiration, and positive energy. That's what I wanted to be—someone as gracious, generous, and fabulous as she was.

I missed her. Like the ground coming up to meet me when I fell off a horse, pain slammed my chest and the air left my lungs with a whoosh. "Erica, am I doing the right thing? Or am I dreaming?" I whispered as I touched her paper cheek with my index finger.

As clear as if she was right in front of me, I heard Erica's voice, "Jane, I believe you have great potential and, with proper support, will go far in the sport of dressage."

I imagined Windsong and me on a similar poster. I didn't want people to recognize me just to be popular. When they saw me and Windsong on a poster, I wanted them to feel the same admiration and respect that I always felt when I gazed on Erica's picture. And if I could inspire just one kid to work a little harder to achieve a dream like Erica inspired me, then my efforts will have paid off.

I also wanted to be the spokesperson for EMA for more than the acclaim. I believed in the organization, in its methods of helping the horses and in its policy of education. I was excited to spread the message, to be a part of such a great thing.

I didn't want to quit school; I had to figure out a way to do all of it. Maybe I couldn't hire a tutor, but like I had mentioned to Cory, there were online colleges. I saw commercials about them all of the time. I pulled my laptop out of the carrying case and keyed it on.

Twenty minutes later, I pressed send and an email zipped to my college adviser's inbox. I shut down the computer, picked up my phone, and called Michelle.

After I hung up, I tucked the phone in my purse. Most of my things were packed for my return to college, so I needed to get only a few more items together. I threw the last of my clothes and toiletries in the bag and carried it down to the foyer. On my third trip down the stairs, my mother got up from the couch. "What are you doing?"

I dropped my last bag on the pile and walked into the living room with my mother trailing behind me. "I have something to say."

My gravity and firm stance had my father clicking the television off.

I looked him in the eye, drawing my shoulders back and lifting my chin. "I thought about what you said and realized that I didn't go about things in a good way. I apologize for deceiving you. It was wrong and childish. But Windsong is my horse, and I have plans and goals. It is my life."

I held up my hand when my father started to rise. He sank back down, his jaw clenched.

"Just listen for a minute," I said, my eyes firmly on his face. "I have made arrangements to move Windsong to a farm that has agreed to employ me and provide living arrangements. EMA is going to sponsor me, supporting my preparation for the Festival of Champions in exchange for certain duties. Michelle is on her way here to pick me up."

My father stood abruptly and crossed his arms as he leaned over me. "What about school?"

Licking my lips and swallowing, I tried not to let his height intimidate me. "I have a meeting with my adviser tomorrow about online courses. I researched it and I can complete a degree at my own pace over the Internet. You have already paid for the next semester, so I will transfer that credit to the virtual college, but in time, I plan on paying you back." As his gaze darkened, I shoved my fists into my pockets to hide their trembling and looked at my mother. Her eyebrows were lifted and her eyes opened wide.

My father rolled his eyes. "How? Mucking stalls doesn't pay that great, last I heard."

I cringed, tearing my eyes from my mom to look around the living room at the big screen television, my father's elaborate surround-sound system, and my mother's delicate and expensive collection of equine art. I wouldn't be living in the lap of this kind of luxury, but I would do okay.

My eye fell on a shiny ceramic figurine of a black horse. I couldn't give up Windsong even if it meant I had to live in the stall next to his to save him. I took a step forward, narrowing my eyes at my father. "Everything is not about money!"

"No, but you won't get far without mine."

I let the air I was unconsciously holding in my lungs stream through my lips. As I looked into his determined eyes, I realized something. He didn't have any faith in me, didn't think I was capable of making it on my own. He still thought of me as his little girl that he had to take care of. With a shake of my head, I took a step back. While I appreciated the sentiment, I didn't agree. I could do this on my own—I would do this on my own.

"I guess we're gonna find out." At the faint sound of a horn, I turned. "I gotta go. I'm sorry if I upset you, Mom."

"Don't go." Mom grabbed my arm. "Let's talk some more, work this out."

I looked over my shoulder. My father still had his arms crossed, his back stiff and straight. When it didn't soften and he showed no sign that he wanted to talk more, to work something out, I shook my head. I gave her a hug and went to pick up my bags.

"Warren!" Behind me, my mother hissed, "Do something. Fix this."

"Jane, wait." Without moving, he tried to call me back. "College is only four years. After you get your degree, I'll buy you another horse. You can pursue your riding while you work at a very good job."

Using my forearm to lever the door handle, I kept moving. "See, that's just it. This *is* a very good job, and the one I want." I kicked the door closed.

His loud angry voice easily came through the closed door. "I'm not giving you your car back!"

CHAPTER

# 21

Michelle helped me load my bags into her little hatchback.

"Thanks for coming." I slipped into the passenger seat and clicked the seat belt closed.

"What a mess. Are you okay?" After looking over her shoulder, she pulled out into the street.

I shrugged. "I guess. I just feel really strongly that this is what I want to do. I still can't believe how crazy my dad is."

Michelle laughed. "He's probably thinking the same thing about you right now."

She was taking me to one of EMA's partner farms. EMA would send rescued horses there for rehabilitation before adoption. There was a room above the barn and I could help with the feeding and barn chores in exchange for boarding Windsong. The farm was small—fifteen horses was its full capacity—but it only had eight horses at the moment.

I kept an eye out for white three-rail fencing but was surprised when Michelle turned into an unmarked dirt driveway. Electric fencing hung from posts that were all askew surrounding a weedy field.

"This is the place?" Michelle's little car bounced so high as we rolled over the deep ruts that I put a hand over my head to protect it from smashing against the ceiling.

The barn was two stories high. The double doors to the hay loft were flung wide open and one hung sideways from a single hinge. The rickety, slatted sliding doors opened on a dirt aisle. Shaggy horses separated by more flimsy white tape fencing trotted to their gates at our approach.

I flipped the seat belt over my shoulder and slowly got out of the car.

"Come on, I'll introduce you to Donna. You'll like her, she's great."

We entered the dark barn and I was surprised to see sturdy new lumber lining the stalls on both sides of the dilapidated building. Only a couple of heads hung over the half doors.

"Up here," a voice called from a narrow stairwell next to an alcove that held metal cans with feed scoops resting on top of their lids. A dusty shelf was tucked in the corner jam-packed with plastic supplement containers.

I followed Michelle up the stairs and stopped dead at the top. A forty-something woman with bristly black hair wielded a broom, attacking the thick layer of dirt like it was fighting back.

"I was giving it a quick sweep. I haven't had anybody up here for a few years. The plumbing works—I just checked—and I switched on the little water heater in the closet next to the bathroom. You'll have to check it in an hour to see if the water is hot."

A section of the hayloft had been walled off to make this room. A worn area rug, a musty couch, and an ancient dresser filled the space. In the farthest corner, a skinny bed with a horse blanket, buckles and all, spread over it was shoved against the wall.

Donna saw my face and grimaced. "I know. It's not great, but I'll help you set it up. It'll look cute once it's clean." She wiped her hand on her pants and held it out to me. "I'm Donna, by the way. It's nice to meet you."

They both helped me carry my bags up the stairs and we made a pile in the other corner. We followed Donna back down the stairs and she gave us a tour, introducing us to the horses and reminding Michelle where each one came from. Michelle made all the appropriate noises about how improved they looked, rubbing noses and patting necks.

I lagged behind them, inspecting door handles and looking in the stalls. They were a nice size and bedded with clean shavings.

Only two stalls were occupied. I stopped in front of one door, clucking at the shaggy brown horse inside. He looked at me suspiciously but didn't stop chewing the delicious-looking hay at his feet. He was thin and had sores on the points of his hips.

I moved to look in the next stall. A taller, thin, Thoroughbred type stepped right over and stuck his head out. "Hi there." I patted his long, thin neck. He perked his ears, lifting his head, begging for a harder scratch. He didn't seem to notice that his skin stretched over protruding bones, all angles and no smooth muscle. He circled the stall and stopped in front of his hay, wide-eyed with energy.

I turned as Michelle put a hand on my shoulder. "I have to go. I'll call you tomorrow. Get some rest."

When her tail lights disappeared down the road, I gingerly climbed the stairs to my new room. I spread a sweatshirt over the grimy-looking pillow and lay down in my clothes. My hands were shaking as I tried to key in Cory's number, redialing four times before getting it right.

"Hey."

I swallowed my words at his cool greeting. My actions were the complete opposite of his advice, would he help me if I asked? I wasn't lying anymore, but there was more to our disagreement than that. There was only one way to find out and I got straight to the point. "Do you think you could help me trailer Windsong to a different barn about a half hour away?"

"Move him? Why?" Suspicious.

Leaving out the details about the condition of this farm, I briefly summarized my plan.

After a painful moment of silence, Cory asked quietly, "Who are you? You left your beautiful house, you're not going back to school, and you're moving your horse? I don't know what's going through your head these days."

With stubborn conviction, I barked into the speaker, "I'm building a future. I know what I'm doing."

"Sounds like you're throwing it away to me."

"You used to believe in me. Is that only when I was the privileged daughter of parents with money? Now that I want to be my own person, make it on my own, you don't want anything to do with me?"

"Quitting college and fighting with your family, your dad, sounds like the actions of a spoiled brat. If I had a dad and he wanted to send me to college, I wouldn't just walk out of his house and throw it all away."

"That's not what I'm doing, and if you don't get it, I guess we have nothing to talk about." I smashed the end button, tossing the phone on the bed.

Leaping up and pacing, I cursed him. I took two deep breaths, battling the nausea that rose up my throat. Cory was always the one I could turn to, he was my rock. I made a fist and smacked my knuckles against my palm. What was his problem? Couldn't he understand what I was trying to accomplish here? I tripped over the curled corner of the threadbare carpet.

Looking around at the naked unpainted walls, the dented and rusty lamp, and the dead flies stuck to the light bulb, I sank back down on the bed. The springs groaned noisily and I had to shift around to find the least lumpy spot. I pressed my fingers over my eyelids to stop the stinging. I wouldn't cry. I had made a good decision. I did know what I was doing. I thought.

I plugged the charger in and connected the phone to it. I held onto it, hoping Cory would call back. With thoughts ping-ponging around in my head, I fell asleep in my clothes on top of the horse blanket, using my coat and bathrobe as covers. Despite leaving the light on in the windowless room, I slept deeply. I awoke to the sounds of whinnying horses and banging buckets. My phone was conveniently still in my hand and I flicked it on to see if I had missed a call. Nothing but the date and time.

I rolled over, stood and slipped my feet right into my barn boots. A whiff of my own breath had me digging out my toothbrush.

Crystal clear water flowed out of the ancient chrome spigot. If the noise the pipes made was any indication, a giant creature was making its way up from the depths of the well. I rinsed and spit quickly, shutting off the water before the monster appeared.

I put on my coat and gloves. Jogging down the stairs, I held the banister in case the rickety boards snapped under my weight and nearly landed on Donna.

A bucket on the top of the stack she was carrying teetered, and I reached to steady it, elbowing her in the side. She flinched, becoming further unbalanced, and when I tried to save her, I stomped on her foot with my thick-soled boots. Finally, I just wrapped my arms around her waist until she stopped wobbling.

I said "I'm sorry" just as she said "Good morning." And we almost started the whole routine over again when I tried to lift half the buckets out of her hands.

"Whoa! Take a step back, girl. I'm not used to so much help."

I stepped back with my hands up, mumbling another apology.

Donna set the stack of buckets down, tugged two free, and handed them to me. "The blue one goes to the little brown horse in the barn, and the green one goes to Marty, the tall Thoroughbred next to him."

Looking in the buckets, I carried them to the stalls. A mixture of textured sweet feed and green pellets half filled each bucket. Three different powders were sprinkled on top. Both horses could have given Windsong a lesson in manners as they waited patiently for me to dump the feed in their bins.

Donna came back in the barn as I jiggled the stall door to make sure the flimsy latch caught.

"Why are these two the only ones in the barn?"

"If the weather is nice, I leave all the horses outside. Saves me cleaning the stalls and saves on shavings. These two have been here only a few days. I want to be able to feed them a lot and have them eat it in peace. It's been a long time since they didn't have to fight for their food." She took the empty buckets from my hands and stacked them together next to the metal feed cans under the stairs.

"They waited so politely for me to feed them, I would never have guessed that they were starved recently."

"What, Marty's bones sticking out all over the place didn't give you a clue?"

"Well, yeah. Can you show me where my horse will go?" I asked with trepidation. I wasn't sure whether Windsong had ever stayed in anything but a show barn. I didn't know how he would make out in these open stalls and with electric fences. It had me worried.

Donna waved an arm. "He can have any stall you want, and you can put your tack here. She pointed to a small area under the stairs that wasn't taken up by feed cans. I followed her out the back door and caught my breath.

Mist floated lazily over gently rolling hills. A dirt lane lined on both sides with wooden posts that held up white electric tape as wide as my leather belt disappeared into the fog. The pastures stretched far back for acres.

"I usually put new horses here, especially if I think they might be nervous." On the right, two smaller pens were framed out, a four-foot-wide space separating them. "Does your guy go out alone or with company?"

"Windsong likes company, but I have to be careful. He's a noodge and a wuss."

Donna cocked her head. "How do you mean?"

I tried to explain his neediness but also his vulnerability and how I couldn't afford for him to get injured.

"We'll put him in one side and we'll put those two next to him. After they all get to know each other, we'll see who gets along. What day do you think you'll be bringing him here?"

"Today, if I can make arrangements. I know you said you try to save on shavings, but can I keep him in at night? I have to be careful, like I said."

She grinned. "You sure can, because now I have you to help with the chores. Let me show you the routine."

She invited me into her house, and over oatmeal and coffee, we discussed how things were going to be done. All eight of the horses came from EMA rescues and the organization gave her money to take care of them. Michelle had arranged for EMA to pay for Windsong, too. I would actually be working off my own room and board. Donna lived alone but worked at the insurance brokerage in town. I would take over most of the barn chores but eat my meals with her.

After breakfast, I called Kate to ask her if she could trailer Windsong over. She said she had a full schedule of lessons, Sunday being her busiest day, but that Cory could borrow her trailer any time. So, I had to explain about my fight with Cory.

"Do you want me to talk to him?" Kate asked sympathetically.

"No, he's been on my dad's side since before Finals. I'll call him in a few days."

"Brandon has a trailer. Why don't you ask him? I can help him load Windsong and your tack. I bet he'll do it for a couple dollars."

He probably would, but what would Cory think? He was already jealous of Brandon. And would Brandon think I was trying to start something with him? I couldn't worry about that right now; I had to get Windsong moved here since I had no car to go there. "Okay. That's a good idea."

I made the call to Brandon. He was happy to help, could leave immediately, and told me I would be seeing my horse in about an hour.

Donna came back in the room carrying a trash bag and a box. When I told her my arrangements, she said, "Great, you can go get a stall ready for him. But, first, I have sheets and a comforter for you and some cleaning supplies."

While I was waiting for Brandon to come, I used some of the stuff Donna gave me. I scrubbed the dresser inside and out. Erica's poster was on top of my clothes in the suitcase. I lifted it out, smoothing the wrinkles with my fingers, and tacked it up over the dresser—where people usually placed a mirror. She certainly brightened the room. As I loaded my clothes in the drawers, I kept stealing glances at her.

I grimaced when I placed shampoo in the bathroom. I told myself that if I could be the inspiration Erica had been, all of this would have been worth it.

I heard Brandon's noisy old diesel clanking down the driveway and thundered down the stairs to meet him. He stuck his arm out the window and waved his beat-up black Stetson, with a toothy grin and a wink for me as the truck rolled to a stop.

His tall, broad-shouldered frame unfolded from behind the wheel. "Hey, girl. I got something for you." He stepped back and opened the side trailer door with a flourish.

Before I could say a word in warning, Windsong poked his head out and whinnied desperately. And then he shook the little two-horse trailer by pawing as hard as he could.

At Brandon's look of alarm, I rushed forward. "I better get him off before he puts a dent in your trailer. Where's the lead?"

I unclipped the trailer tie and dropped the chest bar as Brandon opened the back. "Ready?" he called.

"Just get out of the way. He's used to coming off the slant load forward. I don't know how this is going to go."

Brandon nodded and unhooked the butt bar. Windsong didn't move. I clucked, bumping his nose with a tug on his halter. His feet were planted. Poking his chest with one finger, I commanded, "Back. Go back."

Windsong tipped his head to look behind him. With one back foot he took a tiny step. When it landed solidly on the trailer floor, he took a more confident one. The next one landed lower than he expected on the ramp and he panicked. Flying backward, with me trailing, he shuffled off, rearing when all four feet hit the dirt.

Donna stood on the porch with her jaw hanging open.

"He's a bit of a hot horse," I explained.

"Remember when you first got him? He did the same thing and we were all watching. We thought he was crazy." I couldn't believe Brandon remembered that.

I put Windsong in the stall across from the skinny horses. He paced two circles, stuck his nose through the bars to sniff the air, and took a bite of hay. Then he tried to whinny with his mouth full.

Brandon helped me carry my trunk and other things in and stow them under the stairs. I opened my case and pulled out the stethoscope. Windsong was still carrying on, and I wanted to make sure all was well.

"You're going in there with him like that?" Donna asked from a good three feet away.

"It's all show. He's harmless," I reassured her. As soon as I opened the door, Windsong was on me, nosing my pockets. I gave him a treat and then had to push him away so I could bend down and get his heart rate. Looking at my phone's stopwatch feature, I breathed a sigh of relief. It was within normal range. I stepped out of the stall.

Maybe he would make friends with Marty, who was watching alertly. Windsong wasn't used to being able to put his head over the door. The stall he had lived in had sliding doors with no openings. He lunged forward, misjudging his step and slamming his chest into the wood as he reached toward me to nip my coat.

Donna backpedaled two feet farther from Windsong's snapping jaws. "You can take care of that one, I'm not touching him."

I had forgotten how wild Windsong's behavior might seem to those unacquainted. I rubbed his elegant ebony head fondly. "He's just a big baby. He wouldn't hurt anyone."

"He is beautiful." Donna moved closer, holding up her hand. Windsong touched it with his clean-shaven muzzle, wiggling his lip gently on her palm. With her other hand, she stroked his neck.

As we all walked down the aisle, Windsong nickered, bumping his chest against the door again. "Just keep walking. He's begging. He'll behave when he doesn't see us anymore." I grabbed their arms and propelled them forward.

Standing in front of Windsong's stall later that night, I tried to call Cory. When he didn't pick up, I sighed.

I shook the stall door, testing to see whether Windsong could push or kick it open. It felt pretty solid and he seemed to be comfortably eating his hay. He was staying in tomorrow though, when I went to see my adviser. I was going to watch him closely when I released him for the first time into that electric fencing.

I looked at my phone screen. I guess Cory wasn't calling me back. I guess I was getting the silent treatment again. Well, I needed a ride to school, and if he wasn't going to help me, I would ask someone else. Donna had to work, and Michelle had already done so much for me I was reluctant to ask her to drive me around, too.

Sighing, I keyed in Brandon's number.

I said good morning as I got in the truck and arranged my purse and laptop on the seat between us. Pressing down the lock button, I sat smashed up against the door with my arms crossed and my eyes riveted on the road. I kept the conversation on college and the weather. It should have been Cory taking me instead of Brandon, and I kept chattering to cover my discomfort.

After a few minutes of answering my inane questions, Brandon shook his head. "Jane. You're coiled up tighter than my rope before I toss it over a calf's neck. Relax, I'm happy to help you out."

"And I really appreciate it, but I don't want to give you the wrong impression."

He put his hand on my knee and I flinched. "I know it would take a whole lot of sweet talking to charm you into dating me, but I think I got it in me to try." He sat back, chuckling at my alarm. "At least that's what I told Cory."

"What?"

"I told him I was going to do my best to win you away from his sorry butt. And if he had any brains, he would get over himself and make up with you."

I sat quietly, drawing circles on my pant leg. "He thinks I'm out of my mind. Do you think I'm doing the right thing?"

"Heck, if I qualified for the Rodeo Nationals, nothing would stop me from going. You gotta do it, girl." The deep dimples flashed at me again.

"You're a good friend, Brandon." I molded myself against the door when that provoked the wrong kind of inviting smile.

"I'm at your service, sweetie," he drawled.

We parked. Brandon leaned against the truck. "I'll wait here." His eyes were already roving over the kids walking past, and he tipped his hat at a passel of girls, flashing those dimples. He apparently had a different opinion of the purpose of a college education than Cory did.

My adviser, a professor in the Business Department, waved me in while he wrapped up a phone call. I sat on the edge of the cushioned chair, setting my laptop on the floor next to me. His dark hair had gray starting at his temples. With one eyebrow lifted, he rolled dark brown eyes at me as he repeated himself into the mouthpiece of the phone. He tugged on his tie, loosening the knot.

Smiling in sympathy, I wriggled back on the chair. My knee bounced in a frantic rhythm as I looked around the cluttered office and chewed my nails. The sealed window behind the professor faced the parking lot, and I could see Brandon's cowboy hat. His long, well-worn duster floated in the gentle breeze as he chatted with two girls. He raised his hat, and I could see his dimples from way up here on the second floor.

I chuckled. Those girls didn't have a chance against those blue eyes and that blond hair. Brandon was a foreigner on campus, a cowboy, and he couldn't hide it if he tried. Not just how he was dressed; it showed in the way he walked, how he talked, and even in the way he held his body. He was quite the novelty around here, and two more people stopped, joining the girls hanging around him.

Professor Link placed both hands on the desk and leaned toward me. "How can I help you today?"

With both knees vibrating faster than I could talk, I stuttered, "It's a long story."

"Aren't they all?" He sat, leaned back into his padded desk chair, and crossed his legs. "Lay it on me."

I explained everything—not going into my parents' lack of support at all—and ended with my invitation to the Festival of Champions. "So, I need to study, but I need to train, too." I bit my lip.

He stroked his silver goatee. "That is an amazing story. How often per week do you train?"

I swallowed. "At least five, sometimes six days per week. I have to keep my horse extremely fit; it takes all kinds of strength and power for him to perform upper-level dressage. It's a very athletic sport."

Instead of the expected disparaging argument, he remained thoughtful. "Hmm. I see how being on campus would make that difficult. I was thinking we could tighten your schedule to just a couple of days, but even that wouldn't be enough."

Timidly, I lifted my laptop and set it on my knees, trying to keep them still, and suggested, "I looked online about taking courses on my computer. Do you think there is a possibility that might work? I can take my laptop everywhere with me and study in between my training."

"You might be on to something." He started opening desk drawers and slamming them shut. "Now where is that thing?" he asked himself.

I rose from my chair to look over the desk as he leaned way down, reaching into the back of a bottom drawer. "Got it." He held up a paperback catalog triumphantly.

Flipping the soft cover open, he started scanning pages. "You're a business major, right?"

Holding up one finger and grimacing, "Well, I wanted to ask about that, too."

He stopped. "You want to change your major, right?"

I nodded, still cringing.

"Okay, to what?"

His easy acceptance made my mouth drop open.

He chuckled. "Freshmen do it all the time. What were you thinking about?"

I rubbed my eyebrows, gathering my thoughts. "There's this cool organization, the one I told you about, EMA Rescue, that I want to stay involved with. What degree would a person have who designs their advertising promotions and organizes the confiscation of animals?"

He stared at me silently, and I braced myself for a derisive response.

He started flipping pages again. "Hmm. A business degree with a minor in marketing? No, marketing with a minor in business administration, that way you can take a course or two about the legal end of it." He held the book out to me, marking a page with his thumb. "The university does have that major online. These are some of the courses you will need."

I took the book from his hand. "I keep expecting you to talk me out of my plans," I said with wonder.

"Why would I? You seem to be doing your best to come up with a successful plan. And you are already well on your way to achieving it."

"But my grades were horrendous last semester."

"You'll make them up, Jane. I haven't had a kid in my office with half as much perseverance as you are showing. I am happy to help. In fact, I am thrilled to be at your service. You can call me anytime, even just to chat." His grin was genuine, and my head felt lighter than it had in weeks.

Back at my dorm, Carly, her hands full, held the door open with her butt for Brandon, who was carrying an armload of my belongings from the room to his truck. As I passed her, she wiggled her eyebrows. "Yum. Your cowboys sure are hot."

I laughed. "He thinks the same thing about college girls."

She let the door bang closed and followed me down the sidewalk to Brandon's truck. We both had a bag in each hand. "After you called me last night and told me everything you did, I could barely believe it. I'm really going to miss you."

I sighed. "I know, me too. Do you think I'm crazy?"

"I think you're amazing. And smart, too. You found a way to do everything you need to do. Like I said, I'm really proud of you."

I smiled. "That means a lot. And you better be ready, because every time I need to hear that, I'm going to be calling you."

I hugged her tightly before climbing in the truck.

"What the heck!" She reached up and hugged Brandon, too.

The ride home was so much shorter than the ride to school, or so it seemed. I filled Brandon in on my new major and the courses I had signed up for. I gushed about Professor Link and how great he was. I talked about easily study-ing in between riding and chores. Finally, I paused. "What do you think?"

"Darn, I guess that means I won't get to come back again. I liked college."

Rolling my eyes, I patted his knee. "You mean you liked Carly."

"You know you're the only girl for me," he answered, with deep dimples and false charm.

We were bumping down the driveway to the farm when I noticed a strange car parked near the barn. Donna was at work and hadn't mentioned anyone would be stopping by. It was an expensive black BMW that would have fit in better at my old barn than here.

I thanked Brandon one more time and promised to call him as I slid out of the truck. The barn aisle was empty. I set my laptop on the bottom step and patted Windsong's head as I passed him to look out the back door. Shading my eyes, I surveyed the farm.

A huge red horse was careening down the path, a wispy dust cloud and a man chasing after him. My stomach flipped, and then I darted left and right, finally running to Windsong's stall to yank his halter and lead off the hook. I waved my arms, hoping to stop or at least slow the galloping horse. When he spotted me, he whirled and ran toward the man. Flapping arms and faint curses turned the pounding horse in my direction again.

His eyes wide and neck stretched out, the horse ran straight at me. I had to do something to halt his panicked flight, so I leapt toward him, throwing my arms out and growling like a bear. The regal head flew up, and the horse locked knees, skidding to a halt.

Time stopped and I froze, too, tingling slivers of electricity skittering over my nerve endings. A lightning bolt blaze glowed in the sunlight. He stood square, his triangle-shaped ears sharply pointed at me and his nostrils flaring slightly as he tested my scent. I blinked. Was I seeing a ghost?

"Santos?" I breathed.

When he heard his name, he lowered his majestic head. I held out my hand as I walked toward him. "Santos, easy boy."

He opened his eyes so wide that white circled the dark brown orbs, but he held his ground, lips trembling. He blew gently on my hand, whiskers tickling my palm, and tasted my skin with his big, smooth tongue.

Slowly, I raised my other hand and ran it over the bulging muscles of his shoulder. My fingers floated over stiff, hairless ridges, and I turned my eyes from his for the first time. His shoulders, chest, and lower legs were crisscrossed with gray scars. His mane was long and tangled, and his coat was crusty with dried mud.

Breathing through my mouth, I hissed, "Baby, what happened to you?" Quickly, I slipped Windsong's halter on him with gentle fingers.

Mark Grant trudged up the path, not looking as surprised to see me as I was to see him.

I grinned even though his shoulders slumped. Santos was alive! And here, mysteriously, on the same farm that I wound up on.

"He broke through the fence down there."

"Yikes, let's put him in a stall until Donna comes home."

Mark shrugged. "I don't come here that often. I guess he got excited when he saw me."

I led the horse into the barn and put him in the stall next to Windsong. I threw a few flakes of hay in and dragged the hose over to fill the water bucket. Mark talked disjointedly over my shoulder as I worked.

"Amanda isn't doing well in New York." When I glanced at his car, he quickly assured me, "She's not with me now. I want to get her to ride again. Taking her away from the horses was a mistake."

Standing in the middle of the aisle, he stared in the stall at the giant red horse. I was dying to ask about the injuries, whether Santos was sound, and why he wasn't in training with another rider, but Mark's dejected demeanor and soft voice kept me quiet.

"This is actually the first time I've come here." Hands in his pockets, he kept talking, and I moved closer so I could hear his low words. "As soon as he saw me, he got excited. Whinnying and running. As I turned to leave, he came right through the fence."

"He's been here the whole time?"

He nodded and shrugged. "When I closed the farm, I told Michelle to get rid of all the horses except him. He was Erica's heart, you know." Santos stood with his head over the stall door, studying the man as hard as Mark was staring at him. "Maybe he thinks she's with me."

It did seem like Santos was watching and waiting for something.

With a noisy sigh, Mark turned toward the door. "I guess he's not really suitable for Mandy, though. I have to leave now. Tell Donna I'll pay for the repairs; just let me know what she needs." He turned toward his car and Santos nickered, pawing violently against the stall door.

I stroked the horse's neck and pushed him back in the stall. "Easy, boy." He whirled and charged the door again. I was afraid he was going to break it. He watched Mark's car drive away, and then backed in and pawed, sending shavings flying.

It was painful to watch the horse's anguish. Windsong stuck his nose through the bars, nickering softly in sympathy. Santos arched his neck and touched Windsong's muzzle. Windsong's needy, nonthreatening stance eased Santos's anxiety. He glanced out the barn door one last time and then settled down, chewing hay. Windsong, who loved a stall more than being outside, happily lit into his pile, looking over at Santos now and then.

When Donna came home, I explained what happened. She patted Santos and said, "You miss her, don't you?"

He stepped away from her toward me. I stroked him, feeling so sorry for him. He nuzzled my shirt, twisting his neck to encourage me to scratch his scars.

"Huh, he's not usually very friendly," Donna commented, walking out the back of the barn. I followed her down to Santos's pen. "The beauty of electric fencing is that I can repair most of it myself."

The white tape was pulled off the posts and was laying in the middle of the aisle. Santos must have charged through it, dragging the lines with him as he ran.

"Aren't you worried that he'll just do it again?" I asked as I helped her pick up the pieces.

"He's lived in this pen for over five months and never touched the fence. It clearly was due to Mark's visit. It surprises me that Mark came here. I wonder why."

I shrugged. "He didn't say, just that he wanted to get Mandy riding again."

It didn't take us long to fix the fence, and while we worked, I told her about my online courses.

"That's great, Jane. I'll have to give you the code for my Internet service when we go inside."

Windsong and Santos were touching noses again when we entered the barn.

"They seem to like each other."

I explained how they lived side by side at Erica's for a month. "They stayed close to each other even though they were on opposite sides of a fence."

Donna began preparing the evening grain, showing me her chart and the supplement containers. "Maybe they should live together."

I gritted my teeth. "Windsong can't get hurt."

"Every horse does better with a buddy, plus we would keep a close eye on them. Any marks show up and we wouldn't turn them out together anymore."

I watched both horses eating and wondered if it would be a dramatic squealing and kicking ordeal like sometimes happens when you put two horses together. Or would Santos chase Windsong around, biting his rump and not letting him eat from the same pile of hay? Santos had lived by himself at Erica's. I didn't know why. I wished I could ask her. Or Cory. He had more experience with this type of thing and he knew Windsong well. But then again, he thought selling Windsong was a viable solution, so he might say just throw them together and see what happens. Windsong did like company and did better with a calm friend who didn't react to his neurotic behavior. But what if they hurt each other?

Was it worth the risk?

CHAPTER

# 23

I waited until the next morning to put Windsong and Santos together in Windsong's smaller pen. I carefully put protective wraps on both horses' legs and left their halters on for a quicker capture if things went bad.

I released Santos first, and he walked straight to the hay pile, only flicking an ear at Windsong's desperate whinny that echoed from the barn. Windsong danced and jigged through the gate and raced toward Santos when I unsnapped the lead rope. Skidding to a stop in front of the larger horse, he arched his neck and held out his nose. They sniffed for a moment and then, as if in mutual agreement, took off galloping.

After a joyous lap around the perimeter, they greeted the two rescues over the fence. Both show horses towered over the two skinny animals, but that didn't make much difference to the Thoroughbred. He flexed his neck, prancing a few steps; striking out with a front leg and letting out a squeal. Two minutes later, all four horses were quietly eating hay—Santos and Windsong out of the same pile.

As introductions went, that was an easy one. My body relaxed and I rubbed my dry, tired eyes. I had tossed and turned all night worrying how that was going to go, and it was a piece of cake. So far.

Windsong's neediness kept him close to Santos's side throughout the day, and Santos seemed to like it. I didn't witness one mean expression or a single aggressive posture, and I kept a close watch on them all day.

I rode Windsong in the roped-off area alongside the barn that served as an arena. Since Santos was able to see us, he waited by the gate, only pawing the ground occasionally.

Later, up in my room I waited for my computer to boot up and called Michelle to ask about continuing lessons with Kate. She authorized one per week, so I happily called Kate to arrange it. After setting up a time to haul in on Saturday, I stared at my phone. Should I call Cory to trailer me? I pressed on his name.

"It's me," I cautiously admitted, surprised that he picked up.

"Yeah."

"How are you?"

"I'm fine, and you?" He answered in overly polite tones.

"Come on, Cory. Can't we talk like normal?" I clicked the browser icon on my computer.

"I thought we had nothing to talk about." His voice still cold, still devoid of emotion.

"Are you mad at me for moving Windsong?" I shoved the laptop off my legs, stood, and paced to the dresser.

"No. I'm not mad."

"Then you're okay with what I did?" I leaned one hand on the dresser, looking right in Erica's eye.

"You're doing what you want to do. Why do I have to be okay with it?"

"Cory, I love you. I don't want to fight anymore." I put all the feeling I had into my voice, trying to break through the ice in his.

"You have what you want and you have Brandon to help you with it. Leave me alone." He hung up.

My heart stopped. *Leave me alone.* He couldn't mean that, he was just mad that I asked Brandon. If I told Cory I was paying Brandon, would he see that it was just business?

I redialed, but Cory didn't pick up. I texted the information, but after a half hour, he still hadn't responded. I had my answer. Sighing, I flopped on the bed and wearily called Brandon.

Saturday morning, I leaned heavily on the door jamb of the barn next to my pile of tack as I waited for Brandon and his little trailer. My arms and legs ached from shoveling manure and pushing the wheelbarrow all week, chores

I wasn't used to doing.

I tapped the call history on my phone and counted. Eight unanswered calls to Cory. Eight. I should have known. We got along so well, agreed on most things, were loving and respectful to each other. But when things went wrong and we fought, Cory gave me the silent treatment. More than the silent treatment. He ran away. Through my anger, a tiny finger of fear pierced my heart. What if time wasn't going to fix it? What if he really was breaking up with me for good? Did he really believe I was starting something with Brandon?

I never imagined he would be against this move. But he had a fanatical respect for my dad, probably because he didn't know or see his own father. He also overrated my parents' success because we had a nice house and new cars. He didn't seem to understand that I wasn't being defiant—my father had tried to *sell* Windsong. I was doing what I could to protect my horse.

Besides, even if my father made any effort to hear me and relented, I couldn't go back. I had signed a contract with EMA, had started my new courses, and had to get Windsong to Kate's to continue lessons. If Cory wasn't going to help, Brandon was the only way.

I sent a text to Cory, letting him know I was coming to the farm. I wanted to see him so we could talk in person. I looked at the message list and Cory's name filled the whole screen.

He would come around. I knew his silence meant that he didn't agree with me, not that he didn't care. I would just keep texting. Whatever it took.

After Windsong walked straight on the small trailer, I gave him a handful of his favorite treats. "I'm proud of you, big guy, for braving a new and different ride."

I ran back in to check on Santos, but he was eating quietly in the stall where I put him to wait safely for Windsong's return. "See you in a little bit," I promised, scratching his scars.

I climbed into the truck next to Brandon. "I really appreciate you helping me like this, Brandon."

"Is it working? Do you want to go on a date with me yet?"

I paused as I snapped my seat belt, words stuck in my throat.

"I'm joking. Lighten up. You *are* paying me, you know. So, it's like a job." He chuckled.

After my lesson, I pulled the saddle off, fingering the sticky, wet hair. It would be best to sponge the sweat off with hot water so I wouldn't have to load a damp horse on a trailer in this cool weather. I threw a wool cooler over Windsong's back while I got the water.

As the bucket was filling, Brandon pulled up with the trailer. I nodded to him as he got out of the truck and lifted the bucket.

"Whoa there. Let me get that for you," he said, jogging over.

"I'm fine. I know it's not in your contract." I carried buckets all the time. I didn't need male protectiveness.

He took the handle from me anyhow and flashed those dimples. "Happy to help."

He lifted the full, heavy bucket and carried it as easily as I carried my coffee cup. I squeezed his biceps and pretended to marvel at his brawn. "My hero," I crooned, fluttering my lashes like Olive Oyl always did to Brutus in front of Popeye.

I turned back toward Windsong and stopped dead. Cory was standing next to the black horse, staring at us. He lifted his hat, ran a hand through his hair, and slammed the hat back over his curls. He shook his head, turned on his heel, and strode down the aisle.

"Cory!" I shouted.

"Really, dude?" Brandon rolled his eyes, jerking his chin in Cory's direction.

I took off down the aisle, slowing as I passed Windsong, then zooming ahead. I caught him halfway to the western barn on the top of the hill, his long legs covering ground at a walk almost as fast as I could run.

"Wait!" I clutched his sleeve so he would stop.

He shrugged my hand off but turned around.

My heart pounded from much more than my short run, and I didn't know what to say. Throwing a thumb over my shoulder, I began, "I'm paying Brandon to trailer me."

From the look on Cory's face that clearly didn't explain anything.

"You won't answer my calls," I accused.

Cory did the hat thing. "Seems you have it all figured out and I wish you luck. You don't need me anymore." Without giving me a chance to say anything else, he turned back up the hill.

My feet were rooted to the spot as I stared after him. But I needed him more than ever. I thought about him a million times per day. I missed his solid, sensible presence and his warm, supportive hugs. Nothing came out of my mouth, though. I stood mute, watching his form get smaller and smaller as he strode away.

Days later, I could smell the snow in the air as I cantered a warm-up figure eight. Glancing at the sky, I hoped to finish my ride before those heavy clouds dumped something wet on me and Windsong.

He felt the storm coming, too, jerking into the turns and scooting forward as the wind blew his tail out to the side. This was a conditioning ride, keeping him moving with changes of direction and gait. The impending weather was too distracting for us to work on finely timed movements.

As I led Windsong through the gate, a gust of wind ripped it out of my hands and slammed it all the way open. He balked when I tried to lead him back into the ring to get to it. Obviously, he wasn't interested in any more work today. Finally, I got the gate closed and latched behind us.

Inside the barn, the wind sounded even louder as it swirled around the eaves, making thumping and whistling noises.

I curried Windsong, hoping the massage would relax him. I put his cozy winter blanket on and put him in his stall. It was early yet, and I didn't like to bring him or Santos in until later in the afternoon, but the snow was supposed to begin soon.

He whinnied loudly for Santos, and I went out to get the big red horse. I brought in Marty and Chipper just as the first flakes fluttered down.

Leaning into it, I dragged the barn doors closed and tied them with baling twine to keep them from swinging on their rails. I looked at my watch and decided to feed the outside horses early before the real snow started. I would give them extra hay in their run-in sheds so they could eat out of the weather.

Once everyone was taken care of, I dragged myself up the steep steps to my room. My muscles still weren't used to doing all the chores, and pushing against the wind was especially exhausting.

I heated a mug of water in the small microwave Donna got for me and made hot chocolate. We had also set up a folding table and chair for me to use as a desk. I opened my laptop and scrolled to my current reading assignment.

There were no windows in the room and the howling of the wind was really distracting. I turned up the music on my computer but lasted only thirty minutes before the storm noise compelled me to run down and check on the horses.

Cringing as another gust of wind screamed around the barn, I peeked in at Windsong. He was standing next to the wall by Santos, ears perked, body tense. Santos quietly munched hay, unconcerned about the noise. Maybe he would be a calming influence on nervous Windsong.

I trudged back upstairs, put on my headphones, and continued to do schoolwork until Donna texted me that dinner was ready.

I pulled my coat on, securing the hood over my head. When I slid out the barn door I was surprised that the snow was deep enough already to cover the tops of my boots. I jogged over to the main house, stomping the white stuff off.

The house was snuggly warm, and I left my boots on the rug by the back door. Hot chili steamed in bowls on the table, and Donna was reaching in a cabinet for glasses.

"Get the juice out of the fridge, please."

I did as she asked and poured some for both of us. She set a crusty loaf of bread on the table.

"I'm glad you're here so I don't have to go out and feed the beasts in this weather!" She laughed.

I explained that I fed earlier and dug my spoon into the heavenly food. Refusing ice cream for dessert—too cold to eat frozen treats on a night like this—I stood to clear the dishes.

Donna left cleanup to me and went upstairs for her shower, telling me to be careful in the morning when I went out to feed.

I plodded back to the barn with a hand fastened on my hood to keep it from blowing off. The icy wind pressed me, and I leaned forward and ducked my head like a linebacker blitzing the quarterback. Even though the barn was only a hundred feet from the house, I had to keep looking up to get my bearings in the swirling whiteout.

Finally, I reached up to pull the door handle. My hood blew back and snow dumped on my bare head as I opened the door.

I slammed it shut behind me and tied it with twine, too, although the wind was blowing the doors against the building on that side. Stomping and brushing snow from my head and coat, I spoke to the horses. "Everyone okay in here?"

Windsong answered with a nicker, his head and neck stretched over the low stall door. I handed out treats and checked their hay. "Be thankful you're in here and not out there. Now go to bed and I'll see you all in the morning when this thing is all over."

I left one small fixture on, giving the horses some light to see through the night.

In my room, I made another cup of hot chocolate, turned my little heater up a notch, and climbed under my thick, warm comforter.

I sent Cory a text. "Some storm, huh? I hate snow." Not really expecting an answer, I plugged the phone into my charger and set it on the bed next to me. As I had promised myself, I continued to text and leave voicemails about my day. Back when I was at school, we had communicated by messaging many times a day. Here, I continued to text him as if we weren't fighting, hoping at some point he would cave and send a message back.

I stuck in my ear buds and watched videos on my computer for a while. I fell asleep with my headphones still in my ears.

I opened my eyes, disoriented in the silent dark. The night light was out and my phone wasn't next to me on the bed. I pulled out my ear buds and pushed my computer to the side. I felt around for the charger cord and reeled the phone into my hands. Sitting up, I clicked it on just as I heard a whistling gust of wind and pounding coming from downstairs.

Four in the morning? I turned the switch for the lamp, but nothing happened. Using the light on my phone, I pulled on some clothes and my coat and carefully made my way down the stairs.

The unusual banging sounded again, and I couldn't figure out what it could be. The barn aisle was pitch black; the storm must have taken out the electricity. Walking slowly, I went to Windsong's stall just as the wind screamed, shaking the whole barn.

Windsong's shadowy form whirled around the stall, smacking into buckets and spraying shavings everywhere. He slammed his chest into the rickety stall door, almost rattling the thing off its hinges. The faint light glowed off the whites of his eyes and he blew a fierce blast of air out his nostrils.

"Hey, Windsong. Easy, boy, it's just a storm," I soothed.

Santos and the other two horses stood alert with their backs to the wall. Their ears flicked back and forth as they listened to the rattles and creaks around them.

It sounded like a train was rushing toward the barn. And then it crashed. A loud boom shuddered the building. I ducked, throwing my arms over my head. All four horses bounced in their stalls. Windsong attempted to bolt through his door, smashing his chest against the splintery wood.

I stood up straight, my heart pounding, and stepped cautiously to the cabinet over the feed cans. I pointed my phone in and located the flashlight Donna kept there.

I directed the beam at each horse and into the corners of the barn. Nothing looked out of place. In other words, there were no horrific holes in the walls and the sliding doors were still wobbling on their rails.

I threw some hay to the horses, hoping that eating would distract them. Windsong paced right over his and bolted when loud, metallic thumps came from the front sliders. It took me a moment to realize they were rhythmic and were made from something other than the wind.

"Jane! Open the doors!" Donna's voice was faint.

I ran over, picking at the knot in the string that had tightened from the swaying of the doors. "Hold on, I tied them shut," I called, stamping my foot because my stiff, cold fingers weren't making any progress. Finally, I ran for the scissors we used to open hay bales and cut the darn twine.

I pushed and pulled, inching the doors apart, fighting the piled up snow. Donna and an avalanche of snow spilled through the narrow opening I created.

She stamped her booted feet and shook the snow from her coat. She was in her night clothes.

"The electric is out in the barn," I informed her.

"I know, the house too. Is everyone okay? When that tree came down, I got worried. It's so dark and the snow is still coming down hard. I can't tell where it fell—"

The wind howled, drowning out her last words, and Windsong body-slammed his buckets again, his hooves knocking at the wall. Donna's eyebrows rose in alarm. She walked down the aisle, looking in each stall, and stopped in front of Windsong.

We watched him pace, sweat starting to shine on his dark neck. He paused only to stare suspiciously at the walls and roof before a wild eye would roll back to us. He flung his head over the door, chest bumping it and then whirling to charge around his stall again.

"We all jumped a mile high at that loud crash. I guess that must have been the tree? But the barn seems to be in good shape."

"Thank goodness." Donna ran an appraising eye over Windsong's strained movements, her lips a flat line of concern. "We better go check on the horses outside to make sure it didn't fall on them or their sheds."

"Okay. Let me go get my gloves."

After wrapping our scarves over our faces and tying our hoods tight, we tried to open the back door. After a few moments of tugging, Donna said, "I think the snow is blocking it. Let's just go out the front."

The flashlight didn't penetrate the falling snow, so we were forced to slog out to each of the sheds, ducking through the frozen and ineffective electric fencing.

The five field horses huddled in their shed, heads down and furry backs covered with an inch of snow. A chestnut mare nuzzled my arm with her icicle-coated whiskers. I took off my glove and slipped her a treat from my pocket.

These animals didn't seem to be as tense as the horses inside were. Maybe because they could see the snow and feel the wind, it wasn't the scary unknown. They hunkered together under the roof to wait for the weather to calm.

Our original path was invisible and we pushed against the wind, shielding our eyes from the snow with our gloved hands. It took both of us to move the swinging door a foot so we could slip inside. Once we closed it, Windsong's alarming snorting and banging was louder than the muffled, screaming wind.

I stamped my numb feet and brushed off the snow before I pulled my hood down. I walked to Windsong's stall. The sweat was beginning to foam on his neck, and he flew right past Santos, who was reaching through the bars with his nose.

I asked Donna to hold him so that I could check his vitals. She made a face, but followed me into the stall. I pulled the heavy blanket off, and replaced it with an absorbing wool cooler. He was trembling, and the whites of his eyes flashed in the dim light as I counted heartbeats.

I shook my head. "He's a mess and his heart rate is elevated."

Donna held the lead gingerly, prepared to bolt if Windsong did. "The storm is not supposed to taper off until lunchtime. Maybe you should use that medicine on him? He clearly hates this storm and I don't want him colicking when we couldn't get a vet out here."

Or having a heart attack. Windsong shuddered under my hand. Dr. Clark wouldn't have prescribed the medication if he didn't expect me to use it. Gritting my teeth, I nodded and headed for the supply cabinet.

Donna waited for me to draw the liquid into the syringe and plunge it into Windsong's rock-hard neck. He flinched but didn't waver in his paranoid watch of the walls.

Donna handed me the lead and pulled her hood tight again. "He should feel that in a few minutes. Call me on your cell if anything else happens. I'm going back in to call the electric company." She patted my arm. "We'll find out where that tree came down tomorrow."

I stayed in the stall with Windsong until I saw his muscles start to relax. I thought about how many times he may have been terrified in a storm and I never knew about it because I wasn't there, was only at the barn to ride. Could that explain the times I found his stall totally trashed, with hay and manure and shavings ground together in a terrible mash? I thought I was such a great owner and caretaker, but I never knew how many times my horse and partner may have suffered through night terrors with no one there to help him.

His head lowered, and his ears flickered lazily at the howling wind. I didn't walk out of the stall until his eyelids drooped and his bottom lip hung open slightly. With a gentle pat, I unbuckled the halter. "Go to sleep now, big guy. Don't worry. I'll keep the bogeyman away from you from now on."

I latched his door and headed upstairs. The snowdrift against the barn held the doors in place, so I didn't bother to tie them.

My little heater was electric, so my room was no warmer than the barn below. I pulled on another pair of socks and two dry sweatshirts and climbed under the covers. Just my eyes and hands poked out.

On my phone, I looked up the weather and was shocked to see that sunny skies and a high of fifty degrees were expected on the day after this blizzard.

Seriously? I wished the weather gods could have skipped this storm and gone straight to the sunny skies.

But I refused to complain. I snuggled deeper, slipping my whole head under the comforter. I may never have been so cold before, but Windsong was safe.

CHAPTER

# 25

I woke up to my phone buzzing off my chest.

"Hello?"

Donna's voice was bright and cheery. "Good morning! Breakfast is ready. Have you looked outside?"

"No," I grunted, tactfully not reminding her that I had no windows.

"The tree fell on the arena, landing inches from the barn. If it was a few feet taller, the top would have crashed right in on Santos's and Windsong's stalls. We dodged a bullet there, I'll tell you."

I jumped into my boots and jacket, and ran downstairs. I rushed toward the doors when I hit the bottom but stopped when a chorus of nickers begged for food.

"Alright, alright. I'll feed you before I get my own breakfast." I threw hay to them in their stalls and dumped grain into their tubs.

After wrestling for ten minutes with the back sliding door, I made an opening wide enough to fit myself out. The outside horses had made tracks through the snow and were waiting for me by their feed tubs, or at least where they thought the feed tubs would be under the snow.

Using my gloved hands, I dug through the already wet and heavy melting snow and located the rubber feed pans. I couldn't find the last one, and the little gelding was nickering and pawing for his food, so I dumped it on top of the snow. He scarfed it up with no problem. I carried hay an armful at a time and threw it over the fence for them.

I slogged up to the house, pausing on the porch to survey the fallen tree. The trunk was almost two feet in diameter and it had snapped like a toothpick. The massive cluster of top branches spanned half of the riding arena, obliterating the fence underneath. But what made me slightly nauseous was that the tips of those branches had scraped down the side of the barn. We dodged more than a bullet—it was a bomb.

Inside, I learned that, after getting Michelle's agreement that EMA would help pay for it, Donna had arranged for a tree service to remove the tree. The service would not be able to come for a few days because of the overwhelming number of calls they were getting because of the storm.

After breakfast with Donna, I put the barn horses out for a short time. Windsong studied the fallen tree, and when it didn't get up and move, he took off bucking and running, stopping to rear right in front of Santos. The calm red horse silently walked around him, bent his knees, and rolled happily in the snow. When he rose, he gave a mighty shake, sending droplets of water through the air.

I cleaned the stalls but had to pile the dirty bedding in the barn aisle because I couldn't push the wheelbarrow through the snow and muck outside. There would definitely be no riding for a couple of days, so I concentrated on my schoolwork. It felt eminently satisfying to click send on my first assignment, imagining the paper whirling through cyberspace and landing in my professor's virtual mailbox.

Closing my laptop and setting it on the dresser, I thought about a cappuccino. No way to get one. I dove onto the bed, planting my face on the pillow. If I couldn't have a coffee, a nap was the next best thing.

I awoke disoriented and dug through the covers to find my phone. The lack of a window really messed with my internal clock. I couldn't tell if it was day or night without natural light to judge by. There would be enough time to bring Windsong and Santos in and feed up before dinner. I trudged down the stairs, pulling my beanie low over my ears.

I prepared all the buckets, taking a little longer than Donna usually did because I had to keep checking the chart. I wrote the horses' names on torn scraps of paper and threw them in the buckets to keep them straight. With their keen sense of hearing, the horses were all waiting at the gates for their afternoon meal—all of them except Windsong, who was lying out in the middle of his field.

I took Santos out of the pen first, thinking Windsong would hear the gate and get up. He was still out flat when I returned. I swung the gate open and, without bothering to close it, called his name as I walked toward him.

His head came up when I was within ten feet, and he blinked at me groggily. He straightened his legs, stretching as he rose, and then gave a full body shake. He waited for me to come to him, and I stuck my bare hand under his jacket, feeling for sweat, before I snapped on the lead. His coat was warm and dry.

I closed him in his stall and then dashed to the alcove. I rifled through my trunk and pulled out the stethoscope. Windsong was already down in his stall when I opened the door. I knelt down in the clean shavings, my hands shaking. Placing the circular bell near Windsong's belly, I listened for gut sounds first—silence or a low number of sounds could signal colic. A loud, intense gurgle assaulted my ear and I snatched back the bell.

"Doesn't sound like colic." I moved the listening piece toward the spot behind his front leg. I counted the beats of his heart against my phone's clock. Normal. Heartbeat wasn't elevated at all. I rubbed the bridge of my nose. Was he sick or not?

I couldn't decide on my own and I wasn't going to risk it being a side effect of the medication. I scrolled quickly through my contacts and called Dr. Clark.

He didn't seem surprised to hear from me. "It *is* questionable behavior. The only way to tell for sure is to bring him in for an echocardiogram. I can transfer you to the admittance desk if you would like to schedule that."

"Let me call you back." I paced in front of Windsong's stall. He lifted his head when Santos pounded the door, demanding his dinner. I waited a moment, but he didn't get up.

I called Kate.

After listening to my quick recap, she advised me to take him to the clinic if I was that worried.

Was I that worried? I kept watching, unable to make a determination. I dumped Santos's feed in his bin to quiet his begging. When Windsong heard Santos rattling the pellets around, he rose, shuffled to his feed bucket, and gave it a half-hearted bump with his head. He nickered softly and pawed the air in slow motion.

I set Windsong's feed aside in case he was colicking. Picking up the other buckets, I jogged out to the field and flung the grain into the tubs. By the time I ran back to the barn, Windsong was nodding and nickering more loudly. He wanted to eat, but to be safe, I gave him only a handful of the grain in his bucket. He scarfed that up in seconds and started in on his hay, so I carried on with the feeding, taking hay outside and making separate piles for each horse.

I glanced at Windsong's stall and couldn't see him. He was lying down again.

I tugged out my phone and dialed Michelle. She listened carefully. "Maybe he's just tired, he had a tough night. Or the drug is still in his system making him feel groggy. Wait a few hours before you do anything."

"I'm no expert, Michelle. What if he's having some sort of heart attack? I don't know what that would sound like. The vet said I could bring him in."

"No, don't do that. I can't explain away a million clinic visits to the board of directors, especially when I just promised to pay for that fallen tree so you can ride. That thing is gonna cost almost a thousand dollars! If he gets worse, call me back."

Was this an emergency? I listened to Windsong's heart again. Soft, normal thuds came through the ear pieces. If I held the bell to my own chest, I would go deaf from the thundering of my heart. I considered calling my father, but dismissed the idea quickly. He would probably say "I told you so" or "I'm not paying for it."

I dialed Cory and was not surprised when he didn't answer.

After a few minutes of standing there watching Windsong breathe, I pulled a hay bale over to sit down. It was too low for me to see into the stall, so I brought others enough to stack into a high, comfortable seat.

After a few more minutes, I was bored. I pulled out my phone and played a few games. Donna's call interrupted just as I was tracing the winning string of jellies.

"Dinner is ready."

I explained what I was doing. She came out carrying a covered plate and a soda. I arranged it on a towel. It smelled wonderful, but my stomach wasn't calm enough yet to eat.

Donna looked over the stall door. Windsong groaned, sending clanging alarm bells screaming through my head. He stuck out a front leg, then the other, and hauled himself to his feet as if it was the hardest work he had ever done. He walked to Donna and calmly frisked her for treats. She fondled his cheeks for a moment. "He seems okay, now."

I could barely hear what she said over the ringing in my ears. My hand over my heart, I took a deep breath. I had thought that was the groan of death, and I concentrated on convincing myself that he was alright. He was standing, eating hay; he was not prostrate without a heartbeat.

"I think I'm going to sleep out here tonight."

Donna grimaced. "Are you sure? It's going to get chilly."

No chillier than I was last night with no heater; I could handle it. I shook my head to erase images of sleeping soundly in my bed and finding Windsong cold and stiff when I dumped his breakfast in his feed bin in the morning. "Absolutely." If he was going to stop breathing, I wanted to be right here to pound on his heart until it started up again.

Donna shrugged. "At least, bring a blanket down." She left me to my vigil.

The dinner was still delicious cold, and I ate every speck of it, sipping soda and staring at Windsong's shiny, dark body. He ate his hay, shuffled around his stall, pooped, and drank some water.

After my soda can was empty, I threw the paper plate and can in the trash and ran up to get a blanket. I picked up my laptop, too.

I woke up disoriented, pushing the darkened computer off my lap. And then I remembered and searched for Windsong. He was down. I leapt off the hay bench and reached for the stethoscope. Before I opened the door, I realized Santos was down, too. I stood still, listening. Faint, rhythmic snores were coming from both animals. I spent a minute persuading myself not to disturb them by neurotically collecting Windsong's vital statistics.

I sat on the hay and stared unblinking until Windsong stood up years later. I rubbed my dry eyes, and looked at the time on my phone. Three in the morning, and Windsong was standing over his bucket, hoof floating in the air, hoping I would dump the rest of his food in there. His meaning couldn't be any clearer if he had spoken words.

I scooped up another handful and tossed it in. "You're fine, aren't you. This was all a ruse to drive me crazy." He sniffed my hand, pushing it before taking another bite.

Santos was looking at me with hopeful eyes, and I couldn't leave him with an empty bowl. I threw him a handful, too, and headed up to my bed, dragging my comforter and laptop with me.

A drum roll of raindrops woke me in the morning. It was a cold, soaking rain, and I kept Windsong and Santos inside. I also brought in the two skinny horses, who happily shook out their wet coats and rolled in the dry shavings. They put their heads over their doors and nickered for breakfast, looking like powdered donuts.

I fed the rest of the horses in their sheds where they were escaping the rain. The tree was gone from the riding arena, but the footing was dotted with puddles. Without an indoor, there would be no riding in this weather. Another day off for Windsong. After cleaning the two stalls, I spent the morning grooming.

Windsong was acting completely normal and really needed only a dusting off. He generously allowed me to spend time with the other three, only pawing for treats now and then.

After I vigorously curried Santos, there was enough red hair on the floor to stuff a pillow. I rubbed aloe cream into his scars and began to untangle his mane. After a few frustrating minutes, I stalked to my tack trunk and dug out the pulling blade and thinning shears. I couldn't imagine anyone would complain if I shortened that mess without asking. A half hour later and another pile of hair on the floor, Santos came closer to resembling the superstar sport horse that he was.

Satisfied with my progress, I swept the hair up and planned the same attack on the two rescues.

It was still raining by the time Donna came home from work, and I informed her that I would keep Marty and Chipper—a name I came up with because his coat was the color of a chocolate chip—inside so they would be comfortable.

"If that's okay, I mean."

"Sounds good. How's Windsong?" She went around and petted and loved on each horse, mine included.

"He's seems fine. I guess I got a little paranoid."

She squeezed my arm. "Better paranoid than neglectful. They all look fantastic. You did a lot today. I'm impressed. Come on, let's go eat."

I paused to listen to the steady sound of powerful equine jaws crunching delectable, sweet-smelling hay. It may not be a fancy new show barn, but the horses inside it were feeling pretty coddled right now. Closing the door on my charges, I followed Donna to the house for dinner and smiled. I pulled up my hood with sore, aching arms but there was a bounce in my step.

Finally, the sun was shining and the makeshift arena was dry. I led Windsong into the ring and settled onto his back with a grin. Even a few days seemed like too long to be out of the saddle.

Focused on practicing the most difficult sequence in my freestyle, I didn't pay any attention to Santos when he whinnied loudly. Pushing my leg into Windsong's shoulder, I angled his neck to the side. He reached sideways with his outside front leg for five or six strides before I straightened him, trotted around the corners and pointed him across the diagonal for flying lead changes. Counting in my head, I rocked my weight from one hip to the other, bumping his ribs every four strides. We skipped across the arena, and then I loosened the reins and let Windsong open his stride for a lap around the perimeter.

Looking up for the first time in a few minutes, I was surprised to see Mark standing at the gate. He silently clapped his hands. I slowed Windsong and stopped in front of him.

"Hi." My eyes traveled past his head to the figure feeding treats to Santos.

Mark looked over his shoulder. "Mandy came this time. Actually, I made her come."

My jaw dropped. Cute, outgoing, towheaded Mandy had black-as-night hair, black motorcycle boots, a black studded belt, all covered by a black leather jacket that sported an amazing number of zipper pockets.

"Wow." I couldn't think of any other words.

"I know. City kids, wrong crowd."

She turned and came up next to her dad. "Can we go now?"

The face under all the heavy makeup, the dagger earrings, and the hostile stare were unrecognizable. If Mark hadn't said it was Mandy, I would have politely introduced myself to this stranger. "You grew."

I blanched at the "duh" look she gave me.

"Has Santos run through the fence anymore?" Mark asked, giving Mandy a stern look of his own.

"No, but I've kept him up close with Windsong. They've become friends."

"He looks a little cleaner, thanks."

"No problem."

Mandy maintained an indifferent, detached posture.

"Mandy, would you like to see the latest rescues?" I tried, as I slid down from Windsong.

"No." She didn't even look at me.

"They're next to Santos."

"Stop pretending to be my friend. If you're trying to take my mom's place at EMA, forget it. My dad will stop you. Right, Dad?"

Mark pinched the bridge of his nose. "What do you mean, Mandy?"

"The posters, the ads, the magazine articles. My mom was so much prettier than you. EMA was my mother's rescue, she did everything for EMA, they can't put you in her place. You will never be as good as her."

"I know. It's a great organization. I'm just trying to help EMA. To *honor* your mother," I said in my most soothing voice.

"You have no right to be on those posters and in that magazine. You're nobody. I hate you!"

"Amanda!" Mark put his hands on her shoulders and spun her toward the barn. "That's enough. We'll be leaving now."

Stunned, I was jerked off my feet when Windsong leapt sideways. I grabbed the rein for balance and stopped him from running into Mark's back. Santos was pawing the gate and causing a ruckus that encouraged Windsong to jump and jig.

I circled Windsong in front of Santos as father and daughter entered the barn. Santos galloped the fence line, searching for his family. He finally stopped pawing and dashing about but stared over Windsong's back as they appeared at the other end. He watched as they got in the car and pulled away, and he whinnied loudly one more time.

I knew what he was feeling. Closing my eyes, I remembered. During the one month that I lived in her house, Mandy used to lie across my bed, chattering about sharing clothes and shopping. She was happy to have another girl to talk to, and she often talked about her crush on Shawn. Shawn and I worked hard training for the team championship. Erica, so beautiful and vivacious, treated us like her family. Mandy hung around me, the little sister I never had. And I felt so close to all of them so quickly, even Mark. A half smile teased my lips as I remembered Shawn picking Mandy up and tossing her into the pool as I enjoyed the tingly anticipation of knowing he was coming for me next.

That was all gone. Was Mark going to stop me, request that EMA fire me? Mandy was acting out because she missed her mom, but would her father be influenced by that? A savvy businessman like Mark would look at the results before acting on his grief-stricken thirteen-year-old's words, wouldn't he? Another reason I had better be fantastic at the Festival of Champions.

I needed to see the articles and ads that Mandy was talking about. Were people leaving comments? Would I be able to tell if their reactions were positive or negative?

I worked quickly to take care of Windsong and turn him back out, and then I ran upstairs.

CHAPTER

27

The clicking of the keys as I typed my name into the web browser was the only sound in the room. I took a sip of protein drink and waited for the results.

This couldn't be real. The first hit was an article in *Dressage America* with my image on the cover. I was exiting the arena on Windsong with my fist in the air, a wide, joyful grin on my face. I stared at it. I remembered thinking about Erica and her fans as I rode through the gate because it was the first time I had people cheering for me. I clicked on the link and found the article.

When I finished reading it, I rubbed my hands over my face. The writer used words like "new dressage star," "up and comer," "a role model for the sport." A whole paragraph was about my involvement with EMA Rescue and how I represented the type of horsewoman they believed in. Only one sentence mentioned Erica and her creation of the charity.

I scrolled back to the photographs. Windsong's coat looked like polished ebony; his chiseled head, elegant and expressive. My white-gloved hand was raised to the crowd, which was a multicolored blur in the background. Thank you, Mom and Dad, for all those years of braces and dental visits making my smile glow. It was surreal, like the image was someone else.

My eyes lifted from the screen to the poster hanging on the shabby wall. The pose was nearly the same. Could I ... ?

My phone rang, and I snatched it up when I saw Michelle's name.

"Did you see it yet?" Michelle demanded before I could say hello.

"Yeah, and it's over the top."

"I know. I did a good job getting you into those magazines. It's a major promotional success, if I say so myself."

"Do you think I look good?" As good as Erica? I wanted to say, but didn't have the guts to hear the answer.

Michelle's tone sobered. "You look amazing. Things are shaky this year at EMA with the loss of Erica. Some folks think that the organization will fizzle out without her. Which is why we brought you in, to save it, to keep it going in memory of Erica. Thank you for taking this position. The animals we rescue need us, need this organization to stay afloat."

Recalling Mandy's words, I resisted her praise. "I want to help, but I'm not Erica. I can't be like her. She was an amazing rider, beautiful, charismatic." I shook my head and almost said "I'm just plain Jane Mitchell, dressage kid wannabe."

Michelle's voice softened. "Jane, we chose you because you have those same qualities. I know you're young and unseasoned, making you fit perfectly in our budget, but you will be a good thing for the rescue. Put your big girl pants on, sister. We need you to bring in the donors." Leaving me with that responsibility echoing in my overwhelmed brain, she hung up.

Erica's image practically rode off the wall, and I slipped into the past. I was sitting in the bleachers with Shawn and Mandy watching Erica ride Grand Prix. My heart was in my throat. Her elegance and charisma evoked emotional responses in those who watched. It wasn't a big crowd that day, but the fans applauded the pair with tears in their eyes and love in their voices. She garnered support not by asking for it but by being someone people wanted to follow.

"Erica, what if I don't have any big girl pants?" I mumbled, tapping the scroll button on my mouse.

I read a couple more articles in other magazines, and then I started reading the comments that followed each one. The comments linked to Facebook pages that linked to blogs. I came across one linked to Robert Peterson's name. Knowing that he had praised my riding at Finals, I eagerly opened the article.

My heart dropped with an audible thud when I read his quote: "Jane is a good young rider, but she lacks the mileage needed for open competition. She needs a few more years under her belt before I expect her to be competitive at something like the Festival of Champions."

There it was in black and white. My euphoria fizzled like a struck match in water. I closed out of the browser and shut the lid of my computer. My first instinct was to call Cory. He could bolster my confidence with a few words, cutting to the chase and reminding me of the important things. But he wasn't answering my calls.

I scrolled to Shawn's name.

"Well, if it isn't the beautiful and sexy Jane Mitchell," he answered in a throaty purr. "How are you doing?"

Always the flirt, but it was exactly what I needed right now, to talk to someone who thought I was great.

"I'm not sure, a lot has happened since I spoke with you last."

"I know, I know. Me too. I saw the results of Regionals and Finals, girl. You rock."

I smiled. I couldn't remember one time that Shawn had ever criticized me. "I'm not so sure. I don't have any big girl pants."

After a brief pause, Shawn answered slowly. "I don't know what that means, but I always thought you wore your pants well."

I huffed, "It's just that Robert said I was inexperienced and not competitive enough for the Festival of Champions, and Michelle said she needed me to put on my big girl pants and save EMA. And Windsong is his normal crazy self, so he could spook and blow the whole thing. If that happens, then destroying my parents and infuriating Cory would have all been for nothing. Nothing!"

"Whoa there, Nelly. Slow down. You have to fill in a few of the blanks for me."

He listened without interrupting as I related the events that were making me shake the more I thought about them. The words tumbled out, faster and faster each time he made a sympathetic noise.

When I finally finished, I had to take a few breaths to restore oxygen to my brain. "And so here I am, in a rinky-dink barn trying to get Windsong ready for the biggest show of my life, and my parents and Cory don't believe I can do it, and Michelle is relying on me to win to save EMA."

"Geez, girl. You really know how to load the weight of the world on your own shoulders. Ease up." Shawn laughed.

I smacked my head. What was I thinking, calling Shawn?

"No, sorry," he said, but I could still hear the smile in his voice. "Listen,

I left school, too. My parents weren't happy about it, but after losing Erica, who was more of a mother to me than my own, I didn't want to be there and I was wasting their time and money. Since it would have disturbed their social calendar to argue with me, they agreed to let me drop out for a year or two."

"You do sound better than the last time we talked."

"I came down to Florida with Robert. I've been riding two or three horses a day, doing barn work, and learning so much from him. This is where I belong."

"Shawn, I'm really happy for you. I wish my parents could understand." I sighed.

In my mind I could see Shawn shrugging as he answered. "Erica used to tell me that I would have to get serious someday. I am now. I'm working really hard, but I'm focused. Tune them all out and do what you got to do. That's the Great Shawn Delaney's advice to you, girl."

I smiled. His enthusiasm was infectious. "All right, I'll do what I gotta do, and I hope it's enough."

"I've seen you get ready for a championship. It'll be plenty."

I restarted my laptop, Shawn's last words echoing in my head. *Do what you got to do.* Right. I needed to stop googling my name and reading other people's opinions. I needed to stay focused on my goals. I needed to keep up with my schoolwork. And if I accomplished those things, my success would follow: I would establish myself in competitive dressage, I would save EMA by attracting sponsors, and I would make good grades.

I clicked open my email account. Scrolling past the Facebook messages and Twitter alerts and stopping on the one with my professor's name in the from line, that one I read.

I scanned the contents and then leapt off the bed and did a dance of joy on the threadbare carpet. Pointing my fingers up and wiggling my hips, I shimmied around singing, "Who got an A-plus on her essay? Jane did, Jane did." I did what I had to do and, see, good results were already happening.

I stopped in the middle of the rug. My father thought I couldn't manage riding and school. He should see this grade. Why not? He had ordered me to send him every grade when he thought he could keep tabs on me that way. I forwarded the email to his address with no included message.

Breathing in the smell of success, I wondered who else I could tell. I already knew Cory wouldn't answer, and I would feel silly calling Shawn back about a grade. No one else would really care, especially since it was after ten o'clock at night.

Windsong would be happy for me, and he didn't care what time it was. I opened the door and began to trot down the stairs but was puzzled to find the aisle brightly lit. I had left only one bulb on as a night light. I crept back to my room and searched it for a weapon, and then I remembered the broom at the bottom of the steps. I tiptoed down, grasped the broom handle in two fists, Ninja style, and slowly eased my head around the corner, peeking down the aisle.

CHAPTER

# 28

My muscles instantly relaxed and, leaning the broom back against the wall, I stepped forward. The man and the horse never even noticed me.

Santos had his head and neck over the stall door. His ears were pointed forward and his gaze was fixed on the man who stood six inches in front of his nose. Mark's hands were in his pockets and his attention was just as absorbed by the horse.

Mark spoke in a low tone, "I miss her, too. I'm sorry I left you alone on this farm, but I hated you for a while. If she hadn't been driving you to that stupid horse show, she would not have been in that awful traffic." He rubbed his temples and blew out a sigh.

"But it screwed Amanda up, taking her away from the farm. The city changed my little girl. I want her back, I need her back, and I don't know how to fix it. Erica used to say that you could hear each other's thoughts. Talk to me, Santos. What does Erica want me to do?" Mark's voice cracked on those words, and he covered his face with his hands.

I held my breath, reluctant to interrupt.

Santos stretched his neck and nuzzled Mark's stomach gently. It wasn't his usual door banging and shirt pulling. Mark wrapped his arms around the big bony head and Santos remained still, allowing the man to hold on long and tight.

My throat closed and my heart ached for them.

After a moment, Mark stepped back and wiped his face on his sleeve. "What about you? You're too big for Amanda. What do you want to do?"

I sucked in a breath, trying not to make any noise, but Santos's ears flicked in my direction. He nickered and banged the door. Mark spun around, reddened eyes wide.

His expression sent me over the edge. I choked out a sob, "I'm so sorry."

"Stupid. Talking to a horse, I know." He ground the heels of his palms into his eyes, Adam's apple bobbing as he swallowed hard.

With a watery smile, I shrugged. "I talk to them all the time."

Mark rolled his eyes. "Do they answer?"

"Sometimes." Tugging my coat closed, I moved off the bottom step. "Not in English, more like expressions. For instance," I held my hand out to Windsong, who pushed his nose against my palm. "He clearly said 'Get me a treat.'"

Mark pointed at Santos. "What is *he* saying?"

Reaching up, I scratched Santos's scars. He tipped his head sideways, stretching his neck toward me. When I stopped, he toed the door. "He is saying that, while that feels very nice, he is bored and wants to go back to work."

Mark eyed me suspiciously. "Do you really think that's what he wants?"

"I think he was born to do dressage and that he was famous and people miss him. Some great rider, like Robert Peterson, would kill to have a chance to ride him. Would probably take him to the next Olympics." I slapped my hand over my mouth. Wrong choice of words.

Mark just shrugged. "Erica was qualifying him for the Olympics."

Santos took my jacket in his teeth and tugged me toward him. I rubbed behind his ears and down his cheek. He leaned his massive head against me, so I kept rubbing.

Mark touched the jagged lightning blaze. "He likes you."

"I like him." I kissed the furry red nose.

"Erica used to say he was a snob, didn't like anyone but the family." He glanced at his watch, shaking his head. "It's late, I should go. Mandy and I had a fight, and I just needed a moment. I don't know why I came here."

"I didn't mean to overhear, but I agree that Mandy needs to get back into the horses. Maybe they can help her with, well, you know, your loss."

With a noisy sigh, he agreed. "That's what I'm thinking. But my idea of her feeling connected to her mother by riding Santos probably won't work. I forgot how huge he is."

Pushing that regal ruddy head away from me, I stepped out of Santos's reach. "Bring her here. Some of the rescues need attention. They're not show horses, but they can rekindle her interest." I stalled, realizing I was giving advice to this accomplished, worldly man like I was smarter than him. "I mean, it might work. Ask Donna, though, she would know more."

Reddening under Mark's intense stare, I crossed my arms and braced for his response, wishing I could just keep my mouth shut sometimes.

He nodded, his face losing that lost look and becoming thoughtful. "You may be on to something there." Scratching his head, "I think I'll do that." He opened his arms to me and squeezed me, pressing his lips to my hair. "Thanks. Erica always said you had an uncanny way of knowing the right thing to do," he whispered.

It wasn't until the next day while brushing my hair, standing in front of those two posters, that Mark's words sunk in.

"You thought I made good choices?" I asked Erica's image.

I looked around at the bare barn board walls and the stained, drooping ceiling and compared this place to Erica's gorgeous house and state-of-the-art horse facilities. I had arrived at her place with everything a successful rider needs—provided by my parents. When things were difficult, I ran to my father or to Cory for help. Racking my brain, I couldn't remember one instance when I displayed the good sense Mark had commented on.

Now, Cory believed I was giving up my home and family for a trivial pursuit. For the first time, I had made a choice that the people most important to me didn't agree with. Here I was, basically alone, living in a barn, with no transportation or money of my own. I was hinging my future on one class at one horse show to prove that I was doing the right thing. But when it was all over, win or lose, what would I have proved?

Wobbling with uncertainty, I put out a steadying hand on the dresser.

Too late to change my mind. I had to forge ahead. Straightening, I reached up and stretched mightily. Sucking in as much air as my lungs could hold, I blew it out making a noise low in my throat. I touched Erica's forehead with a finger and said out loud, "I hope you're right."

I sat down, opened my laptop, and started schoolwork.

CHAPTER

# 29

With my eyes still on the computer screen, I answered the phone without looking at the display.

"It's Michelle. I've had a call about a couple of horses. A neighbor has been watching the owner for me for a couple of weeks. We have to go get them before he gets his paycheck. Apparently, he only buys feed when he gets paid and only if he doesn't hit the bars first. If we go right now, we have grounds to take the horses from him or take him to court if he won't sign them over voluntarily."

I sat up, ready to put my feet in my boots. "What do you need me to do?"

"No one I called so far is available with a trailer. Do you know anyone?"

"I can call Kate or Brandon."

"Okay. I'll keep trying my people. Call me back if you get someone." She hung up.

I quickly scrolled to Kate's name and pressed dial.

I explained that we needed her trailer for a rescue.

"Why do people go through the trouble of getting horses if they don't want to take care of them? I'll never understand it. Absolutely! You can count on my help."

"Great. Thank you so much. I'll talk to Michelle and text you the address and time."

Thirty minutes later, Michelle lifted a sheaf of papers from the passenger seat to make room for me in her little silver car.

"Hold these. It will be easier if we can convince the man to sign the horses over to us. Usually the threat of court proceedings is enough to get them to sign. If not, we take him to court."

I settled into the seat, papers on my lap, but before I could snap the seat belt on, Mark's car rolled in the driveway.

"Shoot! Hold on a minute, Michelle." I slid back out and jogged to Mark's window. When it opened, I filled him in on our destination and apologized for forgetting that he was coming by with Mandy.

"A rescue? I've never been on one. Do you want to go with them, Mandy?" She shrugged. "I don't care." But the eager look on her face said otherwise.

Mark rolled his eyes. "I'll make an executive decision. We'll come with you."

He waved Mandy to follow and got out. He stopped with his hand on the back door to Michelle's car. "Maybe I should drive."

Michelle grabbed her stack of documents and slammed her door. "Okay, but let's get a move on. I want to catch him before he finds out we're coming and throws feed in or something."

We all caught her urgency and leapt into Mark's car.

Mark drove fast, but the ride was smooth, even in the back seat. "This is a great car," I commented.

"Thanks, but it won't haul two horses."

I laughed. "Kate is meeting us there with her trailer."

The big luxury car slowed in front of a tired, gray tiny rancher. Behind the house stood a small, barely upright barn surrounded by broken cars and rusty equipment. Inside a sagging barbed wire enclosure, two shaggy, bony, mud-encrusted horses stood side by side. Both were dark brown, and one lifted its head and pricked its ears as we all got out. The other didn't bother to look, its head drooping almost to the ground.

Mandy ran right over to the fence, clucking and holding out her hand. The sleepy horse jerked up its head, looking at her in alarm, but neither horse moved. Mandy bent down and stuck a leg between the wires.

"Hey, kid! Get outta there. That's private property!" a gravelly voice yelled. A screen door banged.

I caught up to Mandy and took her arm. "Wait, Mandy. Give Michelle a minute to talk to the guy. Do what he says so we don't make him mad."

Michelle was talking fast, throwing around terms like "citation" and "court appearance." She was doing her best to wrangle a signature out of the owner.

"Animal abuse is a felony. We won't press charges if you sign your horses over to us. Just think of all the money you'll save on feed."

The gnarled old man practically growled, "They don't eat much. I like having them around. Go away."

Michelle tapped the papers. "My friends will testify as to the horrid state of your animals. I have photographs. We'll be happy to take this to a judge, and you'll have to appear and testify if you want to keep your animals."

Mark stood beside Michelle. "Sir, it's not a crime to give up your animals, but keeping them the way you are is. Do the right thing."

The man's steely gray eyes darted to Mark's wing-tipped shoes and then traveled slowly up his pressed dungarees, over his crisp Oxford shirt, and flicked to the shiny car parked by the curb. "They're mine," he said stubbornly.

Mark coolly withstood the man's frank appraisal. Then his brows drew together, and he reached for his wallet. "What will it take?"

The little gnome began to smile.

Michelle put her hand over Mark's. "That's not how we usually do it, Mark. He doesn't deserve your money."

Mark paused. "No, he doesn't. But if those two horses are lucky, he'll sign the papers and take this wad of cash and go spend it at that bar we passed. And then he'll never get near another animal again. Right, sir?"

The man's jaw dropped lower and lower as Mark counted out the bills, and he licked the spittle from the corners of his lips. His greedy fingers reached for the money, but Mark held it out of his reach. Mark's voice was hard, and he commanded, "Sign the paper."

The man didn't hesitate. He took the pen and signed over ownership to EMA Rescue. He grabbed the cash and then disappeared inside the dilapidated house.

Michelle flung her arms around Mark, accidentally smacking me with the clipboard. "You did it! You're awesome!" She turned to me. "Jane, I thought you said you got someone to come with a trailer?" She tossed the paperwork on the seat of her car and led our little group over to the gate. It looked like the man had kept it together with baling twine. As soon as we reached the fence, Mandy was under it.

With a surprising burst of energy, the two bedraggled beasts ran past her in the tiny paddock, nearly knocking her off her feet.

"Get back here!" I screeched, ducking through the wires and yanking Mandy out of the mud and the path of the panicked animals.

Their long, thick winter coats were matted with crud, disguising how truly thin they were. The dirty, stiff, too small halters had worn patches of hair from behind their ears.

Mandy bent to crawl through the fence, and I gave her a shove when the mare pinned her ears flat back against her skull and made another charge at us.

Dodging the snapping teeth, I slipped in the mud. Two strong arms saved me from falling in the mire, and once I was steady on my feet, Cory lunged in front of me and waved his hat to keep the mare away.

I slithered through the wire and plopped down into the stiff, dead grass on the outside of the fence. The mare retreated to the far side of the pen, pushing the other horse in front of her. I knew my heart wasn't pumping a crazy beat from anything the poor scared animal had done.

What was Cory doing here?

He turned to climb out, the concern on his face quickly disappearing behind a cool mask.

I brushed dirt from my jeans and kept my eyes on Mandy. "That is exactly why your mother kept you from coming to the rescues," I said, a little more sternly than I meant. "We don't know anything about these animals, and their fear can cause them to be dangerous. *Never* go into a pen like that with a strange horse."

Mandy spread her legs and crossed her arms. "I was fine. I just felt bad for the poor things."

Mark cut in, "Mandy, a thank you would have been enough." He turned to Michelle. "What do we have to do to get these horses out of here? This place is disgusting." He held his hand out to Cory. "Mark Grant."

Cory stepped forward and took his hand firmly. "Cory Banks. Kate asked me to come. She couldn't change the lessons she had scheduled. If you'll move your car, sir, I'll back the trailer right up to the gate to make it safer to load these two."

Mark and Cory went to move the vehicles.

Mandy asked, "How are we going to catch them if the mare keeps running away?"

"She's protecting the other horse from us. When Cory comes back, he and I will approach them together. The fewer people in the pen, the better. You wait out here. There will be plenty of time for you to mess with them when we get them safely back to the barn."

Mandy's face tightened, but she didn't insist on helping.

Cory carried two lead ropes and handed one to me. "Ready?"

All of our differences were forgotten as together we eased into the paddock and focused on the two nervous horses we were there to help. The mare stood with her haunches toward us, glaring dully over her shoulder. We walked calmly and slowly toward her. She switched her tail in warning and tossed her head, attempting to move the gelding farther away. His ears were pricked at us, interested in what we had in our hands, but he obeyed the bossier horse and took a step back.

Before we got too close, the mare nipped the gelding on the butt, making him jump forward and run past us. Mud spattered over us as they thundered by. When he reached the end of the small paddock, the gelding whirled around and came back. The mare tried to follow, but her weak legs slipped in the muck, and she went down.

She grunted as her hooves scraped ineffectively against the mushy ground. I slapped a hand over my mouth, cringing while she struggled.

Cory took the opportunity to ease up to the gelding and quietly snapped the lead onto his halter. The gelding allowed himself to be caught when the mare wasn't chasing him away.

I crooned soothing words to the mare but stayed out of the way of her flailing legs, hoping she would get a foothold. She rested a moment flat on her side, with her ribs heaving.

"Easy, girl, I want to help you," I whispered, leaning down to clip on the lead. I tugged gently on her head and she rolled up onto her knees. "Take it easy, go slow."

Something in my voice must have reached her because she watched me steadily as she stretched out her front legs. I leaned with all my weight against the rope helping as she heaved herself up. My hold kept her from sliding backward again. As soon as all four feet were holding her up, she flung around, whinnying to the other horse. He answered with a soft nicker but submitted to Cory's petting comfortably.

"I'll lead him to the trailer first. Keep her right on his tail," Cory told me. He called to Mark and Michelle, "Be ready to hook up the butt bars. If we're lucky, they'll walk right on when they smell the hay."

It took both Mandy and Michelle to wrestle the rusty gate open. The gelding followed Cory until his toes were a step away from the ramp, and then he planted his hooves, his eyes widening in fear. Cory held the rope steady and waited for him to relax his stance.

The mare followed with shaky legs, her breathing heavy. When he halted, she nickered to him. I tried to stop her behind the other horse but the mare spotted the hay net hanging in the trailer and had other ideas.

"Go with it," Cory advised. "Let her go in first if she wants to."

Nodding, I marched in front of her, right up the ramp. She followed, opened her jaws, and chomped down on the hay. I latched the chest bar while Michelle hooked up the butt bar, and the mare was safely on.

The gelding whinnied to her and she answered as best she could with her mouth full of hay. At her encouragement, the skinny brown horse lowered his head and sniffed at the rubber-lined ramp. Bending his legs and examining every step, he tiptoed into the trailer, muscles quivering as the vehicle shuddered gently under his weight.

As soon as his tail was in, Michelle put up the butt bar. Cory latched the chest bar, and the gelding sighed, letting his hooves fully rest on the trailer floor. He leaned on the bar and looked out the side door. Satisfied that he would survive and that the floor would hold him, he finally took a bite of hay.

I dug treats out of my pocket and gave each horse a nugget. I had to push it between the gelding's lips because he didn't seem to know he could take it in his mouth.

Smiling proudly, I turned to Cory. "That was relatively easy. Good horses."

He returned my smile and my heart flipped. Wishing I could throw my arms around him, I leaned in his direction. He tugged his hat down and turned to jump out of the trailer, his face stiffening.

We closed up the doors and lifted the ramp into place. The two triangular rumps were barely visible over the ramp. The tired mare rested her hip against the padded divider. Both heads bobbed as they pulled hay from the net hanging between them.

I couldn't wait to get them back to the barn, into heavily bedded, dry stalls with a pile of sweet green hay and clear, fresh water. My fingers tingled with anticipation to get a brush on those rough coats. I secured the last ramp latch and automatically headed for the truck cab.

"Good idea," Michelle called. "You go ahead with Cory to the barn. I want to knock on this guy's door and see if he has any health records or registration papers for these two."

Mandy piped up, "I want to ride with the horses, too."

Mark nodded. "Fine. I'll follow behind."

I gritted my teeth. There would be no private conversation with Cory. But I held the door open for her and she slid in between us. I tried not to notice Cory's look of relief.

Back at the farm, the gelding hesitated to move backward off the trailer, but the mare knew what she was doing, and so he decided to give it a go. We let them settle each in a stall and Mark agreed to bring Mandy back the next afternoon to spend time with them. As Mark and Mandy climbed into his car, he sent me a grateful nod. He seemed pleased that Mandy was showing so much interest.

Before Cory could say anything, I invited him up to my room for a cup of hot chocolate. Surprisingly, he agreed.

I took two mugs into the bathroom to fill them with water and Cory stood in the middle of the ratty carpet, looking around.

"You can sit on my bed," I said. I put the cups in the microwave and turned it on.

"This place is a dump. My room in my trailer is nicer than this."

I looked at the raw, dust-darkened plank walls, the sagging ceiling, and the one dimly lit lamp on the old dresser. I had stopped noticing my surroundings and had focused on schoolwork and training. A bed and a roof were all I needed.

"The bed's comfortable, try it." The butterflies in my stomach woke up at his heated look.

"I have missed you," he said quietly, but he didn't move toward me.

"I have missed you so much!" I plunged toward him but stopped, stricken, when he took a step back.

"I have always wondered if dating me, if all this," he swept an arm up, "is a rich girl slumming it because she is fascinated by the other side."

My fingers trembled. "The other side?" I stuttered.

"Yeah, you know, I live in a trailer, Brandon, with his beat-up old truck, this decrepit barn. Why aren't you in your new car at your fancy school dating some up-and-comer? Why are you living like your family doesn't have money?"

"Because I have a dream." My jaw tightened. Tension rose in my gut, killing off the butterflies.

He shook his head. "Nothing that couldn't happen while living at home and listening to your father."

The microwave dinged, giving me an excuse to turn away from him. Swallowing, I took the heated water out and stirred in chocolate powder. "You're wrong. And I loved you because you are you, not because of what you have or what your house looks like."

"Right. And now it's Brandon, because he's such a stand-up guy, with a bright future working at the feed store and roping calves."

My eyes lifted and landed on the posters of Erica. My neck clenched and my cheeks burned. I whirled around and strode right over to his tall lanky form and poked him as hard as I could in the chest. *That's right, take a step back now.*

"Maybe you ought to think about your own priorities, dude," I said, glaring up at his face. "*You're* the snob, dating me because I come from money, because I have what you never had, a nice house and a dad, and you're jealous. I believe in what I am doing and after the Festival, you'll see how everything will fall into place. This place," I said, waving a hand around the room, "is a stepping stone to the life I want—not a life revolving around how much money I have in my bank account or what kind of car I drive. But a life where I can make a difference to people and animals, like those two neglected creatures downstairs."

Cory's eyebrows flew up. He took off his hat, ran a hand through his hair, and smashed the hat back down. His mouth was open, but no words came out.

I started to reach for the hot chocolate but then stamped my foot.

Shaking my head, I hissed, "No! You should leave. I don't have anything to apologize for—you do!"

Cory's fists clenched at his sides and his icy blue gaze blazed. With a curt nod, he left.

I stood frozen until the sound of the truck starting penetrated my shock. Tears trickled and I fought them back. No, I wouldn't cry. How could I have misjudged our relationship so badly? I ran down the stairs and out to Windsong's paddock, wiping my cheeks.

Windsong and Santos lifted their heads when I appeared at the gate. Santos immediately walked over and Windsong followed. I rubbed both their noses, letting Santos blow softly on my face and Windsong nuzzle my palm. This was what I needed, not a shallow, false boyfriend.

When Cory and I had first met, he called me Princess. Apparently, his opinion hadn't changed. "Windsong, we'll show him at the Festival. I am *not* just some rich, spoiled brat." And I unbuckled his halter from where it was hanging on the gate. "Come on, we've got work to do."

*CHAPTER*

# 30

Michelle appeared while I was bridling Windsong.

"They look happy in there," she commented. She looked through the bars of the stalls at the new arrivals.

"They settled right in. Both of them drank a half a bucket of water as soon as we put them in a stall."

"That guy was a piece of work. The good news is that they have papers. The mare is a registered quarter horse named Micky's Sunny Swig, and the gelding is her three-year-old son, Micky's Shooter. Michael Beers obviously had a good time naming them."

Holding Windsong's head still, I buckled the noseband. "They're big for quarter horses." They both were about sixteen hands, even though they weighed only about nine hundred and fifty pounds at the moment.

"They have some Thoroughbred in their lineage. Mr. Beers said he bred them for the hunter ring. He had big plans for them but never got around to doing anything. The mare is well trained, but the colt was started and nothing more."

"That explains why the mare was so protective of her son. They seem to be pretty quiet and sensible otherwise."

"They will probably be good candidates for adoption once Donna gets them looking good." Michelle smiled. "Gotta go. I'll talk to you in the next couple of days. Thanks for your help."

After a brief and careful ride in the mucky ring, I brought Santos into his stall, too, and fed dinner. The new horses seemed surprised when I dropped a small amount of grain in their feed bins, but that didn't stop them from licking it up.

Dinner passed quickly. Donna and I discussed the new horses the whole time. She outlined her procedures for new arrivals and instructed me on what their feeding regimen would be.

I occupied my brain with schoolwork until night barn check. Everyone was munching quietly. When I finally laid my head down to sleep, Cory's last look haunted me, making for a restless night.

I woke up bleary eyed and eased my tired body out of bed. I opened my laptop and checked the weather and my email. I had continued to forward my grades to my father and neurotically checked for a response from him. But, like Cory, he was angry, and I was getting the silent treatment from him. I clicked send anyway and waited for the icon to stop twirling before closing the lid.

Rubbing my face and smoothing my hands over my hair, I stood to get dressed. Since it was Saturday, I needed to get the chores done quickly because Brandon was coming to take me for a lesson with Kate. I let gravity boost my momentum and tripped down the stairs in my boots. With my mind on the order of things I had to do, I nearly ran over Mark and Mandy in the aisle.

"Oops! Sorry."

"What are you running from up there? Bats or something?" Mark joked. Mandy wasn't amused and brushed her coat where I had bumped her, like I had soiled it in some way.

"I'm sorry. I'm in hurry to get my work done because I'm taking Windsong out for a lesson." I continued to the feed bins, talking over my shoulder.

"Mandy would like to help with the new horses."

Measuring feed into individual buckets, I just nodded. "'Kay."

"Can she stay with you? I'll come back for her later?" Mark asked.

I straightened, looking at Mandy's back. She stood with her arms crossed and looked in the stall of the new gelding. Her black hair was in a simple pony tail and stuck out of the bottom of a red beanie. She had left her skull earrings and studded belt at home, but the permanent sneer was still in place. "Like I said, I have to leave."

Mark lowered his voice and hunched forward. "She asked to come, and I don't want to do anything to discourage her. Is there any way she can go with you? I'll pay you."

My ears perked up; I needed money, but I wasn't a babysitter. And then I remembered how much Erica did for me, and the Mandy who was my friend last summer. "No way that I'll take your money! She's welcome if you don't mind me dragging her to my old farm and back."

Heaving a sigh, he admitted, "I'd be so grateful. I want her to want this again, you know. I'll be back this afternoon." It looked like he was going to hug me again, but another look at Mandy's stiff back had me leaning away.

"No problem."

After he left, I lifted the stack of feed buckets. Walking past Mandy, I explained, "I have to get all my chores done before Brandon gets here. When we come back, we will have some time to work with the new horses. For now, we'll turn them out into our isolation pen and clean the barn."

I shrugged off the belligerent look she gave me. "Or you could just stand around while I work, but you are not touching those horses without close supervision. We don't know how they will behave." I walked out of the barn to the pastures.

The first two rescues had graduated and joined the group in the first pasture. I put feed in a rubber tub for each horse. The four horses lined up with a minimum of head tossing and tail swishing, confident that everyone would have their own breakfast. I moved down the dirt lane to the two other pastures and was greeted by soft nickers. By the time I was tossing hay into the pens, Mandy was helping.

Knowing Santos had the better manners despite his bigger size, I let Mandy lead him out to the pen, and I followed her with Windsong. Santos nickered and nudged her and lowered his mighty head so that she could unfasten the halter. I pretended not to see when she put her arms around his neck and pressed her cheek into his coppery fur. Since Mark and Mandy had been coming more often, Santos seemed less anxious around them. He stood politely while Mandy pulled his halter off.

She wanted to lead the gelding, so I helped her put a new halter on him, careful not to irritate his raw spots.

"We found out they are mother and son, so wait for the mare and keep him close as you follow me to the pen. His name is Shooter and hers is Sunny."

Mandy handled the horse with confidence, and we released them together into the smallest pen. Both charged directly to the piles of hay we had set out.

Windsong's head flew up at the new arrivals in the adjacent field. Snorting and prancing, he trotted to the fence. Santos followed at a sedate walk. Both horses studied the shaggy pair, who completely ignored them and continued eating. Santos soon lost interest and moseyed back to his pile of hay. Windsong blasted air out his flared nostrils, sounding like a train starting up, then whirled and galloped a circle around Santos, tossing his head until I thought it was going to fly off.

"He's a nut." Mandy watched with wide, shocked eyes.

"You got that right." I laughed.

"I like him. And I really like Shooter, too. I know he doesn't look like him, but for some reason he reminds me of Tucker. A taller, skinnier, browner, younger Tucker. Okay, he's not like Tucker at all."

"Sometimes it's not the looks but the attitude that seems familiar. You must miss Tucker, but we all move on from our first horse. I had to sell my horse Paddy in order to get Windsong. It was hard, but for the best."

Mandy shrugged, "I was ready for a bigger horse anyway."

She blinked rapidly, working to keep the sneer in place. Pretending not to notice, I continued talking. "Shooter seems friendlier than Sunny, and he's a nice height. It was hard to tell if he was a nice mover, but we'll find out more this afternoon. Right now, we have work to get done."

Mandy talked more than she cleaned, but I didn't mind. She told me a little about New York, mentioning that she was sick of the kids there with their constant competition to see who was richer or more popular or the wildest.

"I made some friends, but it got boring after a while. Most of them didn't even own a dog. Besides, Popcorn hated the city. When I took him for walks, he would duck and cringe and dodge the other people walking on the sidewalk. It took him forever to figure out where to pee with so much cement."

"I hardly recognized you that first day you came. Black hair?"

"Everything was so different, I wanted to be different too."

I ripped open a bag of shavings and didn't respond. Really, what could I say?

"It didn't work. I still miss her." There was a pause and a sniff, and I panicked. Was she going to cry? Please, don't.

"Let's go get some hot chocolate up in my room before Brandon gets here."

I filled two cups in the bathroom again, hoping this conversation would go better than the one I had with Cory.

Mandy was in front of my posters. "Why don't you have your poster hanging here?"

Pressing my lips together, I put the cups in the microwave. I looked at Erica's image and smiled. "I talk to her sometimes."

Mandy's head whipped around.

"I know, it's crazy, but I talk to the horses too, remember."

A slow smile lifted her lips. "You're as bad as your horse."

I slipped an arm around her shoulders. "Mandy, you once said that if I worked for EMA, people would forget your mom." I turned her gently toward me. "I will never let that happen, I promise."

I ducked down to look right into her glistening eyes. With a tiny nod, she let me pull her into my arms. We both jumped when the microwave dinged.

CHAPTER

# 31

My promise must have released something in Mandy and she morphed into her old, perky, outgoing self. She didn't protest when I signaled her to climb in the truck and sit between Brandon and me. In fact, her presence kept Brandon from randomly flirting with me.

"You should come more often, Mandy. I am having such a good time with you," I encouraged.

She chattered the entire twenty minutes, and neither of them noticed my nervous silence as we approached the farm. I didn't know what I would do if we ran into Cory. I was the one who told him to leave. I hadn't texted him or left a voicemail—but neither had he. Would he try to talk to me? I was only half sorry for what I had said.

My worries were for nothing. I led Windsong out the back of the barn toward the arena and scanned the parking area. His truck wasn't even there. My heart sank, but then relief lifted my shoulders. It was better this way; I could concentrate on my ride. I would call him later or something.

Always pumped after a lesson with Kate, I loaded Windsong on the trailer inspired once again for another week of training. On the way home, Mandy and I talked about the new horses and what we should do with them. When Brandon pulled into the driveway and we saw that Mark's car was already there, we turned mock frowns on each other.

Mandy pushed past me and ran up to him. "Dad, we haven't had a chance to brush Sunny and Shooter. We can't leave yet," she whined.

"You want to stay longer? I thought you'd be ready after all these hours." Mark's tone was surprised, but he seemed pleased. "Sure. Sure, we can stay as long as you want."

Mandy hopped back and forth from foot to foot, barely containing her impatience as she waited for me to unload Windsong, undress him, turn him out, and put away my equipment.

Mark watched his daughter bounce and then shook Brandon's hand when I introduced them. I didn't think he admired the rust spots that dotted the trailer or enjoyed the soothing sound of Brandon's back ramp squealing, but he didn't say anything until Brandon pulled away.

"I can't believe you put your horse in that thing! Is it safe?" Mark might have been looking at a murder scene. The look of horror on his face was almost comical. When I remembered what Erica's trailer looked like after the accident, I stopped laughing.

"Brandon helps me. I don't even have a car anymore. He gives me rides." I shrugged and carried my saddle and bridle to the barn.

As I passed him on my next trip, I patted Mark's shoulder. "It's not that bad. I'm only going about twenty minutes away."

"What are you going to do when you have to go to New Jersey?"

My head snapped back to him and I stopped. "You know I'm going to the Festival of Champions?"

"Michelle sends the board meeting minutes to me. I've started reading them." He shrugged.

"Oh. I don't have a plan yet. Michelle said she would ask one of the other recipient farms if we could borrow a trailer or try to find someone Windsong could ride along with. We're trying to keep expenses down."

Finally, Mandy and I lifted the halters to capture the filthy newcomers.

We put them on crossties facing each other in the aisle, and I placed a bucket with brushes on the floor. After Windsong's sleek black coat and smooth, muscular body, I was almost reluctant to touch the bony mare's thick, matted hair and angular, lumpy frame.

As long as she could see the gelding, she stood quietly, accepting my ministrations.

"Dad, don't just stand there. Come help."

Startled at her request, he seemed unable to resist her demand. Mandy was currying with a rubber brush, leaving wads of brown fluff on the floor. Mark poked around in the bucket and pulled out an old hair brush.

I giggled and took it from his hand. "Your wife was one of the best riders in the world and you don't know how to brush a horse, do you?"

"I was the money man," he defended himself, but took the body brush I handed him.

I smiled wider when the little girl instructed her worldly father in a very teacher-like voice on how to stroke in the direction the hair grew. Forty-five minutes later, the two horses looked marginally better. Both trotted a circle around the pen when we turned them out, proof that they at least felt better.

Days later, I was cooling out Windsong when Mark's BMW rolled in the driveway. Santos recognized the car and charged to the gate. Windsong responded with a head toss, but I had already shortened my reins and kept him from joining the run.

Mark leaned on the arena gate, waiting for me to stop in front of him. "You're all set for New Jersey," he said. We watched Mandy run to Shooter's gate, calling and clucking to him. "I hired a professional shipper for Windsong. One that uses a tractor trailer rig."

My head whirled back to him. "You did what?"

"I couldn't see you trailering all that long way in that rust bucket from the other day." He chuckled.

I grinned. I *had* worried about Brandon's truck being able to make the trip. This was one big worry lifted right off my plate. "You're amazing! Thank you so much! I'm going to owe you big time. I'll babysit, or whatever you need. Thank you again!" I gushed, finally closing my mouth only when I recalled having said the same thing to his wife the first time I met her. Erica had called on me for help a few days later, and the rest, as they say, was history.

Mandy came over and ducked through the fence, stepping right up to Windsong. She scratched his cheeks and played with his lips. He bobbed his head, trying to convince her to give him some grass or cookies or crackers or whatever she had in her pocket. Her hands were sure as she touched my tall black horse, and I was impressed that his size didn't alarm her.

Then Mark spoke again, distracting me from my memories. "Actually, I booked a spot for Santos, too. I took your advice and called Robert Peterson.

He's very interested in Santos, and since he'll be at the Festival, we arranged for him to try out the horse there."

I looked over at the big red horse, who was staring at us, his neck arched over the gate and his ears pricked forward. I twirled a piece of Windsong's mane around and around my finger and my eyes misted. Santos would go far with Robert. But I would miss him. I would miss his hoof knocking on the stall door at feeding time, miss the way he lowered his regal head to touch my palm, miss his calm, easygoing company for Windsong. My voice was flat. "That will be nice."

Mark grinned because he thought he was giving me good news, but it took all of my strength of will to push the corners of my mouth up. Mark's face fell. "What? You suggested this. You don't think Robert would be good for him?"

Still not meeting his eyes, I said, "I do. Robert's the best." With a shrug of one shoulder, I kept my voice steady. "I'm happy for him."

Mandy's eyes snapped to mine. She recognized a flat-out lie.

Mark put both hands on the fence between us, like an executive at a board meeting. "Okay. I was going to ask a favor. If you would get Santos ready for the trip, you know, ride him, cut his hair, whatever it is you guys do to get him show ready? But if you think it will be too much for you with school and Windsong, that's okay, I understand."

"Ride him?" I looked at Santos, who lifted a hoof and banged the gate. My stomach flipped. I would do anything to ride a horse like him, even if it was for only a few weeks before handing him over to someone else. The ecstasy would be worth the anguish. "I would love to! I mean, I would love to help you by getting him ready to go to Robert."

Still rubbing Windsong, Mandy's face lit up. "I can help. I used to help Mom. Sometimes she would let me walk Santos out at the end of her ride." That explained why she was comfortable with Windsong; he was smaller than Santos.

Mark, who was still standing on the other side of the fence, far from Windsong's reach, raised both eyebrows. "I don't know. Would you really be helping? I don't want to make things harder for Jane."

"Of course." She flipped her hair over her shoulder. "I can handle Santos. Mom used to let me." Her hand perched on her hip, and she did a little head waggle thing.

Mark's lips twitched and our eyes locked. "It would be an honor to ride Santos and to have Mandy's help." I meant it. I would enjoy Mandy's company again, especially since I was basically alone here.

Mandy gave Windsong one last pat and reluctantly moved out of my way, barely hiding a wistful look at my saddle.

I slid down, my fingers already itching for Santos's reins. I realized Windsong was still slightly winded. "Can I let Mandy get on and cool him out for me?" I asked Mark.

With a grin, he nodded.

I handed her my helmet. She started toward Windsong, but I held her back. The helmet was a little loose and I took a moment to tighten the straps around Mandy's chin. She was as fidgety as a horse, eager to get started. She sprung out of my hands and into the saddle like a pro.

"I know how to hold the double reins," she announced as she wove the leather between her fingers. "You don't have to hold him, I got this," she instructed me when I started to walk with her.

And she did have it. Kneading the reins, she signaled Windsong to lower his head down below his knees in the classic stretchy frame used to warm up and cool out dressage horses. Windsong responded happily to her hands and legs and walked calmly forward. Mandy sat tall and straight, rocking in perfect rhythm with his long, powerful strides.

"She's her mother's daughter," I commented. I glanced at Mark. His glistening eyes were riveted on Mandy, and he nodded.

*CHAPTER*

# 32

Standing on the top step of the mounting block, I looked over at Windsong. Even though the pen was not far from the arena, he paced and whinnied like Santos had been taken to another country. Santos watched his antics with idle curiosity, patiently waiting for me to get on.

Butterflies danced in my stomach and my arms were weak with adrenaline. Taking two slow deep breaths, I reminded myself that I was an excellent rider and Santos was a horse. A gigantic, powerful, international horse that hadn't been ridden in months ... but I was an excellent rider.

Santos turned his head to look at me, probably wondering how long it was going to take me to set my butt in the saddle. I patted his neck. Windsong would have moved away from the block three or four times by now, but Santos continued to stand. What a good boy. I stuck my toe in the stirrup and hauled myself up.

Mark had brought over Erica's tack, and a moment of sadness swept over me. The stirrups were set for her long, elegant legs. Sending her a silent prayer, I adjusted them up two holes. "Thank you, Erica, for letting me ride your precious beast. Please ask him to be kind to me."

Santos was both an easy ride and a hard ride. He was easy because he had a very calm, workmanlike attitude, responding without any of the jumpiness I had to deal with when I rode Windsong. But he was hard because his stride was much bigger and bouncier, his body thicker with muscle; even unfit, he was twice as strong as Windsong. I warmed up and then ran through some of my freestyle sequences. Our timing was off, but Santos knew the moves and responded to my aids as if someone had schooled him days—instead of months—ago.

Cooling him down with a calm walk, I again thanked Erica. She trained this horse. His responses, his confidence, his willingness were all a direct result of her work. Mark was right. I felt like she was talking to me through this horse. When Santos halted askew, "Jane, too much left leg." When he stiffened for a moment in the half-pass right, "Soften his jaw." When he inched forward in the *piaffe*, "Square your shoulders." Her voice was so clear in my mind that, when Donna spoke from the gate, I jumped.

"For a moment I thought I was watching Erica."

Blinking away tears, I shook my head. I leaned forward and reached under Santos's neck to scratch those naked scars. He lifted his mane, cocking an ear back toward me. "Such a good boy," I whispered.

The first time Mark came to watch me ride Santos, he made me self-conscious, remembering what Donna had said. I stopped as soon as I noticed him at the gate.

His face pale and his eyes riveted on the big red horse, he rasped, "Keep going. Don't stop."

I did, but I stared at Santos's ears, afraid that if I let my gaze stray to Mark, I wouldn't be able to bear the sight of his sadness.

He surprised me, though, by smiling when I finished and dropped the reins. "I should have done this sooner; he looks great. You look great."

Mandy, looking younger every day with no makeup, her black hair in a ponytail, and a T-shirt hanging over schooling breeches, leaned against the barn door frame. Mandy used to ride her pony following Erica on Santos, mimicking her figures.

Remembering her joy on Windsong and her comment about cooling Santos for Erica, I hoped offering to let her ride him wouldn't mess her up emotionally. She looked a little shaky about seeing me on him.

Her hand trembled as she gathered the reins. I put a hand on her back to steady her as she placed her paddock boot in the stirrup. We both ignored the tears rolling down her cheeks. Santos moved slowly, walking with half the stride and power that he did with me. He knew. He knew he was carrying a child, a family member.

After that, they came almost every day as long as the weather was nice. Mandy always cooled out the horse I was riding. Then I started having her help me tack up both of them at the same time. She would warm up one horse at the walk and trot, and then we would switch mounts, and she would cool one off.

Sometimes Mark helped brush and would stay to watch us ride, and then get bored. We would see him pacing by the car, cell phone glued to his ear, his deep voice drifting over the arena.

We ritually groomed Sunny and Shooter. We couldn't ride them yet. They needed more time to get stronger but were looking and acting better every day.

On the morning of our departure for New Jersey, Mark and Mandy were both at the barn with me waiting for the shipper.

It was so big, it didn't fit in the driveway. Tractor trailers don't look massive until you are standing next to them with your horse, looking straight up the steep ramp to the murky interior. The slender, baseball-hatted driver finished fastening the tall, wooden sides that lined the sharp incline of the ramp. He unlatched a storage compartment in the trailer's belly, and we loaded in the tack and equipment.

He lifted my suitcase and shook his head. "We don't take extra baggage."

"That's not extra. That's mine, I'm going with you." I needed to monitor Windsong's vitals as we traveled.

He shook his head again, stroking his dirty blond beard. "No human passengers."

I pressed my lips together, putting my fists in my windbreaker pockets. "I need to ride with my horse. He has a medical condition."

The bushy eyebrows drew together. "I can't haul a sick horse."

I dug through my tack trunk for the folder that held all of Windsong's paperwork. I showed him the health certificate from the veterinarian that said he was okay to travel.

"Give me that. I have to call the office." He got back in the truck.

Mark came up carrying Santos's paperwork. "What's happening?"

I threw my hands up. "He's saying he can't take Windsong because of his medical condition."

"I thought the exam from the vet covered that." Mark quirked an eyebrow at the cab of the truck.

"Me too. And he's saying I can't ride with him."

Mark just looked at me. "Why would you? We bought you a plane ticket."

"I have to keep an eye on Windsong, take his vitals, to make sure he's handling the trip well." I started pacing a circle, talking to myself. "I should have checked on this. I knew it was important. Now it's too late. I can't let him go on that truck alone. Maybe I can borrow Kate's trailer. Or hire someone else with a trailer. I'm not putting him on there unless I can ride with the guy."

The cab door opened and the little guy leapt down. "I'm sorry. I should have looked closer at the paperwork. I got confused when you said the horse was sick—"

"I never said he was sick," I interrupted him.

"Whatever. The office said he was okay to go, so let's load them up." He handed me my suitcase.

"I have to go with you." I refused to take the handle, crossing my arms.

A firm shake of the head. "Nope. No human passengers." He poked the bag at me again.

"Go right back in that thing and call your office. If I don't go, neither do the horses." I matched his stare, squaring my shoulders and looking down at him.

Mark put a hand on my shoulder. "Now hold on. No need to get hostile. Let me make a call." When I didn't back down, he took the suitcase. "Okay, fella. Wait for me to make the call?"

With one hand on the bill and one hand on the back, the driver fine-tuned the fit of his hat. "Yes, sir. The name is Billy." He held out his hand, immediately respectful to Mark.

Mark shook the proffered hand firmly and, with a nod, said, "Just give me a minute."

I fixed Billy with a steely glare until I realized that, if Mark worked something out, I would have to ride in the truck with this guy for hours on end. I turned my back and tapped my foot instead.

Mandy finished giving apples to all of the horses and walked from the barn. She handed me the half-empty bag. "For Santos and Windsong, when you get to the show grounds."

"Thanks." I bumped her with my shoulder.

Keeping her face averted, she mumbled, "Good luck." And then she threw her skinny arms around my waist, pressing her head on my chest.

"I'll make sure Santos has a good trip. Robert is a really amazing trainer. Santos will be famous again." I patted her back.

She jerked away from me when Mark strode back from his phone call, looking determined. In his best CEO voice, he pointed his phone at the driver. "I spoke to your office, and it's all set. Jane can ride with you." He picked up my bag, shoved it in the storage compartment, and slammed the door shut.

"C'mon, let's get the horses on." Mark hustled Mandy and me to the barn.

I led Windsong out first, and Mandy followed with Santos. Billy jumped in front of me, demanding I give him the lead. "*I* have to put the horses on, company policy."

When I gave him the lead line and stepped to the side, Windsong planted his feet. Billy tugged and tugged. Windsong raised his head high, jumping up and down on his front legs. "Wave your arms behind him," Billy ordered.

Suppressing a smile, I half-heartedly moved my hands. Windsong started marching in place, jerking the lead and inching Billy backward. Santos stood still where Mandy was holding him, watching from a few feet away.

"I can load him for you," I suggested. "He's used to me."

"Can't. Against policy." Billy grunted. Windsong reared, his legs dangling and his head higher than the truck. Maybe he was trying to see what was at the end of that ramp, or maybe he was playing with the strange little man at the end of his rope. But when his hooves landed on the ground, he stopped carrying on.

"See," Billy said, turning and starting up the ramp as if Windsong would follow. Windsong didn't. He turned his chiseled black head to me. It was clear he wasn't going to follow that man anywhere.

"I can put him on. It will take two seconds. No one else will ever know."

Billy didn't hesitate and handed me the lead. Windsong followed me right up the ramp. I backed him into a narrow stall, and Billy attached the trailer ties. Windsong whinnied for Santos, gave the hanging hay net a head butt, and pawed the air. Billy glanced at me as we got to the bottom of the ramp.

"You can handle Santos. He's easy."

Billy studied my face for a moment to make sure I wasn't messing with him. I struggled to keep a serious look. He marched up to Mandy and held a hand out for the lead rope. He eyed the massive horse but then closed his eyes and started toward the trailer. Santos walked up the ramp like a baby lamb.

While Billy fussed around with folding up the sides and closing the ramp, Mark drew me to the side. In a whisper, he spoke quickly, "Hurry up. Get him in the truck and get going and try not to let him call his office. They never agreed to let you ride with him."

"Seriously?" I gave him a quick hug good-bye and ran to the barn. I gathered up my purse and the messenger bag with my laptop and school books in it and was belted in the truck before Billy finished latching things in the back. I waved out the window as we pulled away from the farm until I couldn't see Mark and Mandy anymore.

*CHAPTER*

# 33

After about two hours, we pulled into a rest stop, Billy bragging that state law required a rest after four hours but that his company was so conscientious that they required him to stop every two. He showed me how to open one of the doors on the trailer and then went in search of snacks while I pulled myself in to the horses' compartment.

Windsong and Santos were quietly munching hay in adjacent stalls. I unscrewed the cap on the water can and poured some in a bucket. They both took a sip when I held it high enough for them to reach.

I listened to Windsong's heart and lungs and was thrilled that his numbers were the same as at home. I stroked his neck. He bumped noses with Santos and pushed the hay net around, arranging it for better access. Santos ripped a mouthful through the mesh and chewed steadily. I rubbed his lightning bolt.

Billy slapped a hand on the side of the trailer. "Let's go."

All three of us jumped. "Be good, boys. See you in a few hours." I double-checked that the door was tightly closed and then jogged around to the passenger side. Billy handed me a soda and a bag of sunflower seeds.

"Thanks."

Reading my textbook was putting me to sleep, so I scrolled through websites on my phone. I became absorbed in reading articles on the Festival, and time slipped by. One story mentioned me and Windsong. I read it again, looking up only when the air brakes hissed. Another rest stop.

I emailed the link to my father, tucked the phone in my pocket, and jumped out. Another good report on Windsong's heart. He liked this big rig, and I'm sure having Santos The Solid, standing right next to him was helping, too.

When we were rolling again, I fell asleep, and Billy was parking the truck, shaking me awake in no time. I yawned and requested a burger before heading to the trailer for Windsong's checkup routine.

"They doing okay back there?" Billy asked. We divided the food he had brought back to the cab.

I nodded. "Thanks for dinner."

"Thank *you*. This trip is easy with you taking care of the horses."

"No problem, as long as you don't mind me napping in between. I don't know how you stay awake."

"Secrets of the job." He fixed his hat, setting it back so it looked no different than it did before he touched it.

Sleeping sitting upright in the cab wasn't so bad. I rubbed my stiff neck and bent sideways, trying to crack my back. Windsong pawed as I entered the trailer.

"Good morning, boys. Yes, even though it's still dark out, it's time for breakfast." I unhooked the empty hay net and stuffed it full again. I let each horse take a bite before hanging it. I offered them a drink and unpacked my stethoscope to check on Windsong, though I could tell he was just fine.

I struggled back into the cab after visiting the restroom and brushing my teeth. I was thankful everything was normal in the rear of the trailer. I was too tired to deal with a crisis.

Billy got in and slammed his door. I buckled my seat belt and settled a blanket over my legs. The silence in the cab alerted me to a problem. I looked at the key. Billy's hand wasn't on it. He was glaring at me, his jaw clenched.

"I just got off the phone with my office. I check in before I start in the morning."

Feeling the blood drain from my face and its icy absence spread down my body, I dropped the blanket.

"I see you know what I'm talking about. You lied to me."

"I'm sorry, really. I worry about my horse and this is such an important competition and he's a handful and nervous and the trip is so long—"

He interrupted the flood of words. "Hush. I am trying to figure out what to do. Luckily, I didn't exactly admit you were in the truck. I should just leave you here."

"No! Don't do that." Taking a deep breath, I hoped the oxygen would stimulate my brain. "I'm really sorry," I repeated, unable to come up with anything else.

"Well, sorry won't feed my kids when you make me lose my job. This place is pretty populated; you'll be safe until someone comes to get you." He pointed to the door.

"Wait. Let me just make a phone call. You can't leave me here without knowing someone can come get me, can you? I'm just a kid!" I tugged out my phone, scrolled to Mark's number, and hit the green call button before Billy could respond.

"Where are you?"

"A rest stop called Maryland House," I repeated after asking Billy.

"Good job, you got farther than I expected. Put him on the phone," Mark ordered.

I held the phone out to Billy, chewing my lip. "He wants to talk to you."

Billy held the device to his ear. His expression went from fuming, to outraged, to skeptical, to interested. His response was punctuated alternately with "Uh huh" and "Seriously?" Finally, he said, "Okay," and turned the phone and looked at the screen. "How do you turn this thing off?"

I took the phone out of his hands, wondering if I was getting out.

Billy started the noisy diesel, pulling levers and pressing buttons. The engine screamed to life, the air brakes letting out a loud hiss, and the radio blaring out the country music when he flicked the knob. He shifted into gear and we lurched forward.

I guess I was staying. I slumped into the stiff cushion, resting my head on the seat back until my muscles relaxed.

Within an hour, we were in New Jersey.

The only words Billy said to me after the phone call were, "We're not stopping. It's only two more hours."

I nodded.

When we turned off the highway I pushed my books back into my messenger bag. My excitement grew. We wound through back roads and signs pointed to Hamilton Farm, home of the United States Equestrian Team. Trees lined the road closely because there was no shoulder and I secretly admired Billy's negotiation of the twisting turns and low-hanging branches.

After one particularly tight turn, the truck squealed to a stop on an empty stretch of road.

Leaning forward, eager to arrive, I forgot about the silent treatment. "What's the matter? Are you lost? The sign said it was just ahead."

"No, I'm not lost," came the scathing reply. "You get out here."

"What do you mean?"

"It's just around the bend and I'm not risking anyone seeing you get out of my truck. I could get in a lot of trouble, so you walk from here."

"But I'll duck or something. I promise not to say anything, ever," I pleaded, not convinced he would really kick me out.

"Out. The extra money from that guy is still not worth losing my job."

I started to lift the strap of my book bag, but he stopped me.

"You can leave that. I'll wait for you at the stable and give it back."

I slid out of the truck, hoping that "around the bend" meant a few steps, not a few miles. The instant I was out of the way, Billy put the truck in gear. So, it wasn't my charming personality or apparent helplessness that made him keep me in the truck, but Mark's generous bribe. I watched the big rig roll away with my hands on my hips.

I stayed on the macadam for easier walking and leaned forward, moving at a quick pace. It was beautiful in this area, with soft rolling hills and lots of trees. New Jersey was called the Garden State, and now I knew why. This time of year, in mid-April, everything was blossoming, and yards and pastures were full of color. I made it around the corner and a couple hundred yards ahead, a small but tasteful sign marked the shaded driveway to the show grounds.

I sped up. My chest heaved as I turned in the drive, and I stepped to the side as a car drove past. A few turn-offs led to parking areas, but the main barn was straight ahead. At least, I thought it was the barn. It resembled a quarried stone castle more than a modern steel-sided barn.

I walked through a towering atrium and asked the first official-looking person I saw where horses were unloaded. The gray-haired, fit, fashionable woman pointed me down an aisle and past a schooling arena. Horses were everywhere, being led in crisp show sheets, being ridden in shining tack, and pushing their noses against stall bars. Magnificent horses, every one of them beautiful and expensive looking. My stride slowed and my breathing became shallow. Trying not to be intimidated, I reminded myself of Cory's advice: "Just think of you and your horse." Boy, I wished Cory was walking beside me, although just this once, I might have made him stow the cowboy hat.

I spotted Billy and jogged the last few yards. Windsong whinnied and pawed and jerked on the trailer ties. Billy was standing with a slender girl in a red, white, and blue polo shirt and red ball cap.

"You have to unload the horse and get your truck out of here. You can't stay in the loading zone for so long."

"I'm waiting for the owner. Look at that thing. I'm not touching him." Windsong flung himself against the divider, shaking his head and rattling the clips and ties.

"Until they show up, close the ramp and move your truck out of the loading zone."

"Here I am," I puffed, stopping in front of them.

Another loud scream came from the trailer, accompanied by hoof pounding.

The girl's tight smile didn't reach her eyes, and she waited for the noise to subside. She inspected my scruffy paddock boots and baggy sweatshirt. I guess two days in a tractor trailer hadn't done much for my appearance. "Are you going to unload him yourself? I can get one of the professional grooms." Her tone indicated she doubted I could handle him.

"He's just nervous. Where's Santos?" Knowing Windsong's dependent personality, I would have unloaded him first, keeping Santos in his sight until Windsong was safely in a stall.

"Mr. Peterson's groom already took him to his stall with Robert's string of horses. Should I call someone?"

"No, I'll be fine." I pushed my aching legs up the steep ramp and frowned at the sad, empty stall next to Windsong. A low but desperate nicker greeted me, and I shook the picture of Santos, looking back over his shoulder as some stranger led him away, out of my head.

I rubbed Windsong's cheeks and threaded the chain through the halter, murmuring encouraging words. I carefully stayed to the side of the coco mat, letting Windsong have all the room he needed to negotiate the steep ramp.

I watched proudly as he daintily inched down the slope instead of charging out like he usually would. But when he landed on solid ground for the first time in two days, he reared. I flicked the chain and he came right back down.

The girl pressed her lips together but tipped her head for me to follow her. Windsong left his walking manners at home; instead he jogged slowly beside me, his muscles bunched up tight. The ring of his horseshoes echoed in the cobblestone aisle like a woman's high heels clicking on the terrazzo of a high-scale office building.

With each tap, the butterflies in my stomach woke and got crazier. Being at the home of our country's equestrian team was an honor. *Please don't let me embarrass myself—or anyone else*. I patted Windsong and grimaced, wiping his sticky sweat on my jeans.

Miss USET led us out of the main barn to a smaller more normal-looking barn. Windsong propped and whinnied when he came out into the sunshine. Ears pricked sharply forward, head high, he listened intently. Faint answers drifted out of the barns. Could he tell if one of them was from Santos? Softly nickering, he marched forward.

I was happy when we finally reached his assigned stall. It was bedded deeply, and Windsong kicked shavings everywhere, making a few laps around the space. I tugged the strings off the bale of hay left for us and threw some in the corner. He barely glanced at it but drank deeply from the automatic water bowl.

I was pleased that he took a drink, but his nostrils were still flaring, and I couldn't tell if that was from whinnying so much or if he was short of breath. I needed my stethoscope.

Billy's truck was gone when I returned to the loading zone, but my things were in a neat pile by the door. Carrying as much as I could, I bumbled back to Windsong's stall. He hadn't settled down at all.

I checked his vitals. They were elevated, but not alarming. That would be expected with our arrival and his separation from Santos. There wasn't much I could do; it was too dangerous to take him out when he was in this state. I decided to go collect my show packet and look for Santos.

CHAPTER

# 34

A gazebo-type tent was set up at the back door of the atrium. While I
waited for my paperwork, I looked around at the people laughing and
talking in small groups. It felt weird to be here all by myself. It was
early on arrival day, so more exhibitors would be coming as the day went on.

Michelle should be here somewhere, manning a booth for EMA. I texted
her. Kate was planning on arriving in the morning before my class. Later on, I
was going to school Windsong by myself. I half expected Melinda or Shawn to
get in line behind me, but this wasn't like one of my local shows. I recognized a
lot of faces—riders whose photos had been published in magazines and equine
quarterlies—but I didn't know any of them personally.

I took the large envelope from the clerk and asked her if she knew where
Robert Peterson was stabled. She pointed over her shoulder at one of the wings
of the main barn.

I made my way through the crowd, admiring the glass skylight, which was
the floor of the upper level. I stopped, surprised, when I realized people were
looking down at me. Neat.

I wandered through elaborate stone archways and peered into each stall as
I walked past. Beautiful, well-dressed equines looked back at me, but very few
came forward, no longer interested in the passers-by. The aisle of this barn
was spotless and clear of equipment. Only one groom was carrying a groom
kit into a stall.

I looked into the fourth stall, and there he was. Despite a thorough bath and my meticulous trim job, Santos's coppery coat still wasn't quite as brilliant as the coats' of the other pampered animals. But a few weeks of work and daily grooming would have him up to snuff. Except no product would hide his scars.

"Santos," I whispered, like we were in a church. His ears pricked and he put his nose through the bars. The sliding stall door reached up to the ceiling beam, so he couldn't put his neck out. I slid my whole arm in to reach his chest and scratched the bare skin with my fingernails. He twisted his head up, enjoying it.

The peace was disturbed by clumping boot heels and cheery voices. A group of people came through the archway, Robert in the center with his head turned and arms waving as he related some pertinent piece of information. All heads were cocked toward him so as not to miss a single word. He looked every inch the celebrity. Immaculate white breeches disappeared into tall black boots and a white polo shirt sported a blue-and-red-striped collar. The United States Equestrian Team logo was prominent on the left side of his chest.

I snatched my arm back and shoved both hands into my jeans pockets. It was a long way to the other end of the barn so there was no way to escape his notice. Even if he didn't approve or think I deserved to be here, I had been invited. Raising my chin, I turned and looked him in the eye, bracing my shoulders against the force of his personality.

He stopped talking and walking, and my knees trembled. I leaned back against the stall to steady myself. Santos nuzzled my head and took my ponytail into his mouth. I tried surreptitiously to swat him away, but he tugged and my head bumped the bars. My face heated and the group smiled and chuckled. Finally, I got him to let go, and I ran trembling fingers over my hair, trying to smooth out the lumps.

"Jane." Robert grinned and stepped closer, intending to draw me into a hug. I looked down at my dusty boots and saliva-smeared sweatshirt, not wanting to mar his pristine shirt. He tugged me in anyway, and over his shoulder I could see chins dropping in the whole group. Frankly, mine wanted to hit the floor, too. Robert was hugging me? He said I wasn't seasoned enough to be here. He thought I wasn't good enough.

I did a quick inspection as we parted, thankful I didn't leave any green splotches on him. I picked a few black hairs off his shirt sleeve. "Sorry, I just finished setting Windsong up in his stall and wanted to make sure Santos was settled in and didn't need anything." The red devil nickered softly, pushing his muzzle through the bars. I gently stroked his nose.

"I hear I should thank you for recommending me to Mark Grant. I always envied Erica for getting her hands on Santos before any of us could." He waved absently to the rest of the group.

I kissed that soft velvet but then slapped my hand over my mouth, realizing how unprofessional that must have looked. Santos's hoof bumped the wall and another nicker had me shrugging. I really liked this horse, and I couldn't, wouldn't resist showing it. "He's a really special horse, and you're the best. You'll get him out there again, so the world can see that."

There was an awkward moment. I thought I sounded too much like a teeny bopper. I stuck a fingernail between my teeth but stopped myself before biting down on it. Instead, I made a fist and shoved it into my jeans, and planned on keeping it there.

I shifted my weight and hoped Robert said something soon. Or maybe I should just make an escape now. I looked down the aisle and then back at him.

Robert gave me the warmest smile, and my nervous fidgeting stilled. Softly, he said, "Thanks. I heard you worked with him to get him ready for me. I appreciate that. I have great plans for him."

"He'll do great things. He's so talented and pleasant. Really easy to work with, great focus. Well, you know that. Anyway, you'll love riding him. I know I did. Not that I did anything near what you will, I'm just saying, he's great. Really great." Now was probably a good time to stick my fingers in my mouth to stop the torrent. I touched Santos's nose again and pressed my lips together.

Robert's smile widened. "Kate's not here yet, is she? Meet me in the ring at three. I'll help you with your warm-up ride."

I blinked. "Seriously? I mean, absolutely. I'll be there." Giant, giant advantage to have someone like Robert coach me before a big show like this. He knew my horse, he knew what the judges wanted, he probably even knew exactly whom I was riding against.

"Thank you!" I called, and the group continued down the aisle. Thank you for not making me look like a fool—well, feel like a fool, anyway. I slid the rubber band out of my rat's nest and gave Santos another kiss on the nose. "See you later, big guy. Don't worry, you're going to really like Robert."

I kept looking over my shoulder, and Santos kept his nose pressed to the bars. I finally turned the corner and sighed, resisting the temptation to peek around the wall to see if he had gone back to his hay. The barn at home was going to be awfully quiet without his vibrant personality.

And without Santos boarding there, Mark and Mandy would have no reason to come by anymore. It would go back to being just me and Windsong, alone.

After lunch with Michelle and a couple hours in the EMA booth handing out brochures and talking about our mission, I returned to a quieter Windsong. I tacked him up, led him to the end of the barn, and used a mounting block to climb on. After adjusting my helmet, I steered him past the main show arena, weaving between other horses and pedestrians, nodding with feigned nonchalance at people whom I only knew from pictures in magazines. When Bethany Stillman—a two-time Olympian and top national trainer—said, "Hi, Jane," I nearly fell off of Windsong.

More people addressed me by name, and I stopped at the top of the path that led to the schooling rings. I watched riders school their top-class horses. They looked so smooth and unruffled. My jittery nerves returned.

Did I ever look unruffled on Windsong? I had to maintain fierce concentration and total focus so I could feel the slightest change in his movement, to catch his overreactions before they turned into spooks. I considered letting Robert know that I would be warming up in another ring, one with fewer famous riders—or none if I could find an empty one.

Just then, a fiery chestnut horse with elastic, floating gaits that outclassed all the rest entered the ring. When Santos was in motion, his scars were unnoticeable. Under Robert's capable hands, even his warm-up was mesmerizing. Santos was all business, eyes straight ahead, not distracted by the many horses working around him. As he rounded the near corner, Windsong's gaze locked on the distinct red horse.

Windsong's ribs expanded under my legs. He tested the scent and then whinnied, lurching forward and sliding down the path a few feet. I tightened the reins, trying to control our skid and looking for the safest path.

An answering whinny from Santos surprised me but fueled Windsong's desire to join his friend. He bent his knees, taking fast, tiny steps, mincing forward and tugging on the tight reins. His hooves half slid, half gripped the gravel. Windsong was focused on Santos, not paying any attention to his treacherous descent. He would have leapt to the bottom if I had let up on the reins. I didn't.

Finally, we were safe on level ground and I was able to look up from the ground. Santos was halted on the other side of the fence, ears locked on us. So were most of the other horses.

Robert grinned at me. "Well done." Obviously, he was recalling some of my other unconventional entrances on my crazy horse. He rolled a shoulder toward the gate. "Most people come in from the other side."

A smooth, paved path lined the approach to the gate. It had escaped my notice when I was ogling the horses. My face burned. I nodded and pointed Windsong in that direction.

# 35

This wasn't the first time Robert instructed me, and like the previous times, his directions were clear and on target. Windsong was happy that Santos was in the ring, and he worked without dramatics. I thanked Robert and promised to be on time to warm up for my class with him the next day.

Windsong had other ideas, though, and refused to leave Santos behind. He went sideways, back and forward, shaking his head when I gave him a strong kick. When he continued to try to turn back, I poked him with my spurs. He answered with a half-hearted rear.

Deciding not to be the entertainment again, I slid off and pulled the reins over his head. With a sharp tug, I started up the path. Windsong followed reluctantly, with one last whinny to his friend.

He continued to look for Santos all through his bath and braiding. He ate his dinner while he paced circles and looked for Santos. His heart rate stayed elevated, but it was lower than when he worked. I interpreted that to mean that he was okay, just upset.

After I had dinner with Michelle, I went back to the barn to check on him. His nostrils were slightly flared, and when I counted his heartbeats, the count was the same, elevated. Blowing out a sigh, I decided to stay near the stall with him all night, checking hourly until he settled down.

I called Michelle and told her I was staying here instead of with her in the hotel room. I opened a director's chair in the aisle and settled down for a long night with one of my textbooks and a nervous equine.

One of the grooms doing night check stopped in front of me and explained that she and the rest of the grooms were responsible for checking all the horses. There was no need for me to stay.

"My horse has a heart condition, so I want to monitor him until he calms down. I'll only be here an hour or so," I lied, disguising my unease at Windsong's agitation and my plan to stay here all night.

"Okay. I'm sure that's fine. But you're missing the informal exhibitors' reception in the atrium." She wriggled her eyebrows encouragingly.

"I'll definitely stop in there." I smiled, hoping she would get on her way.

After a boring hour of watching Windsong snatch a bite of hay and pace a circle in the shavings, I took his vitals. They were the same, slightly elevated, but not as high as during work. I decided to make a run to the party, get some snacks, and return within half an hour.

I hustled through the main barn, heading toward the warm glow of light in the center atrium. A low rumble of chatter filled the area. Grooms in jeans and paddock boots took advantage of the wet wipes volunteers were offering. Riders still dressed in their breeches and tall boots were milling around the serving tables against one wall, piled high with sandwiches, salads, and bowls of chips. A tall stack of cups wobbled and a nimble groom caught them before they could tumble.

After filling a plate, I leaned against the smooth tongue-and-groove wall, chewing and watching. I returned a few nods but didn't attempt to talk and eat. I tossed my plate into a trash can and tried to be discreet as I took a selfie with my lips drawn back, exposing my teeth. I was checking for bits of broccoli when a loud clap of thunder made me jump.

I shoved the phone in my pocket and speed-walked to the end of the barn aisle. It hadn't started raining, but the air had that ozone smell. A thunderstorm was predicted but forecasted to be long gone before classes started in the morning. Knowing how Windsong hated storms, I hustled back to his stall. Hopefully, his location in the center of the aisle would help him stay calm.

In my dream, the crowd was cheering, and Windsong was happily prancing under me. Then he lowered his head and kicked out, his hooves drumming the wooden arena fence. He bucked and bucked, I let go, and I was falling, falling.

I awoke with a jerk, grabbing the arms of the chair. I was disoriented and flinched at heavy thumping in the pitch black behind my head. Blinking, I tried to peer into the blackness, but there was not a glimmer of light and I couldn't see a thing.

Gradually, my groggy brain remembered that I was in front of Windsong's stall. The sound of the applause that I had been dreaming about must have been the heavy rain slamming the roof of the barn.

A bright flash of lightning seared my wide-open eyes at the same time a loud clap of thunder shook the building. The pounding started up again, and it was coming from Windsong's stall.

I stood and felt my way to the bars. "Windsong, what are you doing in there?" Not even a shadow of his black body was visible.

Another crash of thunder with an immediate flash of lightning outlined his silhouette. He was standing straight up on two legs. Then it was pitch black again. What the heck?

My hands scrabbled at my pocket, fingers feeling for my phone. Where is it? I threw myself onto my knees, arms outstretched, feeling the aisle floor. More thumping. I smashed my thumb into the chair leg. "Ow." I shook my wrist and inched forward, my knee hitting against my phone.

I clicked on the flashlight feature and aimed it between the iron bars. The glaring light was just bright enough to illuminate the stall. Windsong had paced a trench in his deep shavings and had strewn hay and manure everywhere.

Another clap of thunder and he reared up, pummeling his hooves on the wall like he was trying to climb out. His long, dark silhouette was barely visible against the back of the stall, and a glimmer of white from his eye hovered high up in the air.

I yelped, the phone jerking in my hand. Criminies! He was going to hurt himself, damage a tendon or fall and break his neck. His body slid down the wall, and he whirled around snorting.

"Easy, boy," I whispered ineffectively.

I moved slowly to the door and rolled it open, but the bobbing light terrified him, and he lurched back, bumping his rump into the wall. Inhaling sharply, I slammed the door closed and pounded my palm on my forehead. What do I do?

This was the worst I had ever seen him act. Another explosion of thunder shook the barn and I cringed instinctively. The storm must have been right over the show grounds. I could hear the rustle of movement from other stalls, but none of the horses were pounding on the walls like Windsong was.

I thought of the snow storm and the sound of the tree falling and his wild-eyed craziness then. I had been able to ease his tension only with the sedative. But it wasn't legal to administer medication at a horse show, and it would eliminate us from the competition.

Smacking my hand on my thigh, I tried to prod my paralyzed brain to work. *Do something, Jane!*

Thunder cracked and Windsong's hooves drummed the wall again. The sickening sound of his body sliding down the boards galvanized me to action. I rifled through my trunk, trying to hold the light with my chin. I dropped the phone twice before I found the show program. Windsong thumped and banged, and I ducked away from the ruckus. *Hold on, hold on.*

I flipped through the book and located the information page. Laying it on the floor and holding the page with my knee, I dialed the listed show veterinarian.

A monotone voice answered. "This is an answering service. Please state your name, your location, and the nature of your emergency. I will give the message to the on-call doctor."

I had to raise my voice over the storm and spoke quickly. "My name is Jane. I'm at Gladstone and my horse is flipping out because of the storm."

"I'm sorry. The signal is breaking up," the calm voice returned. "Where did you say you were?"

"Gladstone!" Did she not get that this was an emergency?

"Gladstone? Is that a town?"

"Gladstone. It is an equestrian show grounds. The vet will know what it means." Just write it down, lady. We both knew he was going to call and talk directly to me anyway. Windsong's hooves beat a tattoo just under the iron bars. My stomach turned over.

"Okaaay. And what's the medical emergency?" she asked slowly.

I squeezed my eyes shut against the brilliant flashes of lightning, but I could still hear Windsong's rasping breath and the splash of water as he slammed the bucket. "My horse is nervous due to the storm." How did I explain that he was in mortal danger because of his heart condition? "A heart attack—he could have a heart attack."

"He could, or he is?" she asked, her tone hardening. "This is an emergency line. I won't disturb the doctor if it's not an emergency."

"It is. It is. I'm telling you. He's very frightened, he could die if he doesn't see a doctor soon. He has a heart condition."

"I'll put down heart condition, but I'm warning you, young lady, if this is a trumped-up call, the doctor will bill for a call fee even if he doesn't come out."

"That's fine! Just give him the message. Hurry!" I slid down the wall onto my butt and held the phone tightly so there would be no chance of missing the return call from the doctor.

# 36

I put my hands over my ears to block out the sound of crashing thunder and Windsong's accompanying thuds. I pressed send the instant my phone rang.

In a superfast deluge of words, I explained the situation, including details of Windsong's damaged heart valve, his elevated numbers all afternoon, and his extreme agitation at the storm. There was silence on the other end.

"Doctor, I assure you, this is an emergency. His heart could fail under all the stress. I need you here," I said, doing my best to control the tremble in my voice.

"It is going to take me awhile. Electricity is out all over the area. The rain is coming down so hard, I can barely see the road."

"I understand, but please hurry."

I put my head in my hands, wishing Cory was with me. I thought about calling him, but it was four in the morning, and he still wasn't talking to me.

Horrific images flashed in my mind with every bolt of lightning, each worse than the last. Over the years, I had read occasional stories of a racehorse or event horse dying during competition. My response was always outrage that an owner could let that happen to their animal, disgust that a rider would push their mount until the animal keeled over.

But, now, after having experienced the confusing and nonspecific symptoms of Windsong's condition—a condition we discovered by accident—it was easy to imagine those riders not even knowing their horses were at risk. Windsong's energy and drive never let up when I was riding him. He was strong and fit. He couldn't scare himself to death, could he? He wasn't galloping at full speed;

he was safe in his stall.

I looked up when a faint light floated toward me in the darkness.

"Hi." It was the night groom. "You're still here." Her head whipped around when Windsong's body-slammed the wall. "What was that?"

"My horse. He's a mess."

I stood, and we both peered in the stall. Windsong's eyes glowed back at us, the pink of his nostrils showing, his neck shiny with sweat. I strained my eyes, looking for blood on his dark coat.

"Crud. He's going to kill himself," I moaned. "I called the vet. I didn't know what else to do."

Cathy spoke loudly over the clatter of the heavy rain on the barn roof. "Let's put his halter on. Maybe holding him still and keeping him company will help. My name is Cathy, by the way."

Cathy held her lantern light up so I could see, and I carefully entered the stall. Singing his name and cooing gently, I got the halter over his head and buckled it. I stroked his neck, and my hand came away clammy. I peered at the moisture, relieved that it was not red and that it smelled salty. "Can you get my stethoscope? I left it on the chair."

When the light moved, Windsong snorted and paced a tight, frantic circle around me. He practically disappeared into the dark, his snorting louder than the rain.

Adrenaline made my hands shaky. I carefully placed the earpieces in and put the bell on his side while Cathy held the lead rope. I looked at my phone and had to follow Windsong around a few circles before I got a decent count. I repeated it twice, my nausea increasing with each count. It was higher than I had ever recorded.

His coat was stiff with dried sweat where I stroked his neck. My heart was beating furiously, making me wonder at the stress *his* poor heart was withstanding.

Cathy held him as still as she could, trying to prevent any wall climbing. Windsong quieted slightly, enough to make me wonder whether I had called the vet unnecessarily.

I threw a cotton cooler over his back to absorb some of the sweat and keep him from feeling chilled. I offered him a fresh flake of hay, but he didn't even look at it or the treat in my hand. That worried me more than anything else.

Windsong loved treats, and I was back to feeling impatient for the vet to arrive.

Finally, the veterinarian's pickup truck rolled to a stop at the end of the barn, and he left the headlights pointing down the aisle. A balding, bespectacled man approached us with a reassuring smile. "Ladies, let's take a look."

I led Windsong into the aisle, and he stood in the light.

I told the doctor the current numbers and explained Windsong's history and heart condition. He listened intently. He placed his own stethoscope behind Windsong's leg and listened to the horse's heart himself, commenting that he heard the murmur. He lifted Windsong's lip and pressed a finger against the gums. His hands were gentle as he ran them over Windsong's body, and his voice was soothing to me, so I hoped it helped Windsong.

"His heart rate is elevated and his breathing … Whoa!" The agile man scooted back against the wall. Windsong whirled at another clap of thunder, metal shoes scrabbling on the cement floor, tiny sparks flying from his feet.

"Sorry. Are you okay?" I asked the doctor as I straightened Windsong.

"He is quite jumpy, huh? Anyway, I can hear the irregular heartbeat, and he is highly agitated. I don't really know what that could mean. You say he is a nervous horse. Maybe we give him some time, and then check again. If his heart rate doesn't come down, that may be a sign of something unusual happening with his valve, which could explain the extra agitation he is displaying. Maybe he feels sick or unusual in some way."

I swallowed, raising a shaky hand to my mouth, and sucked in a worried breath. "You think he's having a heart attack?" A stiff wind blew up the aisle. Windsong's tail billowed to the side and he jerked my arm as he scooted past me. I gripped the lead tighter, and turned him around. Cathy flattened herself against the wall to avoid being sideswiped by his rump.

"Not an attack, but something is not right. The increased heart rate, if it continues, may cause that bad valve in the horse's heart to malfunction or may damage it further. He must be calmed. I suggest a sedative." His furry eyebrows shot up in warning. "But there aren't any that are legal in a show after administration."

Chewing a fingernail, I swallowed bile. "How long does the sedative last?"

"It won't clear his system for forty-eight to seventy-two hours, but I usually advise my clients not to administer anything for a whole week before a show."

My class was in less than twenty-four hours. The most important ride of my life. The ride that was going to prove to Robert, to my parents, to Cory—to everyone—that Windsong and I belonged here, that I had what it took to ride at this level, that they should take me seriously as a national contender.

I took a shuddering breath around the lump in my throat, acid burning in my gut. "And if I don't let you give it to him?" I rasped hopelessly.

"It may be hours before the storm is over and he calms down. There is no way of knowing what that valve can handle. Like I said, we can take the risk and give him time to calm down on his own."

An image of Windsong's heart bursting, blood spewing all over the stall, his body sinking to the shavings, eyes rolling back in his head, flashed in my mind. Windsong lying motionless, not breathing. My stomach lurched.

My eyes met the doctor's, his shining with sympathy. He was stroking Windsong's rigid neck, but the horse wouldn't stand still. Windsong turned and looked behind him, and then whipped around to look in another direction. "You think I should give it to him?"

He shrugged. "Your call, but sedating him will practically eliminate the risk of an actual heart attack."

He would live then, but his career would be over. To survive, he obviously needed a quieter life than that of a competition horse. Tears stung my eyes, and I scrunched them shut. What would I tell Michelle? I had signed a contract with EMA that had Windsong's name on it. I would be fired before I could do any good.

And how would I pay for his care if I lost my job? I couldn't sell him or lease him to anyone as a show horse. I couldn't sell him as a trail horse; he was too spooky. Who would buy such an expensive, high-maintenance animal as a pasture pet? No one. That's who. He would wind up at the killer auctions or in some other horrible situation that would kill him dead anyway.

I couldn't let that happen. I had to show in that class. I had to keep my job. I had to be the EMA spokesperson.

I had to tell the doctor no. That was the only way to save Windsong's life. We needed to ride one last class to establish my reputation so that I would have a job and be able to pay for Windsong's care for the rest of his life.

There was a silent flash of lightning, and it was a couple of seconds before thunder rumbled, much quieter now. Windsong lifted his head, scenting the ozone-tainted air, trembling. The headlights backlit his rock-hard, tense stance, head high, nostrils flared, and the whites of his eyes glowing eerily. His legs were splayed and he was ready to escape from the oncoming threat of the storm.

I held up my hand. "Let me call my sponsor." Cathy took the lead rope from my hand, her mouth a grim line.

Quickly, I dialed the number. "Michelle, we have a problem." I told her everything, my voice as shaky as my knees.

"No. You can't drug him. They will eliminate you from the competition. You won't even get to ride him on the grounds again if you do that. Don't do it. Wait for me. I'll get dressed and be there in half an hour." She hung up.

Without looking up, I scrolled through my recent calls. I pressed Kate's name, but she didn't answer. Right, she was already on the plane. It would be hours before I could speak with her.

Hesitantly, I poked at Cory's name, almost canceling the call before his name flashed on the screen. I curled my fingers and let it go through. Please, let him answer. Our disagreement aside, I knew he would understand exactly how I felt and give me good advice.

His recorded voice asked me to leave a message. My lungs deflated with a loud hiss. I leaned my forehead on the stall door. "I need you," I whispered. "It's an emergency. Windsong is really, really upset because of the storm. His heart is under stress and I have to decide to medicate him or not. Cory, *please* call me right back. Tell me what to do." I hung up with a sob.

Holding a tiny hope that he would call back, I took a breath and straightened. I would tell the vet we would wait for Windsong to calm down. Cathy and I would stay with him, soothe him, and he would be fine.

"Jane, what do you want to do?" the kind veterinarian asked, his sleepy, red-rimmed eyes sympathetic.

Windsong's head was high above mine. He twisted his neck to stare into the headlights. Cathy held the rope loosely, letting him look around, instead of fighting him to stand still and adding to his stress.

The strong breeze lifted his forelock, and his nostrils flared, sucking in the crisp smell of ozone. At a loud crack of thunder, he whipped his hind end to the side and yanked Cathy off her feet. She bounced against his shoulder, tightening her grip and using his momentum to regain her footing. His hooves smacked the wall, and he snorted loudly and then scrambled backward away from the misty headlights of the truck.

I ran to his head to take the lead from Cathy. "Windsong, easy, boy." I stroked his neck but blanched as I felt his whole body quiver. His knees were bent and his head cocked sideways. "Easy now, calm yourself."

His ears strained forward and never even flicked in my direction. His eyes were vacant, staring at a distant threat that only he perceived. How long could I watch him suffer this mental anguish? If I didn't sedate him, would there be another, more horrible end to his suffering?

"Windsong, buddy, want a treat?" I wiped my wet cheeks with my sleeve and dug around my pocket. "Please, calm down, buddy."

His head bobbed down, bumping my palm without taking the nugget. An ear splitting crack of thunder snapped through the barn and he flinched, a shudder running through his limbs. I looked at his liquid brown eyes encircled by bloodshot white and his hard, tense muscles. I lightly ran my hand up and down his neck with no response.

Where was Michelle? Why didn't Cory call me? Windsong's metal shoes clipped on the floor as he jigged, his neurosis not abating even a little bit. He was ready to run.

I reached up to stroke that velvety part of his nose, but he didn't even notice.

My parents would say "I told you so." My father, he would shrug with that smug smile. "You should have given up that horse and stayed in school like I said." I wanted to prove him wrong so badly and this show was supposed to do that.

Swiping at my eyes again, I pressed my nose into Windsong's damp neck and breathed in the heady scent of horse sweat and raw fear. Shaking my head, I reminded myself this wasn't about me. Windsong could *die*.

I couldn't—wouldn't—stand here and watch him suffer another second when relief was so readily available. The sedative would make him feel better within moments.

Patting Windsong gently, I signaled the doctor. "Give him the sedative."

CHAPTER

# 37

The doctor injected him, and I walked Windsong back in the stall.

I stroked my poor black dragon, my forehead against his neck. Cathy's and the vet's voices droned, a dull hum in my ears. Gradually, Windsong's neck softened under my forehead. He ignored his hay, standing still. His ears swiveled at the sounds of the storm, but his head began to droop. I gently slid the halter off, and left my boy resting, with one hip cocked and his lower lip hanging. He didn't notice me leave the stall.

"You're safe now, go to sleep, buddy." It was over.

I slumped into the chair, willing my muscles to relax. It was over. Without the results of this show, it would be a long time before I was in this position again. It could be years before I was able to afford a horse of Windsong's talent—no one would be handing a kid like me a great horse without my earning it.

Well, I supposed I could concentrate on school now, and my father would be happy. But he was the only one. I bit my lip thinking of how I would explain what happened to everyone.

Cathy patted my back, the aisle darkening as the vet backed his truck around before pulling away. "I better go make my rounds."

Just as she turned away another set of headlights lit up the aisle and Michelle jumped out of her car. She skidded to a stop in front of Windsong's stall and shined a flashlight at him. "Oh, good, he settled down. See, I told you to just wait."

"No, the vet just left. He's sedated. I won't be showing today."

"What! I told you to wait for me!" She shook her finger at me. "You were like this at Erica's, too, always making a big deal out of everything. Do you know what you just did?"

She started pacing. "I really thought you had matured. I thought that you understood what was at stake. EMA is on the rocks, and if I don't increase revenue, it will shut down because Mark has no interest in it. I have sent him invitations to the meetings, and then the minutes, hoping that he would respond, but nothing." She turned toward me, and I was glad I couldn't see her expression in the dark. "You didn't just end this show, you ended your career with EMA. You may have ended EMA itself. We were counting on you. The board is not going to stand for this. Especially when I tell them I told you not to do it. You ruined everything!"

My arms were wrapped around my chest and I was squeezing my biceps hard. I bowed my head and tears dripped from my cheeks. "I'm sorry. But you didn't see him. Michelle, he was off-the-charts ballistic. He was literally climbing the walls. The vet agreed with me. Even Cathy, the night check girl, agreed with me. I had no choice—I had to do it."

"You made the wrong choice. You should have waited for me! If you weren't standing in front of his stall like a neurotic ninny, you probably would have come down in the morning and would never have known how he was acting."

I squeezed my eyes tight against the image of Windsong flat out on the stall floor. "He probably would have been dead or near to it! I had to, please understand. I know I ruined everything. But I couldn't let him die." Windsong was going to survive, but Michelle's stony expression clearly indicated my dream was dead. My national riding career was over.

Michelle turned back to her car. She said softly, "You're nothing but a drama-loving hypochondriac." The edges of her form blurred as I watched her climb into her little car.

I sank into the chair and pressed my eyes into my already-dampened sleeve.

The rain tapered off and finally ceased as the sun crept up the sky. Windsong stayed quiet, nearly sleeping, the whole time. The screen of my phone was black. The battery had died long ago.

I cleaned out Windsong's trashed stall, gingerly working around the groggy horse. The muck felt like it was full of bricks to my tired muscles. I eased

Windsong to the side to reach the other half of the stall. His legs lurched sluggishly. I spread new shavings out and stroked his neck. "You really blew things this time, hot shot. You get out of showing today ... and maybe forever." One droopy ear flopped toward my voice.

He was still pretty stoned. I gave him just a small amount of hay, even though I didn't expect him to eat it. My stomach grumbled. After freshening his water, I made my way toward the atrium where breakfast was available. Hot coffee and a sweet, decadent donut were in order. Crashing from a sugar high couldn't feel any worse than this, and who cared if I ate well or not? I didn't need to be in peak condition anymore.

The buffet table was covered with a red, white, and blue tablecloth and was pushed back against the wall, but it was empty. My heart sank even lower. I leaned back against the archway and closed my eyes.

"'Morning, Jane. Up early to get ready for the big class?" Robert was standing in front of me holding a steaming cup of coffee in one hand and an oversized muffin in the other.

I looked at the table. It had magically filled with trays of donuts, muffins, and fruit. Two large, shiny coffee urns sat side by side, one labeled decaf and one labeled regular. People were milling about, filling cups and picking out pastries. Was it possible to fall asleep standing up? How did I miss them setting this up four feet away from me?

Robert noisily sipped from his own cup, reminding me that he was waiting for an answer. I forgot about a donut and my stomach flipped over.

"I have to scratch. My horse was drugged."

A piece of muffin fell out of Robert's mouth. "You were sabotaged again?"

He had been involved in the last of the Alison incidents, when she had played tricks on me and Windsong to ruin my time on the Junior Riders team last summer.

Waving my hands, I rushed to explain. "No. No! Windsong was freaked out during the storm, and with his heart and all, I had the vet sedate him."

"Geez, Jane. You scared me there for a second. I'm sorry to hear that. These things happen when you show horses, but there's always next time." Robert wiped his lip on the napkin that was wrapped around the muffin.

I shook my head. "I don't think there will be a next time with Windsong. I won't risk his health to show. I'm going to retire him."

Robert frowned. "Oh, no. I'm sorry. Is that what the vet said?"

"No. I decided it myself." I stood a little taller. "No one agreed with me, I mean, they all thought I should just let him settle down on his own last night so I wouldn't have to scratch. But my show career isn't worth testing the limits of Windsong's heart. I am going to let him lead a quieter life at home." I offered what I thought was a mature, though shaky, smile.

"What a shame! You were a brilliant pair," Robert said thoughtfully.

I couldn't take the sympathy in his eyes, proof that it really was the end. I mumbled an excuse and strode out of the atrium.

Once through the doors, I ran. I found a secluded spot among the trees and leaned my head against rough bark and let the tears flow. It was tiring, all this sobbing. Maybe I was a drama queen, maybe I had ruined my one shot to leap into the big leagues. Maybe I was immature and this whole moving out, leaving college, and defying my father was a series of bad, stupid choices.

I sank to the ground, pushing my back against the tree trunk. Rubbing my temples, I tried to shut out the echo of the announcer's voice as he started the show. My head felt so heavy, I let my chin droop down to rest on my bent knees.

I watched a leaf drift down, swirling in the gentle, warm breeze as it fell. It landed softly next to me right on top of a tiny black ant busy with his daily chores. The leaf moved incrementally as the ant struggled to get it off his body. It was a hundred times his size, yet the ant continued to try. He moved this way and that and finally pushed the burden up and off. He immediately picked up the crumb he had been carrying and scuttled on his way, not letting hardship or an insurmountable obstacle interfere with his goals. What a brave little ant. He was much stronger than me. I closed my eyes, wishing to escape into sleep.

Dampness from the sodden ground seeped through my jeans, making my underwear and then my skin feel cold. I shook off the drowsiness and stood, twisting around to see how dirty my seat looked. Dark brown patches decorated each cheek. The ant was now climbing the tree with his crumb, and I marveled. He seemed to be traveling such a long way, working so hard. Then he ducked into a hole. He made it home with his crumb, probably an amazing accomplishment with all the risks and dangers he had to face. If the ant could carry on, I could, too. I could be as brave as an ant. Windsong and I would find a way on our own. If it took years, then I would keep working at it for years.

I dusted off my pants, swiped at my face, and headed to the secretary's office to officially scratch Windsong. My feet dragged, but I kept pushing one in front of the other until I reached the paper-strewn table. A woman tapped the keys on her laptop and then looked at me. I thought of the ant. Lifting my chin, I pushed the words out.

"Hi. I have to scratch my horse, Windsong, from the Intermediate I class today."

The efficient-looking, short-haired lady smiled gently. "Jane?" When I nodded, she cocked her head sideways. "We heard. You had a heck of a night. I'm really sorry we're not going to see you compete. But you did the right thing. More people should be like you."

Her comment didn't make any sense, and I wondered if she meant I did the right thing by coming to scratch instead of just not showing up at the class.

She flipped pages searching for my entry, and then tucked the top pages underneath when she found it. She smoothed the paper and crossed off Jane Mitchell with four hard strokes of a blue pen. Then she slid her fist over an inch and, using the same four lines, obliterated Windsong's name—from the list, the show, and the rest of my career.

I couldn't take my eyes off the pen, which she dropped to pick up her walkie-talkie. It rolled back and forth over Windsong's name, like a magic wand trying to make the letters completely disappear. Like my career was disappearing.

"Jane. Jane!" Her voice pierced my brain fog. "I have a refund check for you."

That didn't make sense either. "But I'm canceling last minute, usually you keep the entry fees."

She shuffled through some folders and pulled out an envelope with my name on it. "The show committee decided to refund your money because they admire your choice to withdraw instead of chancing your horse's health. There you go." She handed the envelope to me.

"Thanks." At least I could give it back to Michelle for EMA Rescue. That might soften the blow of my cancellation.

Still thinking of what I would say to Michelle, I stepped out the office door and slammed right into a slender middle-aged woman in show clothes.

I grabbed her arms to steady her. "I'm sorry, I wasn't paying attention. Are you okay?"

"Jane, no problem. After the night you had, I can imagine your mind is elsewhere. I'm sorry I won't get to watch you ride, but good luck with Windsong. We are all hoping he's okay." She patted my hand and slipped past my haze of confusion and into the office.

Had we met? I didn't remember ever seeing her before. I shrugged. Maybe she was a friend of Robert's or something. I headed toward Windsong's stall. Maybe it was warm enough to take off his cooler and brush the sweat from his coat. If he was a little more awake, I could take him out for a walk in the sunshine, although that might be pushing it; the doctor said he would be groggy for hours.

Along the path, I was stopped five more times by sympathetic competitors who offered encouraging words. Many others just called out to me. What had they done, made an announcement over the loudspeakers when I was napping? How did all of these people know how I spent my night?

CHAPTER

# 38

I turned down the aisle and Michelle was standing in front of Windsong's stall. I groaned. Here we go. I felt in my pocket for the refund and braced my shoulders. Passing busy grooms tacking up horses and cleaning stalls, I tried to recall all of the brilliant arguments I had come up with.

Michelle hopped from one foot to the other, scanning the aisle. When her eyes locked on me, all the blood drained from my limbs and I couldn't remember a single thing that I was going to say.

I held out the envelope, waving it so she would look at it instead of at me. "I got a check."

"So?" Michelle hugged a clipboard to her chest. "I have been trying to call you for an hour! Where have you been?"

I pulled out my phone. "I forgot it was dead. But the show refunded all of your money. This fiasco didn't cost EMA hardly anything."

She wasn't buying my distraction technique, and I braced to hear another slew of angry accusations.

"Fiasco? Jane, I have to apologize to you. I could not have planned a better goodwill campaign if I had spent months designing it. You're amazing!" She twirled a little circle. "As soon as it was a decent hour, I was on the phone with the EMA board members. Boy, did they make me feel like a jerk. On their instruction, I immediately posted an announcement about your withdrawal everywhere I could. The response was overwhelming. You're a genuine hero, Jane!"

I shook my head, my hand dropping. "I don't understand, I ruined everything, I'm not a hero."

Michelle spoke slowly, putting her hands on my shoulders to keep me focused. "EMA rescues horses. We are all about giving the animals the best care possible. We preach that the horse's welfare comes first. You just put Windsong's welfare before a very good chance of winning this national, prestigious competition. You took our mission statement to the highest level." She hugged me so tight my breath whooshed out with a squeak.

Numb and confused, I had to tell myself to suck air back in to my squashed lungs. "It's still over. I won't compete Windsong again."

"Don't you see? That's the beauty of it. He's already a celebrity, and you are the best representative we could ever have. You're unfired. I'm sorry for, you know, all that before." Her cheeks reddened and she shuffled her feet.

"I still have a job?" I raised an eyebrow. "You'll still pay Windsong's board?" I crossed my fingers.

She nodded enthusiastically. "For the rest of his life."

I clapped my hands together, pressing my fingertips against my lips. Finally, the sunshine streaming through the door penetrated my body and I warmed all over. Grinning, I bounced on my toes, "You won't regret it. I'll work so hard for you! I even changed my major because I want to work for EMA."

"I have no doubt," she squeezed my shoulder.

Her phone rang and she broke eye contact to answer it. While I waited for her to finish her call, I looked in on Windsong. He lifted his nose to the bars and languorously blew air onto my hand. His eyelids drooped and he was chewing hay in slow motion.

Out of habit, I evaluated his stall. The shavings were still clean and fluffy, but a few piles of manure slumped along the back wall. The hay flake was tugged apart in the corner and Windsong had consumed about half of it. His muzzle was dripping, so he had taken a drink. All good signs that he was feeling better. Great signs, in fact, that he was out of danger. I chewed my knuckle, still processing Michelle's change in attitude.

She promised that Windsong would be able to stay at Donna's at EMA's expense. He would be taken care of for life. Things would be different at Donna's, especially with Santos gone. This certainly was a life-changing weekend—just not the changes I had imagined.

Santos would do incredibly well with Robert. I closed my eyes and allowed myself to savor the memory of *passaging* on Santos. I should be grateful I even had that memory and all the memories of showing Windsong. I should stop feeling melancholy over what was ended and look to the future now. EMA was my future, school was my future and someday, my future would include riding another horse at this event.

I needed to shake the disappointment. Things were going to be alright. I would follow Santos's career with Robert like a doting parent keeps tabs on their child. I would ride Windsong without any pressure. I would get my degree and work for EMA. I scrubbed my hands over my face, rubbing off the dried tears.

My name blasted over the loudspeakers and my eyes snapped open. "Jane Mitchell, please report to the secretary's office."

I tightened my grip on the envelope. I hoped they didn't want me to return the check. I glanced over to where Michelle was still on the phone. What would she do if I had to give it back?

Michelle keyed off her phone, smiling furtively. "You better get to the office. Didn't you hear them calling you?"

"Well, yeah, I was waiting for you."

"I've got to get back to the booth. I have a million things to do now—announcements, posts, that kind of thing. You go, have a good time."

I lifted the corner of my lip. How was any of this a good time? I stuffed the check in my pocket. Maybe if the volunteer didn't see it, she wouldn't remember to ask for it back.

I passed shiny horses wearing brilliant white saddle pads and immaculate tack, their riders straightening shadbelly coat collars and buckling belts. I was overcome with melancholy. I knew I should be grateful that EMA was going to keep me, but it would have been great to ride in this Festival. The crème de la crème of dressage was mounting up and showing their stuff.

Misty-eyed, I imagined how breathtaking Windsong would have looked all decked out and full of himself, bristling with energy and spark.

I sighed and pulled the office door open. Kate, Robert, Mark, and Mandy were hovering around the reception table. Mandy was the first to see me and she launched herself at me. "I'm so sorry about Windsong. I loved him." Somehow her demeanor didn't match her words. She was smiling.

I looked over her head. They all were smiling. I knew it was just a show, but really, a little sympathy, please?

Kate threw up her hands. "Where have you been? We've been trying to find you for an hour. I must have called eight times."

"Sorry, my phone battery died. I was walking around thinking." Crying, but they didn't need to know that. "I didn't realize you had arrived."

"We have a proposal for you," Mark said tentatively. He looked for encouragement from the other two adults and actually threw his shoulders back, waiting for me to answer.

Gently pushing past Mandy, I stood in front of the three most confident, effective, powerful people I knew. They avoided my eyes, wrung their hands, and tapped their feet. My heart did a double flip, and I couldn't speak. How bad could it be if these three were too nervous to tell *me* about it?

The worst had already happened, so whatever it was, I could handle it. Anyhow, I was emotionally spent and had no energy left to feel anything. "Go ahead, lay it on me." Shoving my hands in my pockets, I clenched my jaw.

Robert stepped forward. "I know you recommended that Mark send Santos to me, but I think there is a better rider for him. So, I told him no, I would not accept the ride on Santos."

My jaw dropped. I looked at Mark. "That's stupid. Who else? He deserves the best."

Mark's Adam's apple bobbed under my stare, and his eyes darted to Kate. She nodded encouragingly to him. "That's right, he does. And we know of someone else, someone who cares about Santos, and whom Santos gets along with. We think we know who his perfect rider will be."

I fixed him with a glare and he stopped talking abruptly. I stepped forward, pointing at his chest. "I know Santos. And he doesn't like everyone. He may do what he's supposed to because he's such a good boy, but that won't mean he'll be happy. How could you do this to him, to Erica? He needs someone special." I swiped at the tears I couldn't hold back.

Mark took my hand, curling his fingers around mine. "You're right," he said softly. "He needs someone special. He needs you."

I sniffed. "I'll go with him to Robert's, if that's what you mean. As his groom, absolutely." I looked at Robert. "You have to be the one to ride him. You understand him, right?"

Robert shook his head. "No, Jane. *You* understand him. You have to be the one to ride him. We all want you to ride him."

I looked at each one of them. There was no mockery, no amusement in their eyes. They were serious.

Mark shook my hand. "I pulled some strings and it has been approved. You can replace Windsong with Santos and ride him in your class today."

CHAPTER

# 39

Although I didn't think I had an ounce of energy left in my body, a wave of electricity zipped from my head to my toes, turning my limbs to jelly. "Can you repeat that?" My thumping heart must have been visible under my shirt.

Then they were all laughing, and Kate was hugging me. "You can show Santos today! It's all arranged."

Mark released my hand and clapped me on the shoulder. "And you can be the one to train and show him from now on. Mandy suggested it."

I turned to her and her fair cheeks reddened. "I know you love him. And you looked good on him!"

I grabbed her and spun around with her. "You're the best. Thank you."

When I let her down, Mark put his hands on her shoulders. "And we think you two could be contenders for the Olympics."

"Olympics?" I put both hands on my head.

Robert's confident, steady brown gaze pierced my shock. "With my help, of course." He smirked good-naturedly.

"Of course?" My brain felt like it was rotating in circles. Were they for real? My hands dropped down and covered my mouth, but the joy leaked out through my fingers. "I don't know what to say."

Kate turned me around. "Don't talk; get to work. The horse needs to be washed, braided, and warmed up." She checked her watch. "All in two hours." She bustled me out the door with the rest following.

"Thank you," I mumbled, swaying sideways. Kate's hands caught me.

"Have you had anything to eat?"

"Thank you," I repeated and shook my head.

"Will she be able to ride?" Mark asked, his brows drawn together.

"Yes." I nodded vigorously. "I just need coffee."

"Mandy and I will get her some food and meet you at Santos's stall."

I took Mark's hands, smiling. "Thank you," pouring my whole heart into those two words.

He leaned down to peer in my face. "It's just coffee." The corner of his lip lifted at his own joke, but I could tell he knew what I meant.

"Let's go," Kate urged.

Robert patted my shoulder. "I'll meet you at the warm-up ring in an hour."

"Thank you." They were the only words left in my head. The extraordinary circumstances had blasted my synapses clean.

We hustled through the main barn to Santos's stall. I stopped Kate by grabbing her jacket and twisting. "I have to go take care of Windsong. He'll need hay and water by now."

Kate pulled free and kept walking. "It's been taken care of."

"By who?"

Before I took another step, Melinda's distinctive nasal tone drifted out of the stall. "His neck is so long, I'm never going to get done braiding."

A mocking, deep male voice responded, "Stop complaining and keep working. You are such a princess."

"Shut up, spoiled brat. And go easy on the tail hair. Haven't you ever brushed one before?"

I grinned. "Melinda? Shawn?" The stall door slid open, and Shawn stepped out, one hand holding a tail comb. But this was a different Shawn. His deep tan was accented by short dark hair, and a polo shirt stretched tightly over a broad chest. His former leanness had morphed into bulging muscles. My eyes roved over his bronzed arms and long legs. Florida had done him good.

When my eyes met his warm, chocolate brown ones, his lip lifted in a sardonic smile. "At your service, sexy girl."

I laughed and hugged him tight. "What are you doing here? Forget it, I don't care. I'm just glad you are."

He glanced over his shoulder. "Melinda and I wanted to surprise you by coming to watch. We planned the trip weeks ago. Support for our teammate and all. I'm sorry about Windsong, though."

"Me, too," Melinda chimed in. "Jane, get in here and finish your own mane, my fingers can't take any more." Despite her command, she simply held out her arms when I ducked into the stall.

After a tight hug, I offered to take over.

She shook her head. "No, I was just teasing. We already bathed him, and Shawn is supposed to be combing out his tail, but he really is ripping it to shreds. You might want to take over for him before he makes Santos bald."

I took the comb from Shawn. "You bathed my horse—well, I mean, the horse I'm going to ride?"

"Yeah, we've been buzzing around here for centuries. Kate asked us to help when we couldn't find you."

Kate popped her head into the stall. "And I'll finish the tail. Here's Mark with your breakfast. Sit down and eat." She pushed me toward the food.

Robert's tack stall had a rug rolled out on the floor; three-tier saddle racks towered in one corner next to a row of hooks with bridles hanging on them. Everything was spotlessly clean and neatly stowed. Padded folding chairs surrounded a table covered in a silky green cloth. A little vase of fresh flowers stood in the middle. Mark pulled out a chair and placed a breakfast sandwich and a lovely, steaming cup of coffee in front of it.

"Eat," he ordered.

"I'll eat while I tack up."

"Kate has that under control. You need to eat." He pointed at the chair. "And have a rest. I won't have my professional rider blowing her class because she wasn't properly fed."

Although it felt completely unnatural to sit and enjoy a meal before a class, I sank gratefully into the chair, the aroma of coffee and bacon silencing any other protests.

"Jane!" I jumped up and whipped around at my mother's voice, my mouth stuffed with sandwich. I held a hand in front of my full mouth. What were they doing here?

Mom enveloped my stiff form in her arms, and I breathed in the familiar scent of her perfume. "Baby, we're here now." She put her hands on my moving jaw and kissed my cheek. "I've missed you so much, but we're here."

"Mark Grant." Mark shook hands with my father. "Nice to meet you. I'll let you guys have a few minutes by yourselves. Make sure she eats." He slipped out of the stall.

Chewing, I looked over my mother's shoulder at my father, who stood behind her, staring at me. I wasn't sure I had the strength or even the interest to waste on this conversation.

"What are you doing here?" I refused to smile or make this easier. I had reached out to him with every email; I had tried to explain myself. I didn't have time to explain anything right now. Did he think he could just smile that slightly crooked, dear, familiar smile and I would fall into his arms? My vision blurred and I swayed.

My mother slid her hands up and down my arms. "Sit down, finish eating. Warren, stop glaring at her like that. We have been talking to Kate, sweetie. She told us everything. We haven't been able to get you on the phone since yesterday."

"Dead battery." I plopped down onto the fabric seat and took a fortifying sip of coffee.

"First of all, how's Windsong? Is he okay?" my mother asked. She pulled out another chair and settled herself neatly into it.

My father took the chair opposite mine. "We didn't have time to go check on him first. How is he?"

"Don't pretend you care."

"Jane, don't talk like that," my mother protested, but my father put a hand on her arm.

"No, I deserve her venom. Sweetie, I owe you an apology." His eyes looked everywhere but at me. He blew out a big breath like a hot air balloon firing up.

He owed me more than that. How many emails had he ignored? Now, when I needed to focus, he wanted to have an emotional father-daughter talk? I pushed back my chair. "I don't have time for this."

"Please, just give me a minute. I know you're busy." And then he did something I had never witnessed my confident, sometimes overbearing, stern parent do. He bit his lip and repeated softly, "Please."

I perched stiffly on the edge of the chair and waited in silence.

He got up, pacing back and forth in the small space. "I read every email you sent me at least ten times. And just as many times, I wrote a reply but deleted it for sounding stupid. Your mother made sure I saw every article written about you, and I realized how wrong I was. I booked tickets and told your mother to pack. We didn't get Kate's messages until we landed today. And then you wouldn't answer your phone. I thought you were so furious you weren't speaking to me." He swallowed and then leaned his hands on the table, finally meeting my eyes. "I am so proud of you. Will you ever forgive me?"

"I did try to tell you I wasn't blowing off college."

"I know. I wouldn't listen. I was a pompous, puffy-chested, righteous suit and you were smart, focused, and …" His face softened and he smiled as he lightened the moment. "Beautiful."

We stared at each other. My mother sniffed, and even though I wasn't looking at her, I knew she was crying. She cried for everything, no surprise where I got that from.

"You'll let me do things my way?"

He nodded, coming around the table to hug me.

"You're not my little girl anymore," he whispered into my hair.

"I'll always be your little girl. But I have to go right now. I have a job to do."

"I'm going to need a leg up." I smoothed my tailcoat and pulled on my gloves.

Shawn cupped his hands and I put my knee in them.

He nodded. "One, two, three!" I jumped on three and he pushed on my leg, but Santos was so tall, I still couldn't throw my leg over his back. Darn it, I missed my three-step mounting block. I grabbed at his mane and the back of the saddle and clawed my way up.

"Oof!" The air left my lungs as my stomach smacked onto the leather. Shawn used both hands to push on my rump and I wiggled and pulled. Finally, I got my leg on the other side, and Melinda helped put my feet in the stirrups. Santos never moved during the whole fiasco.

Shawn rubbed his hands together. "I love it when Cory's not around."

Rolling my eyes and ignoring a spear of longing, I gathered the reins. I had pulled a braid out during my clumsy ascent. I started to fiddle with it, but Melinda knocked my hands away.

"I'll do it. You look fabulous, even your hair is perfect. That's a good sign for you, Jumpy Jane." Her teasing smile was warm, and she patted Santos's neck. "Knock it out of the park, girlfriend."

"Thank you, Melinda. I never thought I would say this, but you're an awfully good friend."

"Only outside the ring. Someday we'll be in the same class again and I'll be out for your blood." She chuckled.

Melinda and Shawn walked near my knees. We navigated the paths to the warm-up ring. Having them there felt like the team was back together, and I liked it, but I missed the white cowboy hat. How could I be about to ride the most important ride of my whole life and Cory wasn't here? How could I be sitting on the most talented horse ever, and my heart was heavy with missing him?

Michelle was waiting by the entrance gate. "You look great." She held up her hand and I squeezed it.

"Thanks. For everything."

"Hey, Santos." Michelle stroked his chest scars and looked up at me. "I wish Erica was here, but I know she would be glad it was you riding him, now."

"I'm not so sure, but thanks for saying that."

"I'm not just saying it, Erica did. She had a thing for you from the moment she met you. That's why I proposed you as spokesperson for EMA. You're just like Erica, and your actions this weekend prove it. You'll be wonderful today, I'm sure of it."

A lump rose in my throat and I spoke around it. "That's the nicest thing you could have said to me. I will do my best not to disappoint you." We clasped hands again and I rode into the warm-up ring.

Santos was businesslike in warm-up. He didn't look around but kept his eyes trained to the front, undistracted by the noise and other horses. Where Windsong was all electricity and agility, Santos was power, elasticity, fluid movement from figure to figure. I was so nervous my neck was like iron and my back stiff, interfering with my own signals.

I attempted a row of flying lead changes every three strides, but my timing was behind Santos's, and I actually prevented him from completing the last two. Completely disorganized, I hauled him to a walk. He jerked the reins out of my hands, his lips flapping and his stride strong and tense.

Kate waved me over to where she was standing with Robert along the rail. I pointed Santos toward her and right into the path of a cantering horse. I pulled him sideways by the reins, wincing at the dark look from the other rider. Santos ripped at the bit, clearly disgusted with me. Something he had never done in the two weeks that I rode him at home. Kate was going to yell at me, I was ruining this horse, and I had a class in ten minutes.

Carefully looking all around, I navigated Santos to the fence.

Kate stepped up onto the middle rail, raising herself level with me on Santos. Robert put a hand on her back to steady her. "Nervous?" she asked.

Silly question. "Of course," I answered through tight lips, acid burning in my stomach.

"You rode this horse all last week. You practiced your freestyle sequences and he can do them easily. Intermediate I is cake to a Grand Prix horse like him."

"All these people watching and expecting me to be perfect. I can't think," I hissed.

Kate looked around at the unusual number of people leaning on the fence. Most fans usually waited in the stands to watch the actual class instead of gathering around their favorites during warm-up. "Okay. Don't think then, ride from your heart. Santos likes you. Concentrate on your connection to him and let the rest take care of itself." Kate patted her chest. "Feel it."

I glanced at Robert and he nodded agreement. With a deep, fortifying breath, I cautiously rode into the center of the arena. Signaling a canter, I eased around a corner, pointed the giant red body across the diagonal and began skipping the flying lead changes. Change, one, two, three, change, one, two, and three, or four. Wait, ahhh, I missed it again. I patted Santos's neck and turned the corner for another try, but Kate was jumping up and down. I realized she was waving me to the gate. A tremor traveled from my lips to my fingertips. It was time.

I rode out the gate and Kate began buffing my boots and wiping Santos's lips and bits.

"Kate, I couldn't get the changes! What am I going to do?" I couldn't control the quiver in my voice.

Kate smiled, cool, confident, and encouraging. "Jane, you know what to do. Stop worrying. Ride like I taught you, listen to your horse, and, most of all, have fun."

Certainly, they were words I had heard before. But like a balm on a wound, I needed to hear them again. I gave a solemn nod, trying to imitate Kate's cool, calm confidence.

I gathered Santos's reins and moved toward the show ring. All eyes were fastened on me. I pasted a stiff smile on my mouth but didn't connect with any of them. I was longing for a set of mesmerizing, steady blue ones peering from under the brim of a white cowboy hat. Grins and wishes of good luck poured out of people, meant to encourage me but adding to the liquid feeling in my knees.

I walked Santos in the gate and picked up a trot at the corner. Santos lifted his legs in a floating, powerful gait, eating up the ground and making the faces outside the ring a blur. My body automatically adjusted to the motion of his strides, and I focused on his ears.

Matching my breathing to his rhythm, I massaged the reins with my fingers. He softened his jaw and then his neck. My hands became steadier, and my back absorbed and followed the motion. Santos relaxed. He rocked his weight back and organized himself for the first corner. I smiled. He was a pro, and incredibly trained. My smile widened and I lifted my chin.

Shawn and Melinda stood next to Michelle, and both gave me a thumbs-up and bright, encouraging smiles as we passed them. I wanted them to enjoy my performance. I grinned at them.

Next to them, my father stood behind my mother, his arms around her protecting her from stray elbows. Both were wearing matching misty-eyed expressions. I wanted to prove to them that I had chosen the right path. I pressed my seat bones more firmly into the saddle, adjusting my posture to make myself taller, more elegant.

I rounded the corner, and Kate and Robert were both nodding. Kate raised her eyebrows and silently clapped her hands, bubbling with excitement. She had designed this freestyle. I wanted to do it justice just to please her and thank her for all of her hard work. I wanted Robert to see that I had determination, if not seasoning, and prove to him that he had made the right choice. I squared my shoulders.

Mandy stood on a rail of the fence in front of Mark. Cupping her hands around her mouth, she called, "Go, Jane and Santos!" Mark's chin rested on her shoulder and his arms were around her. He grinned and nodded. My chest swelled. I blew them a kiss and then beamed my love and appreciation. I wanted to justify Mark's support and show Mandy that I deserved to ride her mother's horse.

My gaze roamed over the other spectators along the fence. My eyes snagged on Alison's pale blond head. Surprise punched me in the gut and my new determination faltered. What was she doing here? She had been banned from horse showing as a result of her sabotage attempts during the North American

Team Championships. I didn't think she was even allowed on the show grounds as a spectator, but there she was.

In morbid fascination, I waited for a scorching belittlement delivered in her sneering snotty voice, but her eyes never rose to mine. They were riveted on Santos, the appreciation of a horse lover written plainly on her face. Despite her animosity toward me, she clearly was a fan of Santos. I wanted her, and all his other fans, to see his brilliance and heart.

Recalling the grace and joy that radiated from Erica as she rode Santos, I fingered his coppery mane. He swelled with purpose and showmanship when he entered a show ring, warming the hearts of his fans as he responded to Erica with pleasure. I wanted the spectators to see me in that way, a promising partner for Santos, following in Erica's footsteps.

Santos's ribs lifted my legs as he pulled in a deep breath and let it out slowly. He was preparing himself as we approached our starting mark. He knew we were about to perform. I wanted to be the best partner to him that I could be.

I signaled Santos to halt. My eyes inadvertently strayed to the gate as they did every time I was about to begin a test. My brain knew Cory wouldn't be there, but it was a habit.

I saw the white cowboy hat. My throat closed. I waited for the brim to lift, not daring to hope that it could be. Boot on the bottom rail, denim-clad knee bent, the cowboy lifted his hat, ruffled dark curls, and set it back down just so. His chest was heaving, as if he had run a long way.

Finally, the face came up and electric eyes as blue as the sky met mine and a grin that could stop a heart filled mine until I had to slap a palm to my breast to keep it from bursting out. He folded his hands as if in prayer and his lips formed the words "Forgive me."

I nodded vigorously. He was here! Placing my hand back on the reins, I grinned. My jitters melted away.

He pointed to me and then laid his hand on his chest. He loved me.

I threw him a kiss. "For them, Santos," I whispered. "Let's dance." With confidence and joy radiating from my heart, I lifted my arm to signal our music.

# About the Author

As in every industry, the professional equestrian world is filled with all types. While writing a fiction novel, I sometimes get bogged down in portraying a scene realistically or ideally. The truth is that no matter how good hearted the owner or rider, they sometimes make bad decisions due to emotions, ignorance or just plain unaware. Teenagers are especially known for not being reasonable. Just recently, one of my long time students, who is now an Equine Business graduate of Del Val College and a professional herself, commented on a young teen who was schooling her horse on her own. "She wouldn't stop cantering him. Now I know why you would yell at me to give my horse a break. I was like that when I was that age too." I smiled in appreciation of her becoming aware, years after her horse suffered all of her unintentional abuse. He survived, thrived and is still strong and in training at the age of sixteen. I hope I was able to strike a balance between real and what you want to read and enjoy. Every partnership is personal, and every rider is human, and every equine athlete is still a horse. As I observe good riding and bad at the horseshows I attend, I remind myself to be tolerant. I don't know what that horse's personality is, or what issues the pair has had to overcome just to get there and ride down the centerline. Most riders try their best, but have a long way to go in their education. Their horse seems to be forgiving of mistakes, otherwise they would be on the ground. So do your best, always be open to learning, and appreciate your horse on the good days and the bad. That's what I plan on doing. Visit me at tonimaribooks.com and tell me your story.

Look for more by this author at tonimaribooks.com

Made in the USA
Lexington, KY
13 February 2017